HIGH COURT CASE SUMMARIES

D1192494

CIVIL PROCEDURE

Keyed to Marcus, Redish, Sherman
and Pfander's
Casebook on Civil Procedure,
5th Edition

WEST®

A Thomson Reuters business

Mat #41039836

© West, a Thomson business, 2005
© 2010 Thomson Reuters
  610 Opperman Drive
  St. Paul, MN 55123
  1–800–313–9378
Printed in the United States of America

ISBN: 978–0–314–26566–1

Table of Contents

Alphabetical Table of Cases

CHAPTER ONE

Choosing a System of Procedure

Band's Refuse Removal, Inc. v. Borough of Fair Lawn

Instant Facts: After the Borough of Fair Lawn (D) adopted an ordinance requiring a town garbage collection contract as a prerequisite for obtaining a garbage collection permit, Band's Refuse Removal, Inc. (P) filed suit to declare the ordinance unconstitutional and compel the issuance of a permit.

Black Letter Rule: A judge must serve as an impartial arbiter of parties' claims without advocating any particular position.

Kothe v. Smith

Instant Facts: The court sanctioned Smith (D) for settling the case against him after trial had begun, despite the court's instruction to entertain settlement negotiations *before* trial.

Black Letter Rule: Courts may not use their sanction powers to force litigants to settle otherwise legitimate claims.

Band's Refuse Removal, Inc. v. Borough of Fair Lawn

(Garbage Collector) v. *(Town)*

62 N.J. Super. 522, 163 A.2d 465 (App. Div. 1960)

A JUDGE'S EXCESSIVE INVOLVEMENT IN A TRIAL VIOLATES DUE PROCESS

■ **INSTANT FACTS** After the Borough of Fair Lawn (D) adopted an ordinance requiring a town garbage collection contract as a prerequisite for obtaining a garbage collection permit, Band's Refuse Removal, Inc. (P) filed suit to declare the ordinance unconstitutional and compel the issuance of a permit.

■ **BLACK LETTER RULE** A judge must serve as an impartial arbiter of parties' claims without advocating any particular position.

■ **PROCEDURAL BASIS**

On appeal to review a judgment for the defendant.

■ **FACTS**

After advertising for bids for garbage collection in May 1957, the Borough of Fair Lawn (D) awarded the town contract to the Capassos. In August, the Borough passed an ordinance that required all garbage collectors to operate with a permit and limited the issuance of permits to those who held a contract with the town, effectively precluding anybody other than the Capassos from thereafter collecting garbage in Fair Lawn. Band's Refuse Removal, Inc. (P) held a contract with a local electric plant to collect garbage and applied for a permit. The Borough (D) denied the application. Band's Refuse (P) filed a complaint in state court challenging the ordinance as illegal and unconstitutional, seeking an order compelling the Borough (D) to issue a permit. The Borough (D) and the Capassos, who had intervened, answered that the ordinance was legal because the contract was awarded under a competitive bidding process. In the meantime, a grand jury investigation was conducted against various Borough (D) officials concerning alleged improprieties in the bidding process for Borough (D) garbage collection contracts. In response, Band's Refuse (P) amended its complaint to contest the Capasso contract, alleging it arose outside the competitive bidding process and was tainted by fraud. Around the same time, the trial judge issued a pretrial order defining the issues for trial and narrowing the scope of the plaintiff's fraud allegation.

Before trial, the judge communicated with the plaintiff's counsel by telephone concerning the production of various witnesses at trial. During that conversation, the plaintiff's counsel informed the judge that he was considering dismissing the amended counts and proceeding on the original cause of action. The judge informed counsel that if that happened, he would have no choice but to declare the contract between Band's Refuse (P) and the electric company void. Six days before trial, the judge scheduled a hearing with counsel to discuss the production of various witnesses for trial. Although the Capassos' attorney could not attend, the court proceeded with the hearing. At this hearing, the Borough's (D) attorney first learned of the *ex parte* telephone conversation with the plaintiff's counsel. The plaintiff's counsel explained that his evidence concerning fraud on the defendants' part was scarce, which prompted consideration of dismissal. The judge then read a prepared statement explaining that because of the indictments brought and various newspaper accounts suggesting fraud, the public interest required that the court consider the fraud allegations and stating that the Borough (D) had failed to adequately investigate the legality of the Capasso contract to protect the public interest. The judge then appointed amicus curiae to present evidence and represent the public interest at trial.

At trial, the judge was intimately involved, including issuing subpoenas to witnesses, collecting and reviewing evidentiary documents, offering exhibits, and examining and cross-examining witnesses. When questions of admissibility arose, the judge issued a ruling. In all, of the thirty-two witnesses testifying at trial, the judge called twenty-seven of them, many of whom were allowed to testify over objections of counsel because the witnesses were not named in response to discovery requests. Eleven days into trial, the judge, on his own motion and over the Capassos' objections, expanded the issues litigated beyond those identified in the pretrial order to include noncompliance with state statutes governing competitive bidding. The next day, the court permitted the Borough (D) to change its defense that the ordinance and contract were valid and file an amended answer and cross-claim alleging fraud against the Capassos and seeking recovery of all money paid under the contract. The Capassos objected to this change of position as a violation of their fundamental rights. The judge denied the Capassos' request for additional time to investigate and obtain discovery related to the Borough's (D) new defense. After trial concluded, the judge entered an order declaring the Capasso contract void *ab initio*, finding all payments made under the contract illegal, finding the Borough (D) permit ordinance illegal and void, and awarding the Borough (D) over $300,000 against the Capassos. The Capassos appealed.

■ ISSUE

Does a judge commit prejudicial error by prejudging issues to be determined at trial, excessively investigating and calling witnesses on his or her own initiative, introducing new issues into a trial without notice to the parties, and permitting a party's change of position without affording an opponent reasonable time to respond?

■ DECISION AND RATIONALE

(Goldmann, J.) Yes. A judge must serve as an impartial arbiter of parties' claims without advocating any particular position. Here, the Capassos challenge the trial judge's conduct throughout the litigation. First, the Capassos take exception with the judge's *ex parte* communication with the plaintiff's counsel discussing the production of witnesses and the court's statement that dismissal of the fraud counts would require the court to declare the plaintiff's contract void. The approach taken by the judge suggests that he had predetermined the ultimate issue to be determined at trial, although no evidence had yet been presented or considered. Clearly, the court must consider all evidence presented at trial before making its decision.

Second, the Capassos challenge the judge's excessive participation in collecting and reviewing documentary evidence, subpoenaing, calling, and examining its own witnesses, and introducing evidence necessary to his examination. While a trial judge generally may interrogate a witness to qualify or elicit information and may call witnesses on its own initiative under special circumstances, the judge in this case crossed the line from impartiality into advocacy, apparently concerned with the public interests involved. Due process requires that a court maintain the appearance of impartiality and not unreasonably involve itself in the participation of a trial. By his actions, the judge served more as an advocate for the public than an unbiased tribunal adjudicating the parties' claims. This violation is compounded by the failure to inform the Capassos in advance of the names and addresses of the court's witnesses, which would have been required had an opposing party sought to call the witnesses. The potential harm of surprise is just as great regardless of who calls an unidentified witness. The court committed prejudicial error.

Third, the judge also committed error by introducing new issues for trial beyond those previously established by his pretrial order. These issues were introduced without notice to the Capassos, who were afforded no reasonable time to consider the issues litigated. "The function of a trial judge is to serve litigants by determining their disputes and the issues implicated therein in accordance with applicable rules and law." The court may not infuse new issues not raised by the parties without affording them a full and fair opportunity to address those issues.

Finally, the judge erred in refusing to allow the Capassos reasonable time to address the Borough's (D) change of position in the course of trial. Although it was appropriate to permit the Borough's (D) change in light of the additional information uncovered as a result of the grand jury investigation, fairness requires that the Capassos, who up to that point had proceeded under the understanding that the

Borough (D) had supported the legality of its contract, be afforded the opportunity to prepare a defense to the new claims asserted against them. Reversed and remanded.

Analysis:

Although the judge's motives were honorable, his excessive involvement in preserving the public interest is the root of the errors in this case. The judge acted within his authority to appoint amicus curiae to protect those interests. Had the judge remained uninvolved and the amicus curiae engaged in the same activities, there likely would have been no error relating to his participation.

■ CASE VOCABULARY

ADVOCATE: A person who assists, defends, pleads, or prosecutes for another.

AMICUS CURIAE: A person who is not a party to a lawsuit but who petitions the court or is requested by the court to file a brief in the action because that person has a strong interest in the subject matter.

CROSS CLAIM: A claim asserted between codefendants or coplaintiffs in a case and that relates to the subject of the original claim or counterclaim.

EX PARTE: Done or made at the instance and for the benefit of one party only, and without notice to, or argument by, any person adversely interested; of or relating to court action taken by one party without notice to another, usually for temporary or emergency relief.

IMPARTIAL: Unbiased; disinterested.

VOID AB INITIO: Null from the beginning, as from the first moment when a contract is entered into. A contract is void ab initio if it seriously offends law or public policy, in contrast to a contract that is merely voidable at the election of one party to the contract.

Kothe v. Smith

(Patient) v. *(Physician)*

771 F.2d 667 (2d Cir. 1985)

A DEFENDANT CANNOT BE SANCTIONED FOR SETTLING DURING RATHER THAN BEFORE TRIAL

■ **INSTANT FACTS** The court sanctioned Smith (D) for settling the case against him after trial had begun, despite the court's instruction to entertain settlement negotiations *before* trial.

■ **BLACK LETTER RULE** Courts may not use their sanction powers to force litigants to settle otherwise legitimate claims.

■ **PROCEDURAL BASIS**

On appeal to review a district court order imposing sanctions.

■ **FACTS**

Kothe (P) sued Smith (D) in federal court for medical malpractice. Prior to trial, the district court judge ordered the parties to entertain settlement discussions and recommended a settlement of between $20,000 and $30,000. The judge warned the parties that if a comparable settlement were reached after trial had begun, he would impose sanctions as needed. During settlement negotiations, Dr. Smith (D), through his malpractice insurer, offered to settle for $5,000, which offer was refused by the plaintiff. Kothe (P) demanded settlement in the amount of $50,000, although her counsel had informed the court that she would settle for as low as $20,000. When the case ultimately settled for $20,000 one day after trial began, the court sanctioned Smith (D). Smith (D) appealed.

■ **ISSUE**

May a court sanction a party for settling a claim only after trial has begun, when the court previously ordered the parties to enter into pretrial settlement negotiations?

■ **DECISION AND RATIONALE**

(Van Graafeiland, J.) No. Although voluntary pretrial settlements are to be encouraged, trial courts are not permitted to use a threat of sanctions to coerce involuntary settlements. Courts may not use their sanction powers to force litigants to settle otherwise legitimate claims. Here, the court committed an especially prohibited act because it sanctioned only Smith (D), although Kothe (P) had never offered to settle her claims for anything less than $50,000. Smith (D) cannot be required to increase his settlement offer merely because the judge believed it to be too low. Similarly, Smith (D) should not be penalized because his counsel, upon considering the evidence presented during the first day of trial, reevaluated his client's case and chose to accept a settlement at that time. Judgment vacated.

Analysis:

Under Federal Rule of Civil Procedure 16, a federal judge may direct counsel for parties to attend a mandatory pretrial conference to help facilitate settlement of all claims. It is generally understood that, within a court's discretionary powers, the judge may issue other orders that may help the parties reach a voluntary settlement. Nothing in the federal rules, however, permits a judge to exert any influence that may render a settlement the product of duress, coercion, or intimidation. Settlements must remain voluntary.

■ CASE VOCABULARY

PRETRIAL CONFERENCE: An informal meeting at which opposing attorneys confer, usually with the judge, to work toward the disposition of the case by discussing matters of evidence and narrowing the issues that will be tried.

SANCTION: A penalty or coercive measure that results from failure to comply with a law, rule, or order.

SETTLEMENT: An agreement ending a dispute or lawsuit.

CHAPTER TWO

The Rewards and Costs of Litigation—of Remedies and Related Matters

Fuentes v. Shevin

Instant Facts: Fuentes (P) defaulted on an installment sales contract and the secured property was taken from her without a hearing.

Black Letter Rule: Before a person may be deprived of property, due process requires that he or she be provided with notice and a hearing to contest the validity of the deprivation.

Mitchell v. W.T. Grant Co.

Instant Facts: Mitchell (D) purchased merchandise on credit from Grant (P), and Grant (P) seized the property when it claimed Mitchell (D) had defaulted on the sales contract.

Black Letter Rule: A system of pre-hearing seizure that minimizes the risk of a wrongful interim possession is constitutional.

North Georgia Finishing, Inc. v. Di–Chem, Inc.

Instant Facts: Di–Chem (P) obtained an order freezing North Georgia Finishing's (D) bank account, pursuant to a statute authorizing garnishment upon an affidavit of a creditor.

Black Letter Rule: Due process requires that official seizure proceedings have a provision for a hearing or other safeguards against mistaken repossession.

Connecticut v. Doehr

Instant Facts: DiGiovanni obtained an order attaching Doehr's (P) home on the basis of an affidavit alleging that Doehr (P) had committed assault and battery on DiGiovanni.

Black Letter Rule: Due process requires either a hearing or a showing of exigent circumstances before prejudgment seizure of property may be ordered.

Carey v. Piphus

Instant Facts: Piphus (P) was suspended from school without a hearing and brought an action under the Civil Rights Act.

Black Letter Rule: A deprivation of procedural due process rights that does not result in any actual injury is actionable only for nominal damages.

Smith v. Western Electric Co.

Instant Facts: Smith's (P) petition for protection from tobacco smoke in the workplace was dismissed for failure to state a claim upon which relief may be granted.

Black Letter Rule: Injunctive relief is available if irreparable harm is otherwise likely to result and the plaintiff has no adequate remedy at law.

Venegas v. Mitchell

Instant Facts: Mitchell (P) agreed to represent Venegas (D) in a civil rights suit, and Venegas (D) agreed to pay a contingent fee.

Black Letter Rule: Contingent fee agreements are upheld in civil rights cases, even if the resulting fee is more than the attorney's fees awarded by the court.

Fuentes v. Shevin

(Debtor) v. *(State Attorney General)*
407 U.S. 67, 92 S.Ct. 1983 (1972)

SEIZURE OF PROPERTY REQUIRES NOTICE AND AN OPPORTUNITY TO BE HEARD

■ **INSTANT FACTS** Fuentes (P) defaulted on an installment sales contract and the secured property was taken from her without a hearing.

■ **BLACK LETTER RULE** Before a person may be deprived of property, due process requires that he or she be provided with notice and a hearing to contest the validity of the deprivation.

■ **PROCEDURAL BASIS**

Appeal from judgments of three-judge federal district courts that upheld the constitutionality of state statutes.

■ **FACTS**

Fuentes (P) purchased a stove and a stereo under a conditional sales contract. The contract stated that Fuentes (P) was entitled to the possession of the items purchased as long as she continued to make regular monthly payments. Fuentes (P) made payments as required, but a dispute developed over the servicing of the stove. The seller alleged that Fuentes (P) refused to make the remaining payments and obtained a writ of replevin by submitting forms to the clerk of the local small-claims court. The property was seized the same day the writ was obtained.

The Florida statute that authorized the issuance of the writ stated that a writ of replevin would be issued on the allegation of a claimant that he or she was entitled to the property. The claimant was required to post a bond and to file a complaint to commence a court action for repossession. The complaint would be served on the defendant at the same time that the property was taken from his or her possession. There was an opportunity for a hearing *after* the property was seized.

The case also involved a challenge to a Pennsylvania pre-judgment seizure statute. The Pennsylvania statute was similar, except that there was no requirement that there *ever* be a hearing on the claims for possession of the seized property.

■ **ISSUE**

Are the pre-judgment seizure statutes constitutional?

■ **DECISION AND RATIONALE**

(Stewart, J.) No. Before a person may be deprived of property, due process requires that he or she be provided with notice and a hearing to contest the validity of the deprivation. The purpose of the hearing is to ensure that property is not seized unfairly, or as a result of a mistake. The purpose of the notice requirement is to make certain that there is a meaningful opportunity to exercise the right to the hearing. The notice and hearing must be granted at a time when the deprivation of the property still can be prevented. The right to a hearing after the seizure is therefore insufficient for due process purposes. A later hearing, or a damage award, cannot undo the arbitrary taking. The requirements in the Florida and

Pennsylvania statutes of a bond and an allegation that the claimant is entitled to the property are only a test of the strength of a claimant's convictions, not a substitute for a prior hearing.

Prior cases have upheld seizures of property prior to a hearing in limited circumstances. In those cases, the seizure was directly necessary to secure an important governmental or public interest, and there was a special need for prompt action. In addition, the person initiating the seizure was a governmental official. In the cases involved here, there is no governmental or general public interest at stake, but only the interests of private creditors. It does not matter that Fuentes (P) and the other appellants do not have full legal title to the property seized, or that their deprivation may be only temporary. The length and severity of the deprivation may have some bearing on the type of hearing to be afforded, but not in determining the basic right to a hearing. Fuentes (P) also had a significant property interest in her continued possession of the goods she purchased, and that interest is protected by the due process clause. It is also irrelevant that the goods purchased were not necessities, as the Fourteenth Amendment speaks only of "property" generally. Reversed.

■ DISSENT

(White, J.) The hearings in cases such as these would generally be limited to the question of whether the buyer has defaulted. The likelihood of a mistaken claim of default does not seem to be sufficiently real or recurring to justify the broad constitutional requirement announced by the majority. The majority's opinion probably will not give debtors more protection than they already have, and probably will reduce the availability of credit, or make it more expensive.

Analysis:

The specifics of a pre-seizure hearing do not appear to be of great concern to the majority. The Court does nothing more than provide general language about an opportunity to contest the seizure. The statutes at question, on the other hand, provided no protection whatsoever to the holder of the property. This complete lack of protection may have made the Court hesitant to promulgate overly specific guidelines, since the transition from no debtor protection is a dramatic one.

■ CASE VOCABULARY

DETINUE: A common-law action to recover personal property wrongfully taken by another.

REPLEVIN: An action for the repossession of personal property wrongfully taken or detained by the defendant, whereby the plaintiff gives security for and holds the property until the court decides who owns it; a writ obtained from a court authorizing the retaking of personal property wrongfully taken or detained.

TROVER: A common-law action for the recovery of damages for the conversion of personal property, the damages generally being measured by the value of the property.

Mitchell v. W.T. Grant Co.

(Debtor) v. *(Seller of Goods)*
416 U.S. 600, 94 S.Ct. 1895 (1974)

PRE–HEARING SEIZURE AUTHORIZED BY A JUDGE IS CONSTITUTIONAL

■ **INSTANT FACTS** Mitchell (D) purchased merchandise on credit from Grant (P), and Grant (P) seized the property when it claimed Mitchell (D) had defaulted on the sales contract.

■ **BLACK LETTER RULE** A system of pre-hearing seizure that minimizes the risk of a wrongful interim possession is constitutional.

■ **PROCEDURAL BASIS**

Appeal from an order of the Louisiana Supreme Court upholding the validity of a state statute.

■ **FACTS**

Mitchell (D) purchased several items on credit from W.T. Grant (P). Grant (P) claimed that Mitchell (D) defaulted on the credit agreement and brought an action against Mitchell (D). Grant (P) requested sequestration of the property Mitchell (D) purchased. The sequestration statute relied on by Grant (P) allowed a creditor to obtain sequestration upon submission of an affidavit to a judge stating that it was within the power of the defendant to conceal, waste, or remove the property. Only someone who claimed a possessory interest in the property could submit the affidavit. Grant (P) followed the procedure of the statute, stating that it had reason to believe that Mitchell (D) would encumber, alienate or otherwise dispose of the merchandise purchased. The judge signed an order granting Grant (P) possession of the merchandise during the pendency of the proceedings and ordering Grant (P) to post a bond. Grant (P) posted the bond. The order was signed without notice to Mitchell (D).

■ **ISSUE**

Was the Louisiana sequestration statute constitutional?

■ **DECISION AND RATIONALE**

(White, J.) Yes. A system of pre-hearing seizure that minimizes the risk of a wrongful interim possession is constitutional. The statutory scheme at issue in this case is significantly different from the procedure found unconstitutional in *Fuentes v. Shevin,* 407 U.S. 67 (1972). The Louisiana statute sets out specific facts that must be alleged before a sequestration order will be granted. The affidavit must be presented to a judge, as opposed to a clerk, so there is judicial supervision of the process. The statute requires that a hearing be held immediately, and the writ dissolved, unless the plaintiff proves the grounds for the issuance of the writ. If the writ must be dissolved, the party whose property was wrongly sequestered is entitled to damages and attorney's fees. There is less danger that the writ will be issued by mistake. Affirmed.

■ **CONCURRENCE**

(Powell, J.) The Court is withdrawing from the reasoning of *Fuentes v. Shevin*. It is fair to say that that case is overruled. The broad rule adopted by the Court in that case was unnecessary. The replevin statutes at issue in that case could have been invalidated on other grounds.

■ **DISSENT**

(Stewart, J.) The majority is overruling *Fuentes v. Shevin* without admitting it. This case is constitutionally indistinguishable from *Fuentes.*

■ **DISSENT**

(Brennan, J.) *Fuentes v. Shevin* requires invalidation of the Louisiana statute.

Analysis:

As a practical matter, the most significant difference between the Louisiana statute and the laws invalidated by *Fuentes v. Shevin* is the requirement that the plaintiff prove his or her claim at a hearing. Otherwise, the difference between the two statutory schemes lies in the exact nature of the hoops a plaintiff must jump through: instead of mere conclusory allegations, the plaintiff must make certain claims set out in the statute, and the order must be approved by a judge, not a clerk. In theory, a judge could reject an affidavit as insufficient, but a skilled plaintiff should know how to frame an affidavit to meet the requirements of the local judge.

■ **CASE VOCABULARY**

PENDENTE LITE: [Latin, "while the action is pending."] During the proceeding or litigation; contingent on the outcome of litigation.

SEQUESTRATION: A judicial writ commanding the sheriff or other officer to seize the goods of the person named in the writ. This writ is sometimes issued against a civil defendant who has defaulted or has acted in contempt of court.

North Georgia Finishing, Inc. v. Di–Chem, Inc.

(Purchaser of Goods) v. *(Garnishor)*

419 U.S. 601, 95 S.Ct. 719 (1975)

CREDITORS' SEIZURES REQUIRE SAFEGUARDS AGAINST MISTAKE

■ **INSTANT FACTS** Di–Chem (P) obtained an order freezing North Georgia Finishing's (D) bank account, pursuant to a statute authorizing garnishment upon an affidavit of a creditor.

■ **BLACK LETTER RULE** Due process requires that official seizure proceedings have a provision for a hearing or other safeguards against mistaken repossession.

■ **PROCEDURAL BASIS**

Appeal from an order of the Supreme Court of Georgia upholding the validity of a state garnishment statute.

■ **FACTS**

Di–Chem (P) brought an action against North Georgia Finishing (D) alleging that North Georgia (D) owed over $51,000 for goods purchased from Di–Chem (P). A state statute authorized the issuance of a writ of garnishment if a plaintiff submitted an affidavit that set out the amount claimed and stated that the plaintiff had reason to believe that the money would be lost if a writ did not issue. Di–Chem's (P) president filed such an affidavit, and the clerk of court issued a garnishment summons to North Georgia's (D) bank, freezing North Georgia's (D) bank account. The state courts rejected North Georgia's (D) constitutional challenges to the statute.

■ **ISSUE**

Was the Georgia garnishment statute constitutional?

■ **DECISION AND RATIONALE**

(White, J.) No. Due process requires that official seizure proceedings have a provision for a hearing or other safeguards against mistaken repossession. The seizures in *Fuentes v. Shevin,* 407 U.S. 67 (1972), were carried out without any such safeguards and were thus invalid. By contrast, the sequestration statute found constitutional in *Mitchell v. W.T. Grant Co.,* 416 U.S. 600 (1974), required an affidavit that clearly set out the allegations supporting the sequestration and the posting of a bond. The order was also issued by a judge, and a post-seizure hearing was held immediately.

The Georgia statute at issue here has no protections against improper seizure. There is no requirement of a bond or other security, and the order is issued by a clerk, not a judge. The statute does not require that the affidavit be based on the personal knowledge of the affiant, and it requires only conclusory allegations of fact. There is also no provision for an immediate hearing. The statute does not comport with due process requirements. Reversed.

■ **CONCURRENCE**

(Stewart, J.) It does not appear that the Court has overruled *Fuentes v. Shevin.*

■ **CONCURRENCE**

(Powell, J.) Procedural due process would be satisfied by a requirement that security be posted and that the need for the seizure be established before a neutral officer. Due process also requires a prompt post-seizure hearing in which the garnishor bears the burden of showing the need to continue the garnishment.

■ **DISSENT**

(Blackmun, J.) *Fuentes,* a constitutional decision, should not have been decided when there were two vacancies on the Court. The Court now engages in a case-by-case analysis of the state statutes.

Analysis:

In *Fuentes v. Shevin,* the Court spoke clearly of the need for notice and a hearing prior to seizures. The opinion in *Fuentes* was clear about the need for notice *before* the seizure, yet that requirement appears to be waived if there is a guarantee of a hearing *after* the seizure. The language in *Fuentes* stating that the availability of a remedy cannot undo a wrong seems to be ignored in this case.

■ **CASE VOCABULARY**

GARNISHMENT: A judicial proceeding in which a creditor (or potential creditor) asks the court to order a third party who is indebted to or is bailee for the debtor to turn over to the creditor any of the debtor's property (such as wages or bank accounts) held by that third party. A plaintiff initiates a garnishment action as a means of either prejudgment seizure or post judgment collection.

Connecticut v. Doehr

(Enforcer of the Statute) v. *(Defendant in a Civil Suit)*

501 U.S. 1, 111 S.Ct. 2105 (1991)

EXIGENT CIRCUMSTANCES MAY JUSTIFY A PRE–HEARING SEIZURE

■ **INSTANT FACTS** DiGiovanni obtained an order attaching Doehr's (P) home on the basis of an affidavit alleging that Doehr (P) had committed assault and battery on DiGiovanni.

■ **BLACK LETTER RULE** Due process requires either a hearing or a showing of exigent circumstances before prejudgment seizure of property may be ordered.

■ **PROCEDURAL BASIS**

Appeal from an order of the Second Circuit Court of Appeals finding that a Connecticut statute was unconstitutional.

■ **FACTS**

DiGiovanni (D) alleged that Doehr (P) committed assault and battery on him. DiGiovanni (D) obtained an order attaching Doehr's (P) real property in accordance with a Connecticut statute that authorized pre-judgment attachment of real estate. The statute did not require a pre-attachment hearing, notice to the property owner, or a bond or other security if the attachment should prove to be wrong. DiGiovanni (D) submitted an affidavit that alleged that the facts set out in his complaint for assault and battery were true. Neither the affidavit nor the complaint alleged that the assault and battery were connected to Doehr's (P) property. Nonetheless, a judge issued an order that stated that there was probable cause to sustain the validity of DiGiovanni's (D) claim, and an order was issued attaching Doehr's (P) property. The attachment order was the first notice that Doehr (P) had of the attachment. The order informed Doehr (P) that he had the right to a hearing to contest the attachment. Instead of requesting a hearing, Doehr (P) brought an action against DiGiovanni (D) that claimed the Connecticut statute was unconstitutional. The district court granted summary judgment for DiGiovanni (D), but the Second Circuit Court of Appeals reversed, holding that the Connecticut statute violated due process.

■ **ISSUE**

Was the Connecticut attachment statute constitutional?

■ **DECISION AND RATIONALE**

(White, J.) No. Due process requires either a hearing, or a showing of exigent circumstances before prejudgment seizure of property may be ordered, and here there was neither. Prejudgment attachments were unknown at common law. When the remedy was allowed, it was generally in situations in which the property owner threatened to take some action that would render the property unavailable. The remedy also is generally available only to creditors. Moreover, the attachment of real estate affects significant property interests. The owner's ability to sell or alienate the property is impaired, his or her credit rating could suffer, and title to the property is impaired. Although the deprivation of property is not complete or permanent, and may not amount to an actual physical deprivation, even temporary or partial deprivations of a property interest are sufficient to trigger due process concerns.

The risk of erroneous deprivation of a property interest is great under the Connecticut statute at issue here. There is no clear definition of "probable cause" that supports the issuance of an attachment order. Only a minimal affidavit need be filed, and the complaint supporting a claim may be conclusory, rather than setting out detailed facts. The assault and battery claim at issue here is not uncomplicated and does not lend itself to documentary proof. Thus, safeguards provided by the statute, including a post-attachment hearing, do not adequately reduce the risk of error in this case.

The interests advanced by an *ex parte* hearing are minimal. DiGiovanni (D) had no prior interest in the property, and there was no allegation that Doehr (P) was about to take any action that would make the real property unavailable to satisfy a judgment. There is no governmental interest that affects the analysis. But even with safeguards such as a hearing or a requirement of exigent circumstances, the risk of an erroneous deprivation is high. A bond, however, would provide protection in the event a seizure was erroneous. Most statutes that allow prejudgment seizure of property require a bond, and a bond requirement has been discussed by the Court in consideration of other pre-judgment seizure cases. A bond would not eliminate the requirement of a hearing, but would provide additional protection for the property owner. Affirmed.

■ **CONCURRENCE**

(Rehnquist, C.J.) The holding in this case is limited to situations in which a plaintiff had no prior interest in the property. It does not apply to situations such as mechanic's liens, in which an interest is created by operation of law.

■ **CONCURRENCE**

(Scalia, J.) Prejudgment attachment is not a remedy recognized at common law.

Analysis:

Cases in which the Court upheld the validity of prejudgment seizures of property typically involved the ownership of property that was related to the controversy, such as a secured creditor's repossession of merchandise. Those cases also generally involved personal property, which can be moved or even destroyed, as opposed to real property. In this case, there was no factual connection between Doehr's (P) home and his alleged assault and battery of DiGiovanni (D). In addition, although real property can be sold, the transaction often is far more involved than disposing of personal property.

■ **CASE VOCABULARY**

EX PARTE: Done or made at the instance and for the benefit of one party only, and without notice to, or argument by, any person adversely interested; of or relating to court action taken by one party without notice to the other, usually for temporary or emergency relief.

LIEN: A legal right or interest that a creditor has in another's property, lasting usually until a debt or duty that it secures is satisfied.

SUMMARY JUDGMENT: A judgment granted on a claim about which there is no genuine issue of material fact and upon which the claimant is entitled to prevail as a matter of law. This procedural device allows the speedy disposition of a controversy without the need for trial. *See* Fed. R. Civ. P. 56.

Carey v. Piphus

(*School Principal*) v. (*Student*)
435 U.S. 247, 98 S.Ct. 1042 (1978)

DAMAGES ARE NOT PRESUMED IN CIVIL RIGHTS CASES

■ **INSTANT FACTS** Piphus (P) was suspended from school without a hearing and brought an action under the Civil Rights Act.

■ **BLACK LETTER RULE** A deprivation of procedural due process rights that does not result in any actual injury is actionable only for nominal damages.

■ **PROCEDURAL BASIS**

Appeal from a judgment of the Seventh Circuit Court of Appeals.

■ **FACTS**

This case is a consolidation of two cases. In the first case, Carey (D), principal of a high school, saw Piphus (P) and another student smoking what he believed to be marijuana. Piphus (P) was suspended without a hearing, although two meetings with school officials, Piphus's (P) family, and a legal aid representative were held to explain the suspension. Piphus (P) obtained a temporary restraining order readmitting him to school. In the other case, Brisco (P), a sixth-grade student, wore an earring in defiance of a school rule against male students wearing earrings. Brisco (P) also was suspended without a hearing, but was readmitted after he obtained a preliminary injunction.

Piphus (P) and Brisco (P) brought actions for violations of their civil rights. The district court held that the rights of both students had been violated but did not award damages. The court also found that the two were entitled to declaratory relief and deletion of the suspensions from their school records, but did not enter an order grating that relief. The district court ordered the complaints dismissed. The Seventh Circuit Court of Appeals reversed and remanded, holding that the district court should have granted declaratory and injunctive relief. The court also held that Piphus (P) and Brisco (P) should have been allowed to present evidence regarding the pecuniary value of each day they missed from school due to the suspension. The court's holding stated that Piphus (P) and Brisco (P) would not be able to recover damages for missed school time if it were shown on remand that they would have been suspended even if a proper hearing had been held. The court of appeals also held that Piphus (P) and Brisco (P) would be able to recover "nonpunitive" damages, simply because they had been denied procedural due process.

■ **ISSUE**

Are plaintiffs in civil rights actions entitled to recover damages without proof of monetary loss?

■ **DECISION AND RATIONALE**

(Powell, J.) No. A deprivation of procedural due process rights that does not result in any actual injury is actionable only for nominal damages. An action for deprivation of civil rights is analogous to a common law tort action. Tort actions award damages to compensate for proven injuries. Damages are presumed only in limited cases, such as defamation *per se*. A defamatory statement is, however, much more likely to cause emotional distress than a deprivation of procedural due process rights. It is not reasonable to

---

assume that every deprivation of procedural due process, however small, is inherently likely to cause distress. Such a deprivation may not even be apparent until counsel is consulted, making the likelihood of distress small. Furthermore, a deprivation of rights may be justified, but the procedures used to impose that deprivation may be deficient. In such a case, the distress actually may be attributable to the justifiable deprivation. If the deprivation is justified, there can be no compensation.

In an appropriate case, there may be damages that flow from the denial of procedural rights. In those cases, the plaintiff may seek to recover damages. Those damages will not, however, be presumed. Similarly, punitive damages may be available to a plaintiff in a civil rights case, but the facts in this case do not support an award of punitive damages. Although there may be no compensable damages in certain cases, however, there may nonetheless have been a deprivation of rights. Traditionally, common law courts have awarded nominal damages to vindicate deprivations of rights that are not shown to cause actual injury. The right to procedural due process is an absolute right that does not depend upon the merits of the substantive assertions. Thus, if a plaintiff cannot prove actual damages, he or she may recover nominal damages. Reversed and remanded.

Analysis:

The Court's reasoning in this case could be considered dicta: there was no award of compensatory damages, and there was no finding that the reasons for the suspensions were proper or improper. The Seventh Circuit remanded the case to allow Piphus (P) and Brisco (P) to present evidence on the monetary damages they suffered. When the case reached the Supreme Court, there had been no award of damages, presumed or otherwise.

■ CASE VOCABULARY

NOMINAL DAMAGES: A trifling sum awarded when a legal injury is suffered but when there is no substantial loss or injury to be compensated.

PRELIMINARY INJUNCTION: A temporary injunction issued before or during trial to prevent an irreparable injury from occurring before the court has a chance to decide the case. A preliminary injunction will be issued only after the defendant receives notice and an opportunity to be heard.

TEMPORARY RESTRAINING ORDER: A court order, usually preserving the status quo, forbidding the opposing party from taking some action until a litigant's application for a preliminary or permanent injunction can be heard. A temporary restraining order may sometimes be granted without notifying the opposing party in advance.

Smith v. Western Electric Co.

(Employee) v. *(Employer)*
643 S.W.2d 10 (Mo. Ct. App. 1982)

IF A PLAINTIFF WILL SUFFER IRREPARABLE HARM, AN INJUNCTION MAY ISSUE

■ **INSTANT FACTS** Smith's (P) petition for protection from tobacco smoke in the workplace was dismissed for failure to state a claim upon which relief may be granted.

■ **BLACK LETTER RULE** Injunctive relief is available if irreparable harm is otherwise likely to result and the plaintiff has no adequate remedy at law.

■ **PROCEDURAL BASIS**

Appeal from an order dismissing a petition for failure to state a claim upon which relief can be granted.

■ **FACTS**

Smith (P) was a nonsmoker employed by Western Electric (D). He brought an action that alleged that he was suffering serious health effects as a result of his exposure to tobacco smoke in the workplace. Smith (P) claimed that Western Electric (D) tried to find a place for him to work where he would not be exposed to smoke, but was unable to do so. Smith also claimed that Western Electric (D) failed to implement its own policy on smoking in the workplace. Smith (P) alleged that Western Electric (D) finally told him he could either continue to work in the same location while wearing a respirator or go to work in the smoke-free computer room, which would have entailed a decrease in pay. Smith (P) chose the respirator, which proved ineffective.

Smith (P) alleged that he had exhausted all avenues of relief available through Western Electric (D), that he had no adequate remedy at law, and that he was suffering and would continue to suffer irreparable physical injuries and financial losses unless Western Electric (D) improved working conditions. The trial court dismissed the petition for failure to state a claim.

■ **ISSUE**

Did Smith's (P) petition state a valid claim for relief?

■ **DECISION AND RATIONALE**

(Dowd, J.) Yes. Injunctive relief is available if irreparable harm is otherwise likely to result and the plaintiff has no adequate remedy at law. Smith's (P) allegations set out a valid claim under Missouri law, which imposes a duty on an employer to provide employees with a safe workplace. Smith (P) further alleged that his health has deteriorated and will continue to deteriorate, which is an allegation of irreparable harm. While money damages may be compensation for a harm that is done, monetary compensation is inadequate for a harm that could have been prevented. An injunction is the appropriate remedy.

The Occupational Safety and Health Act does not preempt Smith's (P) claim. That law states specifically that it does not preempt common law claims for injuries or diseases arising out of employment. In addition, a state court may assert its jurisdiction over a safety or health issue for which there is no OSHA standard. Reversed.

Analysis:

The procedural posture of this case—an appeal from a dismissal for failure to state a claim—requires the court to consider only the allegations in Smith's (P) petition and to regard those statements as true. Western Electric's (D) response, if any, to the allegations is not considered. The appellate court also does not look at other factors that a court would take into account in making a decision after a trial, such as the credibility of witnesses. The likelihood of Smith's (P) ultimate success is not at issue here.

■ CASE VOCABULARY

INJUNCTION: A court order commanding or preventing an action. To get an injunction, the complainant must show that there is no plain, adequate, and complete remedy at law and that an irreparable injury will result unless the relief is granted.

OCCUPATIONAL SAFETY AND HEALTH ACT OF 1970 (OSHA): A federal statute that requires employers to (1) keep the workplace free from recognized hazards that cause or are likely to cause death or serious physical harm to employees, and (2) comply with standards promulgated by the Secretary of Labor.

PREEMPTION: The principle (derived from the Supremacy Clause) that a federal law can supersede or supplant any inconsistent state law or regulation.

Venegas v. Mitchell

(*Civil Rights Plaintiff*) v. (*Attorney*)
495 U.S. 82, 110 S.Ct. 1679 (1990)

CONTINGENT FEE CONTRACTS ARE ALLOWED IN CIVIL RIGHTS CASES

■ **INSTANT FACTS** Mitchell (P) agreed to represent Venegas (D) in a civil rights suit, and Venegas (D) agreed to pay a contingent fee.

■ **BLACK LETTER RULE** Contingent fee agreements are upheld in civil rights cases, even if the resulting fee is more than the attorney's fees awarded by the court.

■ **PROCEDURAL BASIS**

Appeal from an order of the Ninth Circuit Court of Appeals affirming an award of attorney's fees.

■ **FACTS**

Mitchell (P) agreed to represent Venegas (D) in a civil rights suit. The agreement provided for payment of a contingent fee to Mitchell (P) of 40% of the gross recovery from the suit. The contract further provided that Mitchell (P) could apply for court-awarded attorney's fees, and that any award from the court would be applied to offset the contingent fee. Venegas (D) obtained a judgment for $2.08 million and Mitchell (P) was awarded $75,000 in attorney's fees. Mitchell (P) and Venegas (D) signed a stipulation that allowed Mitchell (P) to withdraw as counsel on appeal. Mitchell (P) then asserted an attorney's lien of $406,000, representing his share of the forty-percent contingent fee. Venegas (D) claimed that the fee was excessive and that Mitchell (P) should be limited to the $75,000 awarded by the court. The district court refused to disallow the fee, finding it reasonable, and the court of appeals affirmed.

■ **ISSUE**

Is a contingent fee arrangement valid in a civil rights case?

■ **DECISION AND RATIONALE**

(White, J.) Yes. Contingent fee agreements are upheld in civil rights cases, even if the resulting fee is more than the attorney's fees awarded by the court. There is nothing in the civil rights acts or in their legislative history to indicate that private fee arrangements are prohibited. Several Supreme Court cases have implicitly recognized that private fee arrangements may co-exist with court-awarded fees. An award under the civil rights laws belongs to the plaintiff, not his or her attorney, and there is no reason to believe that the plaintiff may not assign part of that award. Depriving plaintiffs of the option to pay an attorney more than the court-awarded fees could make it more difficult to obtain competent counsel in civil rights cases. Both lower courts rejected Venegas's (D) claim that the contingent fee was unreasonable. The Court now has no reason to disturb that conclusion. Affirmed.

Analysis:

A frequent argument against contingent fees is that they can result in a windfall to an attorney who secures a very large recovery, such that the fee received is disproportionate to the work involved. The

---

counter-argument is that such windfalls are rare, and that the very large recovery can be attributed to the efforts of the attorney, who should be rewarded for his or her great skill. A contingent fee also carries an element of risk to it. No matter how solid a case may appear to be, a jury can reject a claim for an almost infinite variety of reasons, leaving both the plaintiff and his or her attorney with nothing.

■ CASE VOCABULARY

CONTINGENT FEE: A fee charged for a lawyer's services only if the lawsuit is successful or is favorably settled out of court.

LODESTAR: A reasonable amount of attorney's fees in a given case, usually calculated by multiplying a reasonable number of hours worked by the prevailing hourly rate in the community for similar work, and often considering such additional factors as the degree of skill and difficulty involved in the case, the degree of its urgency, its novelty, and the like.

CHAPTER THREE

Describing and Defining the Dispute

Gillispie v. Goodyear Service Stores

Instant Facts: Gillispie's (P) complaint alleged that the defendant trespassed, assaulted her, and caused her to be arrested, but the defendants' demurrer to her complaint was sustained.

Black Letter Rule: A complaint must contain a statement of the facts that constitute a cause of action.

United States v. Board of Harbor Commissioners

Instant Facts: The United States (P) filed a complaint alleging that the defendants discharged oil into a river; the defendants moved for a more definite statement.

Black Letter Rule: A complaint is sufficiently definite if the opposing party is fairly notified of the nature of the claim against it.

McCormick v. Kopmann

Instant Facts: McCormick's (P) complaint included an allegation that Kopmann (D) caused her husband's death and another that his death was due to his own intoxication.

Black Letter Rule: Factual allegations may be pleaded in the alternative, regardless of any inconsistencies.

Zuk v. Eastern Pennsylvania Psychiatric Institute of the Medical College of Pennsylvania

Instant Facts: Zuk's (P) copyright infringement action was dismissed, and the court sanctioned him and his attorney.

Black Letter Rule: Sanctions may be imposed against an attorney who fails to make a reasonable inquiry into the facts and law that govern a case.

Mitchell v. Archibald & Kendall, Inc.

Instant Facts: Mitchell (P) was injured during a robbery attempt while he was parked in a public street waiting to enter Archibald & Kendall's (D) premises.

Black Letter Rule: A motion to dismiss for failure to state a claim is decided on the basis of the facts pleaded in the complaint, not legal conclusions that may be alleged or drawn from the pleaded facts.

Tellabs, Inc. v. Makor Issues & Rights, Ltd.

Instant Facts: The plaintiff alleged a violation of the PSLRA by the defendant, and the defendant moved to dismiss for failure to state a claim.

Black Letter Rule: A complaint alleging securities fraud under the Private Securities Litigation Reform Act will survive a motion to dismiss only if a reasonable person would deem the inference of scienter cogent and at least as compelling as any opposing inference one could draw from the facts alleged.

Cash Energy, Inc. v. Weiner

Instant Facts: Cash Energy (P) filed a complaint alleging that officers of a corporation were liable for acts done by the corporation.

Black Letter Rule: A court may order that a complaint be amended to add greater specificity in order to promote substantial justice.

Swierkiewicz v. Sorema, N.A.

Instant Facts: Swierkiewicz's (P) employment discrimination complaint was dismissed for failure to allege facts sufficient to state a prima facie case.

Black Letter Rule: A prima facie case is an evidentiary standard for trial, not a rule of pleading.

Bell Atlantic Corp. v. Twombly

Instant Facts: Telephone and Internet subscribers sued their local telephone companies for allegedly entering into a conspiracy to create monopoly power in their respective markets in violation of § 1 of the Sherman Act.

Black Letter Rule: Federal Rule of Civil Procedure 8(a)(2) requires a "short and plain statement of the claim showing that the pleader is entitled to relief," in order to "give the defendant fair notice of what the . . . claim is and the grounds upon which it rests."

Shepard Claims Service, Inc. v. William Darrah & Associates

Instant Facts: Darrah's (D) attorney misinterpreted an agreement extending the time in which to answer a complaint and Shepard (P) moved for a default.

Black Letter Rule: A motion to set aside a default will be granted if the plaintiff will not be prejudiced, the defendant has a meritorious defense, and the defendant's conduct was not willful.

David v. Crompton & Knowles Corp.

Instant Facts: Crompton & Knowles (D) moved to amend its answer to change an allegation that it was without sufficient information to deny.

Black Letter Rule: An answer that a defendant is without knowledge sufficient to admit or deny an allegation in a complaint will be deemed an admission if the matter is something peculiarly within the control and knowledge of the defendant.

Wigglesworth v. Teamsters Local Union No. 592

Instant Facts: Wigglesworth (P) brought an action against Local 592 (D) for violations of the Labor Management Reporting Disclosures Act; Local 592 (D) counterclaimed for defamation and abuse of process.

Black Letter Rule: A counterclaim that would not rely on the same evidence as the claim in the plaintiff's complaint is a permissive counterclaim, and there must be an independent basis for federal jurisdiction over a permissive counterclaim.

David v. Crompton & Knowles Corp.

Instant Facts: Crompton & Knowles (D) moved to amend its answer to change an allegation that it was without sufficient information to a denial.

Black Letter Rule: Leave to amend a pleading will be denied if it would result in undue delay and prejudice to the other party.

Goodman v. Praxair, Inc.

Instant Facts: Goodman (P) sued a company that he believed was the successor to a lobbying company with which he had contracted, but he had actually sued the successor's parent company; the defendants moved to dismiss the complaint after Goodman (P) added the subsidiary, arguing that by then it was barred by the statute of limitations.

Black Letter Rule: Under Federal Rule of Procedure 15(c), an amendment that changes the party against whom a claim is asserted relates back to the date of the original pleading if (1) the claim in the amended complaint arose out of the same transaction that formed the basis of the claim in the original complaint, (2) the party to be brought in by the amendment received notice of the action such that it will not be prejudiced in maintaining a defense to the claim, and (3) it should have known that it would originally have been named a defendant were it not for a mistake concerning the identity of the proper party.

Gillispie v. Goodyear Service Stores

(Assault Victim) v. *(Alleged Assailant)*
258 N.C. 487, 128 S.E.2d 762 (1963)

A COMPLAINT CANNOT SET FORTH LEGAL CONCLUSIONS

■ **INSTANT FACTS** Gillispie's (P) complaint alleged that the defendant trespassed, assaulted her, and caused her to be arrested, but the defendants' demurrer to her complaint was sustained.

■ **BLACK LETTER RULE** A complaint must contain a statement of the facts that constitute a cause of action.

■ **PROCEDURAL BASIS**

Appeal from an order sustaining the defendant's demurrer.

■ **FACTS**

Gillispie (P) served a complaint on Goodyear Service Stores (D) and other defendants. Her complaint alleged that Goodyear (D) and the other defendants trespassed on Gillispie's (P) property, assaulted her, caused her to be seized and exhibited as a prisoner, and caused her to be confined in a public jail. Gillispie's (P) complaint also alleged that the defendants' actions were deliberate and malicious, and that as a result Gillispie (P) was damaged in the amount of $25,000. The court sustained the defendants' demurrer to Gillispie's (P) complaint but granted her leave to file an amended complaint.

■ **ISSUE**

Was Gillispie's (P) complaint legally sufficient?

■ **DECISION AND RATIONALE**

(Bobbitt, J.) No. A complaint must contain a statement of the facts that constitute a cause of action. Gillispie's (P) complaint stated legal conclusions, but did not set out the facts on which these conclusions were based. "Assault" and "trespass" are legal conclusions, or the results of certain facts. There is no factual basis to which the court could apply the law. Affirmed.

Analysis:

The modern trend is for courts to be lenient in reviewing pleadings, on the theory that the essential purpose of an initial pleading, such as a complaint, is to provide notice to the defendant that he or she is being sued and some idea of why. Even under such liberal pleading practices, Gillispie's (P) complaint probably would be deficient. There was no allegation as to when or where the acts complained of took place, and there was no way of knowing if her claims were time-barred, or even if her case is in the proper venue.

■ **CASE VOCABULARY**

AMENDED COMPLAINT: A complaint that modifies and replaces the original complaint by adding relevant matters that occurred before or at the time the action began. In some circumstances, a party must obtain the court's permission to amend its complaint.

DEMURRER: [from the French *demorer*, "to wait or stay."] A pleading stating that although the facts alleged in a complaint may be true, they are insufficient for the plaintiff to state a claim for relief and for the defendant to frame an answer. In most jurisdictions, such a pleading is now termed a motion to dismiss, but the demurrer is still used in a few states, including California, Nebraska, and Pennsylvania.

LEGAL CONCLUSION: A statement that expresses a legal duty or result but omits the facts creating or supporting the duty or result.

NOTICE PLEADING: A procedural system requiring that the pleader give only a short and plain statement of the claim showing that the pleader is entitled to relief, and not a complete detailing of all the facts.

SECUNDUM ALLEGATA ET PROBATA: [Latin, historical.] According to what is alleged and proved.

United States v. Board of Harbor Commissioners

(Environmental Law Enforcer) v. *(Oil Spillers)*
73 F.R.D. 460 (D. Del. 1977)

A COMPLAINT MUST GIVE THE DEFENDANT NOTICE OF THE CLAIM

■ **INSTANT FACTS** The United States (P) filed a complaint alleging that the defendants discharged oil into a river; the defendants moved for a more definite statement.

■ **BLACK LETTER RULE** A complaint is sufficiently definite if the opposing party is fairly notified of the nature of the claim against it.

■ PROCEDURAL BASIS

Decision on a motion for a more definite statement.

■ FACTS

The United States (P) filed a complaint against SICO (D) and NASCO (D) that alleged that the defendants, "or each of them," owned and operated facilities from which oil was discharged into the Delaware River from June 25 to November 23, 1973, "or took actions which caused such oil to be discharged." SICO (D) and NASCO (D) alleged that the complaint was deceptively vague because it did not specify which defendant was responsible for the discharge, how much oil was discharged, what the cost of removal was, and the actions that caused the discharge. SICO (D) and NASCO (D) moved for a more definite statement of the claims against them pursuant to Fed. R. Civ. P. 12(e).

■ ISSUE

Was the complaint deceptively vague?

■ DECISION AND RATIONALE

(Latchum, C.J.) No. A complaint is sufficiently definite if the opposing party is fairly notified of the nature of the claim. A motion for a more definite statement is granted if a pleading suffers from unintelligibility, rather than a want of detail. The allegations, together with the rest of the complaint, gave SICO (D) and NASCO (D) fair notice of the allegations against them. The additional information sought is more properly the subject of discovery. Motion denied.

Analysis:

The allegations against SICO (D) and NASCO (D) were sketchy, but it is important to note that the case is dealing only with a complaint, the initial document that starts a lawsuit. This is not the document upon which the case will be decided. Further details always remain to be fleshed out in the course of litigation. In addition, the court explained that allegations must be considered "together with the other averments in the complaint." In other words, one paragraph, read in isolation, could not determine the sufficiency of the complaint in what was probably a very complex action.

■ CASE VOCABULARY

DISCOVERY: The act or process of finding or learning something that was previously unknown; compulsory disclosure, at a party's request, of information that relates to the litigation; the facts or documents disclosed. The primary discovery devices are interrogatories, depositions, requests for admissions, and requests for production. Although discovery typically comes from parties, courts also allow limited discovery from nonparties.

McCormick v. Kopmann

(*Widow*) v. (*Truck Driver*)

23 Ill. App. 2d 189, 161 N.E.2d 720 (1959)

ALTERNATIVE FACTUAL CLAIMS ARE ALLOWED

I'LL BE ALRIGHT TO DRIVE... I JUST NEED A FEW MOMENTS TO COLLECT MYSELF.

■ **INSTANT FACTS** McCormick's (P) complaint included an allegation that Kopmann (D) caused her husband's death and another that his death was due to his own intoxication.

■ **BLACK LETTER RULE** Factual allegations may be pleaded in the alternative, regardless of any inconsistencies.

■ **PROCEDURAL BASIS**

Appeal from a judgment against Kopmann (D).

■ **FACTS**

McCormick's (P) husband was killed when his automobile collided with a truck operated by Kopmann (D). McCormick (P) brought suit against Kopmann (D), alleging that he negligently drove his truck across the center line of the highway and that McCormick's (P) husband was exercising due care. McCormick (P) also brought suit against Huls (D), the owner of the tavern where her husband drank beer before the accident. She alleged that Huls (D) sold her husband alcoholic beverages that made him intoxicated, and that his intoxication caused her husband to collide with Kopmann's (D) truck. Judgment was entered against Kopmann (D), but in favor of Huls (D). Kopmann appealed, arguing that McCormick's (P) complaint should have been dismissed because it contained inconsistent allegations. The allegation against Kopmann (D) stated that McCormick's (P) husband was free from contributory negligence, which allegation could not be reconciled with the allegation that he was intoxicated.

■ **ISSUE**

Can a plaintiff's complaint include inconsistent allegations?

■ **DECISION AND RATIONALE**

(Reynolds, J.) Yes. Factual allegations may be pleaded in the alternative, regardless of any inconsistencies. The evidence introduced at trial will determine the theory under which a plaintiff is entitled to recover. Each count of a complaint stands alone, and inconsistent statements in one count cannot be used to contradict the allegations in another count. Alternative pleading is not permitted, however, if the plaintiff knows which set of facts is true. Here, there is nothing that indicates that McCormick (P) knew which version of the facts was true. Affirmed.

Analysis:

Alternative pleading promotes judicial economy by having all of the claims that arise out of a particular incident heard at one time. McCormick (P) could have brought separate suits, but both cases would have required much of the same evidence, increasing the costs and burden of litigation. Trying both cases together could have worked to Kopmann's (D) benefit if he had succeeded in proving that Huls

(D) was to blame for the accident, since the contributory negligence of McCormick's (P) husband would have barred her recovery against Kopmann (D).

■ CASE VOCABULARY

ALTERNATIVE PLEADING: A form of pleading whereby the pleader alleges two or more independent claims or defenses that are not necessarily consistent with each other, such as alleging both intentional infliction of emotional distress and negligent infliction of emotional distress based on the same conduct.

DRAM–SHOP ACT: A statute allowing a plaintiff to recover damages from a commercial seller of alcoholic beverages for the plaintiff's injuries caused by a customer's intoxication.

WRONGFUL–DEATH ACTION: A lawsuit brought on behalf of a decedent's survivors for their damages resulting from a tortious injury that caused the decedent's death.

Zuk v. Eastern Pennsylvania Psychiatric Institute of the Medical College of Pennsylvania

(*Psychologist*) v. (*Medical College*)

103 F.3d 294 (3d Cir. 1996)

SANCTIONS MAY BE IMPOSED FOR FRIVOLOUS LITIGATION

■ **INSTANT FACTS** Zuk's (P) copyright infringement action was dismissed, and the court sanctioned him and his attorney.

■ **BLACK LETTER RULE** Sanctions may be imposed against an attorney who fails to make a reasonable inquiry into the facts and law that govern a case.

■ **PROCEDURAL BASIS**

Appeal from an order of the district court sanctioning Zuk (P) and his attorney upon dismissal of Zuk's (P) copyright infringement suit.

■ **FACTS**

Zuk (P) brought a copyright infringement action against the Eastern Pennsylvania Psychiatric Institute (EPPI) (D). He was represented by Lipman (P), who had never handled a copyright infringement case before. The suit alleged that EPPI (D) infringed Zuk's (P) copyright in certain films made by Zuk (P) while he was on the faculty of EPPI (D) by lending out copies of the films without Zuk's (P) permission. EPPI (D) moved to dismiss and notified Lipman (P) that it intended to move for sanction under Fed. R. Civ. P. 11(c)(1)(A), on the ground that Lipman (P) had failed to conduct a reasonable inquiry into the facts and the law. The court granted EPPI's (D) motion to dismiss, finding that Zuk (P) had no copyright in the films, that the copyright belonged to EPPI (D), that EPPI's (D) use was not an infringement, and that the statute of limitations had expired. The court later entered an order imposing sanctions on both Zuk (P) and Lipman (P), finding them jointly and severally liable to EPPI (D) for attorney's fees in the amount of $15,000. There was no finding of bad faith. Zuk (P) settled his liability for $6,250.

■ **ISSUE**

Was the imposition of sanctions against Lipman (P) proper?

■ **DECISION AND RATIONALE**

(Rosenn, J.) Yes. Sanctions may be imposed against an attorney who fails to make a reasonable inquiry into the facts and law that govern a case. The trial court's award of sanctions is governed by Fed. R. Civ. P. 11, which authorizes sanctions against the attorney and the party represented. Rule 11 of the Federal Rules of Civil Procedure authorizes the imposition of sanctions to deter misconduct, whether such conduct is willful or merely negligent. Other fee-shifting laws, such as the provisions of the Copyright Act, or 28 U.S.C. § 1927, authorize the imposition of fees against either the attorney or the party, but not both. The imposition of sanctions is left to the discretion of the court, so an award of sanctions will be reviewed for abuse of that discretion.

The trial court found that an adequate investigation into the facts of the case would have resolved the statute of limitations issue, and no lawsuit would have been filed. The court also found that a minimal amount of research into the copyright laws would have shown that Zuk's (P) claims were unwarranted. Lipman (P) could have presented his argument as a case of first impression, but did not do so. Lipman (P) and Zuk (P) made a claim for ownership of the films themselves, which is not so easily resolved. EPPI (D) contended that Lipman (P) and Zuk (P) made a faulty argument on the issue of ownership of the films, but the trial court did not address this argument.

In determining the type of sanctions imposed, the court should consider all of the possible options. Since the purpose of the sanctions is to deter, rather than to compensate the opposing party, options such as a fine paid into the court should be considered. Money sanctions are not forbidden, but they are not encouraged. The court also should look at the sanctioned party's ability to pay, the attorney's history of the sanctioned type of behavior, the other party's need for compensation, the degree of frivolousness, and the willfulness of the conduct. Remanded.

Analysis:

Sanctions cannot be imposed just for losing a case. Lipman (P) made one claim, regarding Zuk's (P) ownership of the films, which was found to be less clearly resolved than the copyright infringement claims. Although the district court found that Zuk (P) did not own the films, the ownership issue was not relied upon in imposing sanctions. Thus, one reasonable argument does not appear to be enough to avoid sanctions, if the rest of the case is frivolous.

■ CASE VOCABULARY

COPYRIGHT INFRINGEMENT: The act of violating any of a copyright owner's exclusive rights granted by the federal Copyright Act, 17 U.S.C.A. §§ 106, 602. A copyright owner has several exclusive rights in copyrighted works, including the rights (1) to reproduce the work; (2) to prepare derivative works based on the work; (3) to distribute copies of the work; (4) for certain kinds of works, to perform the work publicly; (5) for certain kinds of works, to display the work publicly; (6) for sound recordings, to perform the work publicly; and (7) to import into the United States copies acquired elsewhere.

DERIVATIVE WORK: A copyrightable creation that is based on a preexisting product, such as a translation, abridgment, musical arrangement, fictionalization, motion-picture version, or any other recast or adapted form, and that only the holder of the copyright on the original form can produce or give permission to another to produce.

FRIVOLOUS: Lacking a legal basis or legal merit; not serious; not reasonably purposeful, as in a frivolous claim.

FRIVOLOUS CLAIM: A claim that has no legal basis or merit, especially one brought for an unreasonable purpose such as harassment.

FRIVOLOUS SUIT: A lawsuit having no legal basis, often filed to harass or extort money from the defendant.

JOINT AND SEVERAL LIABILITY: Liability that may be apportioned either among two or more parties or to only one or a few select members of the group, at the adversary's discretion.

SANCTION: A penalty or coercive measure that results from failure to comply with a law, rule, or order, such as a sanction for discovery abuse.

Mitchell v. Archibald & Kendall, Inc.

(Truck Driver) v. *(Property Owner)*

573 F.2d 429 (7th Cir. 1978)

A COMPLAINT MUST SET OUT FACTS IN SUPPORT OF A CLAIM

■ **INSTANT FACTS** Mitchell (P) was injured during a robbery attempt while he was parked in a public street waiting to enter Archibald & Kendall's (D) premises.

■ **BLACK LETTER RULE** A motion to dismiss for failure to state a claim is decided on the basis of the facts pleaded in the complaint, not legal conclusions that may be alleged or drawn from the pleaded facts.

■ **PROCEDURAL BASIS**

Appeal from an order dismissing Mitchell's (P) complaint for failure to state a claim for which relief may be granted, pursuant to Fed. R. Civ. P. 12 (b)(6).

■ **FACTS**

Mitchell (P) drove a load of goods to Archibald & Kendall's (A & K) (D) premises in Chicago. When he arrived, the loading dock was occupied. A & K (D) employees told Mitchell (P) to stay in his truck and wait on a public street adjacent to A & K's (D) warehouse, until the truck could be unloaded. While Mitchell (P) was waiting in his truck, two men approached the truck and demanded money. Mitchell (P) refused to comply and one of the men shot him in the face with a shotgun. Mitchell (P) brought suit.

Mitchell's (P) complaint against A & K (D) alleged that A & K (D) knew or should have known of the high risk of a criminal attack and assault in the vicinity. A & K (D) employees allegedly knew of various criminal acts, including an armed robbery of a truck driver while parked on A & K's (D) premises. Mitchell (P) was not informed of the risks of a criminal assault while parked in the area. Mitchell's (P) complaint alleged that A & K (D) breached the duty to maintain its premises and adjacent areas in a reasonably safe condition, to provide a reasonably safe means of ingress and egress, to exercise reasonable care to protect Mitchell (P) from the criminal acts of others, and to provide a reasonably sufficient number of employees to afford reasonable protection to invitees. Mitchell's (P) complaint was dismissed for failure to state a claim for which relief may be granted pursuant to Fed. R. Civ. P. 12 (b)(6), because Illinois law does not impose a duty to keep invitees safe off the landowner's premises. Mitchell (P) argued on appeal that there were sufficient facts to support his claim, and he noted that "premises" does not have a fixed definition under Illinois law. Mitchell (P) also argued that the public street on which he was injured could be found to be a part of A & K's premises.

■ **ISSUE**

Was dismissal of Mitchell's (P) complaint proper?

■ **DECISION AND RATIONALE**

(Pell, J.) Yes. A motion to dismiss for failure to state a claim is decided on the basis of the facts pleaded in the complaint, not legal conclusions that may be inferred or drawn from the pleaded facts. The argument that the street area was a part of A & K's (D) premises sets out a new theory of liability not in the complaint. The complaint did not allege that the public street was a part of A & K's (D) premises,

---

and so the court must determine whether Illinois law imposes a duty to keep invitees safe while they are near a landowner's property. This is the issue as framed by the complaint. It is not the court's function to determine whether "premises" could include an adjacent public street, since the complaint alleged an injury occurring off the premises. Illinois law imposes a duty to keep invitees safe from third-party criminal activities, but only while the invitee is actually on the landowner's property. There is no duty to keep invitees safe while off the premises. Affirmed.

■ DISSENT

(Fairchild, C.J.) Mitchell (P) was injured after following A & K's (D) instructions regarding where to park and wait. These instructions increased the danger to Mitchell (P) and, under these circumstances, Illinois courts would find a duty to Mitchell (P).

Analysis:

This case demonstrates that a complaint must do more than provide notice to a defendant: it must set out legally sufficient facts to constitute a cause of action. The court seems to suggest here that Mitchell (P) could have avoided dismissal of his complaint merely by striking the words "adjacent areas." The question would then have been whether the facts of the case supported the allegation that Mitchell was on the premises when he was attacked, and whether the adjacent street could be considered part of A & K's (D) premises.

■ CASE VOCABULARY

ERIE DOCTRINE: The principle that a federal court exercising diversity jurisdiction over a case that does not involve a federal question must apply the substantive law of the state where the court sits.

INVITEE: A person who has an express or implied invitation to enter or use another's premises, such as a business visitor or a member of the public to whom the premises are held open. The occupier has a duty to inspect the premises and to warn the invitee of dangerous conditions.

WELL–PLEADED COMPLAINT: An original or initial pleading that sufficiently sets forth a claim for relief— by including the grounds for the court's jurisdiction, the basis for the relief claimed, and a demand for judgment—so that a defendant may draft an answer that is responsive to the issues presented. A well-pleaded complaint must raise a controlling issue of federal law for a federal court to have federal-question jurisdiction over the lawsuit.

Tellabs, Inc. v. Makor Issues & Rights, Ltd.

(Manufacturer) v. *(Stock Purchasers)*

551 U.S. 308, 127 S.Ct. 2499 (2007)

ALL INFERENCES MUST BE CONSIDERED IN DETERMINING WHETHER "SCIENTER" IS SHOWN

I did it! I'm finally higher than the standard for scienter under the PSLRA!

stus.com

■ **INSTANT FACTS** The plaintiff alleged a violation of the PSLRA by the defendant, and the defendant moved to dismiss for failure to state a claim.

■ **BLACK LETTER RULE** A complaint alleging securities fraud under the Private Securities Litigation Reform Act will survive a motion to dismiss only if a reasonable person would deem the inference of scienter cogent and at least as compelling as any opposing inference one could draw from the facts alleged.

■ **PROCEDURAL BASIS**

On certiorari to the United States Court of Appeals for the Seventh Circuit.

■ **FACTS**

Tellabs (D) manufactured fiber optic network equipment. Tellabs' (D) shareholders brought a class action suit against the company and its president and CEO under the Private Securities Litigation Reform Act (PSLRA), alleging that the defendants deceived the public about the true value of Tellabs (D) stock.

The PSLRA requires plaintiffs to state with particularity the circumstances constituting the alleged violation and the facts establishing scienter—i.e., the defendant's intention to deceive, manipulate, or defraud. In particular, the plaintiffs must state with particularity the facts giving rise to a strong inference that the defendant acted with the required state of mind. The defendants in this case brought a motion to dismiss under Fed. R. Civ. P. 12(b)(6), alleging that the plaintiffs did not meet this standard. The federal district court granted the motion, but the Seventh Circuit reversed, concluding that the shareholders had sufficiently alleged the company president/CEO's requisite state of mind.

■ **ISSUE**

Did the court apply the correct analysis in determining whether the plaintiffs alleged a violation of the PSLRA with sufficient particularity to withstand a motion to dismiss?

■ **DECISION AND RATIONALE**

(Ginsburg, J.) No. A complaint alleging securities fraud under the PSLRA will survive a motion to dismiss only if a reasonable person would deem the inference of scienter cogent and at least as compelling as any opposing inference one could draw from the facts alleged. In determining whether this standard is met, the court must consider more than whether the complaint alleges facts from which a reasonable person could infer that the defendant acted with the required intent. The court must engage in a comparative evaluation, considering not only the inferences urged by the plaintiff, but also any competing inferences rationally drawn from the alleged facts. The strength of an inference cannot be decided in a vacuum. The inquiry is inherently comparative: How likely is it that one conclusion, as compared to others, arises from the underlying facts? Because the lower courts did not have an opportunity to decide the case under this standard, the judgment below is vacated.

■ CONCURRENCE

(Scalia, J.) The majority's test is flawed. To establish the strong inference required by the PSLRA, the inference of scienter must be more plausible than any opposing inference, not just equal to it.

■ CONCURRENCE

(Alito, J.) I agree with Justice Scalia's approach, which aligns the pleading test under the PSLRA with the test that is used at the summary-judgment and judgment-as-a-matter-of-law stages.

■ DISSENT

(Stevens, J.) It is unlikely that Congress intended to adopt a standard that made it more difficult to commence a civil case than a criminal case, but the Court's approach here is more stringent than a probable-cause determination. Judges are accustomed to applying the probable-cause standard, and it should be applied in this context as well.

Analysis:

In the securities context, "scienter" is described as the mental state consisting of an intent to deceive, manipulate, or defraud. The PSLRA requires that, in alleging scienter under the PSLRA, the plaintiff must, "with respect to each act or omission alleged to violate this chapter, state with particularity facts giving rise to a strong inference that the defendant acted with the required state of mind." 15 U.S.C. § 78u–4(b)(2). The plaintiff cannot simply point to a false statement and declare that the defendant "must have known" that the statement was false, based upon his or her position within the company. But at the pleading stage, without the benefit of discovery, plaintiffs often do not have access to witnesses or documents that might prove the defendant's state of mind in making the false statement, so the standard is a difficult one to satisfy.

■ CASE VOCABULARY

INFERENCE: A conclusion reached by considering other facts and deducing a logical consequence from them.

PROBABLE CAUSE: A reasonable ground to suspect that a person has committed or is committing a crime or that a place contains specific items connected with a crime. Under the Fourth Amendment, probable cause—which amounts to more than a bare suspicion but less than evidence that would justify a conviction—must be shown before an arrest warrant or search warrant may be issued.

SCIENTER: A degree of knowledge that makes a person legally responsible for the consequences of his or her act or omission; the fact of an act's having been done knowingly, especially as a ground for civil damages or criminal punishment.

Cash Energy, Inc. v. Weiner

(Property Owner) v. *(Corporate Officer)*

768 F.Supp. 892 (D. Mass. 1991)

EVEN NON–FRAUD CLAIMS MAY REQUIRE GREATER SPECIFICITY

■ **INSTANT FACT** Cash Energy (P) filed a complaint alleging that officers of a corporation were liable for acts done by the corporation.

■ **BLACK LETTER RULE** A court may order that a complaint be amended to add greater specificity in order to promote substantial justice.

■ **PROCEDURAL BASIS**

Decision on a motion to dismiss for failure to state a claim on which relief may be granted.

■ **FACTS**

Cash Energy (P) owned property that it claimed was contaminated by the storage or transfer of chemical solvents on a site adjacent to Cash Energy's (P) property. Cash Energy (P) brought suit under the Comprehensive Environmental Response, Compensation, and Liability Act (CERCLA) to recover cleanup costs from the corporations. Cash Energy (P) also sued four officers of the corporation individually, claiming that the four "actively participated in and exercised control over the affairs" of one or more of the corporate defendants. Weiner (D) and the other corporate defendants moved for dismissal for failure to state a claim for which relief may be granted.

■ **ISSUE**

Does Cash Energy's (P) complaint state a valid claim against the corporate officers?

■ **DECISION AND RATIONALE**

(Keeton, J.) No. A court may order a complaint to be amended for greater specificity in order to promote substantial justice. Such an order is authorized by Fed. R. Civ. P. 8 (f), which states that pleadings shall be construed to do substantial justice. The federal rules require specificity of pleading in fraud cases, and courts have required specificity in analogous cases. In certain other non-fraud cases, many courts have developed a similar requirement for greater particularity of pleading. Such cases include forfeiture cases and antitrust cases, because of the drastic nature of the remedy sought. The rules of pleading are increasingly read to require a greater degree of specificity than in the past.

CERCLA cases, while not analogous to fraud, do involve a drastic remedy, and the potential costs of defending against a non-meritorious claim are substantial. It is a reasonable prediction that higher courts will extend the specificity of pleading requirement to CERCLA cases, so this court will require specific pleading in CERCLA cases unless there is a contrary indication in legislation or precedent. Cash Energy's (P) complaint will therefore be dismissed unless an amended complaint is filed that details the factual basis for the allegations against Weiner (D) and the other individual defendants.

Analysis:

Rule 8 (f), on which the court relies for making its ruling, could be read as a rule of construction to be followed by the courts, as opposed to instructions to the drafters of pleadings. Taken with the general

---

leniency of the pleading requirements in the Federal Rules of Civil Procedure, the rule reads like a direction to give a pleader the benefit of the doubt and allow a pleading to stand unless it clearly is inadequate. It could also be read as only giving a court discretion to make sure individual pleadings are adequate, but not the authority to make a blanket rule governing pleadings in certain types of cases.

■ **CASE VOCABULARY**

CERCLA: Comprehensive Environmental Response, Compensation, and Liability Act of 1980. This statute holds responsible parties liable for the cost of cleaning up hazardous-waste sites. 42 U.S.C.A. §§ 9601 *et seq.*

Swierkiewicz v. Sorema, N.A.

(Former Employee) v. *(Insurance Company)*

534 U.S. 506, 122 S.Ct. 992 (2002)

DISCRIMINATION COMPLAINTS DO NOT NEED TO STATE A PRIMA FACIE CASE

■ **INSTANT FACTS** Swierkiewicz's (P) employment discrimination complaint was dismissed for failure to allege facts sufficient to state a prima facie case.

■ **BLACK LETTER RULE** A prima facie case is an evidentiary standard for trial, not a rule of pleading.

■ **PROCEDURAL BASIS**

Appeal from an order of the Second Circuit Court of Appeals, affirming dismissal of Swierkiewicz's (P) complaint.

■ **FACTS**

Swierkiewicz (P), a fifty-three-year-old native of Hungary, brought an employment discrimination suit against Sorema (D). His complaint alleged that he was demoted and that his former position went to someone younger and less experienced than he was, but who was a French national (as was the CEO of Sorema (D)). Swierkiewicz (P) alleged that he was terminated after he outlined his grievances. Swierkiewicz's complaint also alleged that he was terminated on account of his national origin and age. The district court dismissed Swierkiewicz's (P) complaint because it did not adequately set out a prima facie case of employment discrimination. The Second Circuit Court of Appeals affirmed, holding that Swierkiewicz's (P) complaint should have alleged facts sufficient to constitute a prima facie case, as detailed in *McDonnell Douglas Corp. v. Green,* 411 U.S. 792 (1973): (1) membership in a protected class; (2) qualification for the job; (3) an adverse employment decision; and (4) circumstances that support an inference of discrimination. Swierkiewicz (P) appealed.

■ **ISSUE**

Was Swierkiewicz (P) required to allege a prima facie discrimination case in his complaint?

■ **DECISION AND RATIONALE**

(Thomas, J.) No. A prima facie case is an evidentiary standard for trial, not a rule of pleading. The Court has never stated that the requirements for proving a prima facie case of discrimination set a standard for pleading. A requirement of greater specificity in pleading discrimination cases conflicts with Fed. R. Civ. P. 8 (a)(2), which requires only "a short and plain statement of the claim showing that the pleader is entitled to relief." That statement must simply give fair notice of the plaintiff's claim and the grounds for that claim. Notice pleading relies on liberal discovery rules and summary judgment motions to define disputed facts and dispose of unmeritorious claims. Rule 8 (a) applies to all civil actions, with limited exceptions. Those exceptions have not been extended to other types of cases.

Other provisions of the federal rules are linked to the simplified pleading standard. The rules state that no technical forms of pleading are required and that all pleadings are to be construed so as to do substantial justice. A complaint should be dismissed only if it is clear that no relief could be granted under any set of facts that could be proved consistent with the allegations. Under a notice pleading system, such as that of the Federal Rules of Civil Procedure, it is inappropriate to require a prima facie case to appear in the pleadings. The *McDonnell Douglas* standard does not apply in all cases, and the exact case that must be established may vary in different situations. The precise requirements of a prima facie case are flexible, and the precise formulation of the case may not be developed until discovery has uncovered relevant facts and evidence. Reversed and remanded.

Analysis:

The Court's opinion seems to diminish the importance of pleading, making it just a preliminary to the actual case. The Federal Rules of Civil Procedure support this minimization, by cautioning against overly technical readings of pleadings. As pointed out by the Court, the sample complaints attached to the rules are notable for their brevity. The factual allegations in many of those sample complaints are limited to one or two sentences and avoid going into any sort of detail.

■ CASE VOCABULARY

EXPRESSIO UNIUS EST EXCLUSIO ALTERIUS: [Law, Latin.] A canon of construction holding that to express or include one thing implies the exclusion of the other, or of the alternative. For example, the rule that "each citizen is entitled to vote" implies that noncitizens are not entitled to vote.

PRIMA FACIE CASE: The establishment of a legally required rebuttable presumption; a party's production of enough evidence to allow the fact-trier to infer the fact at issue and rule in the party's favor.

PROTECTED CLASS: A group of people who benefit from protection by statute, such as Title VII of the Civil Rights Act of 1964, which prohibits discrimination based on race, sex, national origin, or religion.

Bell Atlantic Corp. v. Twombly

(*Local Telephone Companies*) v. (*Telephone and Internet Subscribers*)

550 U.S. 544, 127 S.Ct. 1955, 167 L.Ed.2d 929 (2007)

EVEN SHORT AND PLAIN STATEMENTS REQUIRE SUFFICIENT FACTUAL ALLEGATIONS TO SUPPORT THE CLAIM

■ **INSTANT FACTS** Telephone and Internet subscribers sued their local telephone companies for monopoly power in their respective markets in violation of § 1 of the Sherman Act.

■ **BLACK LETTER RULE** Federal Rule of Civil Procedure 8(a)(2) requires a "short and plain statement of the claim showing that the pleader is entitled to relief," in order to "give the defendant fair notice of what the ... claim is and the grounds upon which it rests."

■ **PROCEDURAL BASIS**

Supreme Court review of a Second Circuit decision reversing the federal district court's dismissal of the complaint.

■ **FACTS**

A group of telephone and Internet subscribers sued their local telephone companies, alleging that the companies were violating antitrust laws by agreeing not to compete with each other and to exclude other potential competitors in their market areas. The plaintiffs further alleged that as a result of this "parallel" conspiracy, each local company benefited from monopoly power in its own market. The district court dismissed the complaint on the pleadings, but the Second Circuit reversed, finding that the plaintiff's allegations satisfied the "short and plain statement" requirement of Rule 8 of the Federal Rules of Civil Procedure. The Supreme Court granted certiorari to address the proper standard for pleading an antitrust conspiracy through allegations of parallel conduct.

■ **ISSUE**

Did the plaintiffs properly allege an antitrust conspiracy claim under § 1 of the Sherman Act?

■ **DECISION AND RATIONALE**

(Souter, J.) No. Federal Rule of Civil Procedure 8(a)(2) requires a "short and plain statement of the claim showing that the pleader is entitled to relief," in order to "give the defendant fair notice of what the ... claim is and the grounds upon which it rests." *Conley v. Gibson*. But the plaintiffs have failed to satisfy that requirement in this case. Although *Conley* suggests that a complaint should not be dismissed unless it appears beyond doubt that the plaintiff can prove no set of facts that would support his entitlement to relief, a better standard is that once a claim has been stated adequately, it may be supported by showing any set of facts consistent with the allegations. *Conley*'s oft-quoted "no set of facts" language does not establish the minimum standard of adequate pleading to govern a complaint's survival.

Although detailed factual allegations are not required, a plaintiff must provide more than labels, conclusions, and a formulaic recitation of the elements of a cause of action. Factual allegations must raise the right to relief about the speculative level, if the allegations are taken as true. Applying these general standards to § 1 requires that the factual allegations must suggest more than parallel behavior; they must suggest that an actual agreement was made. We do not require heightened fact pleading of specifics, but only enough facts to state a claim to relief that is plausible on its face. Because the plaintiffs here have not nudged their claims across the line from conceivable to plausible, their complaint must be dismissed. Reversed.

■ **DISSENT**

(Stevens, J.) Does a judicial opinion that a charge is not plausible provide a legally acceptable reason for dismissing the complaint? I think not. As we previously held in *Swierkiewicz*, a notice pleading system does not contemplate a court's passing on the merits of a litigant's claim at the pleading stage. Although private antitrust litigation can be enormously expensive, and there is a risk that jurors may think that parallel conduct proves that the parties acted pursuant to an agreement when they in fact made similar, independent decisions, those concerns do not justify dismissal of an adequately pleaded complaint. The Court has announced a new rule today that does not even purport to respond to a congressional command. The transparent policy concern that drives this decision is the interest in protecting antitrust defendants, who are often some of the wealthiest companies in the economy.

Analysis:

The defendants moved the court to dismiss the plaintiffs' claims for failure to state a claim under Fed. R. Civ. P. 12(b)(6). Rule 12 (b) provides that "[e]very defense to a claim for relief in any pleading must be asserted in the responsive pleading if one is required." However, the Rule goes on, a party may assert the following defenses by motion, as in this case: "(1) lack of subject-matter jurisdiction; (2) lack of personal jurisdiction; (3) improper venue; (4) insufficient process; (5) insufficient service of process; (6) failure to state a claim upon which relief can be granted; and (7) failure to join a party under Rule 19." A motion asserting one of these defenses generally must be made before the defendant files its answer, unless no responsive pleading is required, in which case it can be raised at trial. "No defense or objection is waived by joining it with one or more other defenses or objections in a responsive pleading or in a motion."

■ **CASE VOCABULARY**

ANTITRUST LAW: The body of law designed to protect trade and commerce from restraints, monopolies, price-fixing, and price discrimination. The principal federal antitrust laws are the Sherman Act (15 U.S.C.A. §§ 1–7) and the Clayton Act (15 U.S.C.A. §§ 12–27).

CONSPIRACY: An agreement between two or more persons to commit an unlawful act that causes damage to a person or property.

MONOPOLY: Control or advantage obtained by one supplier or producer over the commercial market within a given region; the market condition existing when only one economic entity produces a particular product or provides a particular service. The term is now commonly applied also to situations that approach but do not strictly meet this definition.

SHERMAN ACT: A federal statute, passed in 1890, that prohibits direct or indirect interference with the freely competitive interstate production and distribution of goods. This Act was amended by the Clayton Act in 1914.

Shepard Claims Service, Inc. v. William Darrah & Associates

(*Claims Adjuster*) v. (*Insurance Brokerage*)

796 F.2d 190 (6th Cir. 1986)

DEFAULTS ARE LIBERALLY SET ASIDE

■ **INSTANT FACTS** Darrah's (D) attorney misinterpreted an agreement extending the time in which to answer a complaint and Shepard (P) moved for a default.

■ **BLACK LETTER RULE** A motion to set aside a default will be granted if the plaintiff will not be prejudiced, the defendant has a meritorious defense, and the defendant's conduct was not willful.

■ **PROCEDURAL BASIS**

Interlocutory appeal from an order denying Darrah's (D) motion to set aside a default.

■ **FACTS**

Shepard (P) brought an action against Darrah (D) for non-payment for services rendered. The secretary for Darrah's (D) attorney secured by telephone an extension of time to answer. A confirmatory letter was drafted and signed by the secretary with counsel's permission. The letter stated that the time to answer the complaint was "45 days from February 22, 1985." On April 10, no answer had been filed, so Shepard's (P) attorney requested entry of a default against Darrah (D). On April 19, Darrah (D) filed a notice of retention, and an answer was filed on April 26. In response to Shepard's (P) motion for a default, Darrah (D) submitted affidavits from its attorney and the attorney's secretary. The affidavits stated that their understanding of the extension of time was that it would run forty-five days in addition to the normal time in which to answer. The confirming letter was a "misstatement" of what the secretary and counsel believed the arrangement to be. Counsel stated that he did not review the confirming letter and did not know of the entry of default until April 29. The district court was unpersuaded and denied the motion to set aside the default. The court found that Darrah's (D) attorney engaged in culpable conduct when he allowed his secretary to make arrangements for the extension and then failed to review the confirmatory letter.

■ **ISSUE**

Did the district court abuse its discretion in refusing to set aside the default?

■ **DECISION AND RATIONALE**

(Lively, C.J.) Yes. A motion to set aside a default will be granted if the plaintiff will not be prejudiced, the defendant has a meritorious defense, and the defendant's conduct was not willful. The decision whether to set aside an entry of default is left to the discretion of the court, but there is still a strong preference for trials on the merits. Since no judgment was entered, this case is governed by Fed. R. Civ. P 55 (c), which allows the court to set aside a default for "good cause shown." If there is no showing of prejudice to the plaintiff and the defendant has shown a defense that is good at law, without regard to the likelihood of success, it is an abuse of discretion to refuse to set aside a default unless the default is due to the willful failure of the defendant to appear and plead. If a default judgment, as opposed to just

---

a default, has been entered, the judgment will be set aside only if the criteria set out in Fed. R. Civ. P. 60 (b) are met. However, this case is governed by Fed. R. Civ. P. 55 (c).

Analysis:

Refusal to set aside a default may mean a denial of justice based on an oversight. Many, if not most, deadlines to interpose an answer are missed due to clerical errors, misunderstanding about time limits, or simple mistake. Entry of a default serves to prevent a defendant from having his or her defense heard, even if the defense was such that the plaintiff actually had no claim. The standards for setting aside a default once a judgment has been entered are more stringent, because a plaintiff may have begun to take action in reliance on the judgment, and in recognition of the fact that the defendant probably had ample time to set aside the default and put in an answer before the judgment was entered.

■ CASE VOCABULARY

DEFAULT: To fail to appear or answer; to enter a default judgment against (a litigant).

DEFAULT JUDGMENT: A judgment entered against a defendant who has failed to plead or otherwise defend against the plaintiff's claim; a judgment entered as a penalty against a party who does not comply with an order, especially an order to comply with a discovery request. Also termed *judgment by default*.

David v. Crompton & Knowles Corp.

(Injured Worker) v. *(Manufacturer)*
58 F.R.D. 444 (E.D. Pa. 1973)

AVERMENTS OF INSUFFICIENT KNOWLEDGE ARE DEEMED ADMISSIONS IF THE PARTY KNEW THE FACTS

■ **INSTANT FACTS** Crompton & Knowles (D) moved to amend its answer to change an allegation that it was without sufficient information to deny.

■ **BLACK LETTER RULE** An answer that a defendant is without knowledge sufficient to admit or deny an allegation in a complaint will be deemed an admission if the matter is something peculiarly within the control and knowledge of the defendant.

■ **PROCEDURAL BASIS**

Decision on a motion for leave to amend an answer.

■ **FACTS**

Crompton & Knowles (D), the defendant in a products liability action, moved to amend its answer. The answer originally stated that Crompton & Knowles (D) was without sufficient information to admit or deny David's (P) allegation that it designed, manufactured, and sold the machine that injured him. Crompton & Knowles (D) moved to amend its answer to deny that it designed, sold, or manufactured the machine because it was manufactured by Hunter, a company that Crompton & Knowles (D) purchased after the machine was manufactured. Crompton & Knowles (D) claimed that it learned after answering the complaint that the contract by which it purchased Hunter did not make it liable for claims of this kind.

■ **ISSUE**

Is the averment of lack of knowledge an admission?

■ **DECISION AND RATIONALE**

(Huyett, J.) Yes. An answer that a defendant is without knowledge sufficient to admit or deny an allegation in a complaint will be deemed an admission if the matter is something peculiarly within the control and knowledge of the defendant. The rules provide that such an answer normally is a denial, but a party is not allowed to make a denial of sufficient information with impunity. The terms of Crompton & Knowles's (D) agreement to purchase Hunter is something uniquely within the control and knowledge of Crompton & Knowles (D), so the allegation will be deemed admitted.

Analysis:

The averment that a party is without sufficient information is a way for a defendant to remain within the bounds of truth when pleading, by not explicitly denying something without knowledge while at the same time avoiding potentially damaging admissions. The rule that an averment of insufficient knowledge acts as an admission if the party knew the truth or had control over the truthful information is almost a type of sanction on a party that fails to make a thorough investigation into its own fact base. While the rule may seem harsh, especially in complex lawsuits when there is limited time to investigate before making an answer, it does discourage parties from forcing their opponents to prove facts that they really knew all along.

■ **CASE VOCABULARY**

ADMISSION: Any statement or assertion made by a party to a case and offered against that party; an acknowledgment that facts are true.

DENIAL: A refusal or rejection, especially a court's refusal to grant a request presented in a motion or petition; a defendant's response controverting the facts that a plaintiff has alleged in a complaint; a repudiation.

Wigglesworth v. Teamsters Local Union No. 592

(*Union Member*) v. (*Union*)
68 F.R.D. 609 (E.D. Va. 1975)

PERMISSIVE COUNTERCLAIMS REQUIRE AN INDEPENDENT BASIS FOR FEDERAL JURISDICTION

■ **INSTANT FACTS** Wigglesworth (P) brought an action against Local 592 (D) for violations of the Labor Management Reporting Disclosures Act; Local 592 (D) counterclaimed for defamation and abuse of process.

■ **BLACK LETTER RULE** A counterclaim that would not rely on the same evidence as the claim in the plaintiff's complaint is a permissive counterclaim, and there must be an independent basis for federal jurisdiction over a permissive counterclaim.

■ **PROCEDURAL BASIS**

Decision on a motion to dismiss a counterclaim for lack of subject matter jurisdiction.

■ **FACTS**

Wigglesworth (P) brought a federal action against Local 592 (D) under the Labor Management Reporting Disclosures Act, 29 U.S.C. § 401 *et seq*. There was no diversity of citizenship between Wigglesworth (P) and Local 592 (D); jurisdiction was based solely on the existence of an issue of federal law. The complaint alleged that Wigglesworth (P) was denied his rights at union meetings in September and October 1974. Local 592 (D) counterclaimed for defamation and abuse of process, alleging that Wigglesworth (P) committed defamation by reason of remarks he made at a press conference when he filed his complaint. Local 592 (D) also alleged that Wigglesworth's (P) lawsuit constituted abuse of process.

■ **ISSUE**

Did the court have jurisdiction over Local 592's (D) counterclaim?

■ **DECISION AND RATIONALE**

(Warriner, J.) No. A counterclaim that would not rely on the same evidence as the claim in the plaintiff's complaint is a permissive counterclaim, and there must be an independent basis for federal jurisdiction over a permissive counterclaim. A compulsory counterclaim, by contrast, which arises out of the same transaction as the original complaint and would rely on the same evidence, may be asserted regardless of whether there is a basis for federal jurisdiction. Local 592's (D) counterclaim is permissive because it is based on occurrences that happened several months after the events in Wigglesworth's (P) complaint. Proof of the allegations in the counterclaim would not rely on the same evidence used to establish or refute the allegations in Wigglesworth's (P) complaint. Local 592's (D) claim that the motion to dismiss for lack of subject matter jurisdiction is untimely is without merit. Challenges to a federal court's subject matter jurisdiction may be brought at any time. Fed. R. Civ. P. 12 (h)(3). Motion to dismiss granted.

Analysis:

Subject matter jurisdiction cannot be waived or conferred by agreement of the parties. If a court does not have subject matter jurisdiction over an action, anything it does with regard to that action is a nullity.

Most courts will hear challenges to their jurisdiction at any stage of the proceedings, even if so much time has elapsed that a dismissed claim could not be brought in any other forum.

■ **CASE VOCABULARY**

ABUSE OF PROCESS: The improper and tortious use of a legitimately issued court process to obtain a result that is either unlawful or beyond the process's scope.

COMPULSORY COUNTERCLAIM: A counterclaim that must be asserted to be cognizable, usually because it relates to the opposing party's claim and arises out of the same subject matter. If a defendant fails to assert a compulsory counterclaim in the original action, that claim may not be brought in a later, separate action (with some exceptions).

PERMISSIVE COUNTERCLAIM: A counterclaim that need not be asserted to be cognizable, usually because it does not arise out of the same subject matter as the opposing party's claim or involves third parties over which the court does not have jurisdiction. Permissive counterclaims may be brought in a later, separate action.

SLAPP: A strategic lawsuit against public participation—that is, a suit brought by a developer, corporate executive, or elected official to stifle those who protest against some type of high-dollar initiative or who take an adverse position on a public-interest issue (often involving the environment). Also termed *SLAPP suit.*

SUBJECT MATTER JURISDICTION: Jurisdiction over the nature of the case and the type of relief sought; the extent to which a court can rule on the conduct of persons or the status of things.

David v. Crompton & Knowles Corp.

(Injured Worker) v. *(Manufacturer)*
58 F.R.D. 444 (E.D. Pa. 1973)

MOTIONS TO AMEND MAY BE DENIED IF PREJUDICE WOULD RESULT

■ **INSTANT FACTS** Crompton & Knowles (D) moved to amend its answer to change an allegation that it was without sufficient information to a denial.

■ **BLACK LETTER RULE** Leave to amend a pleading will be denied if it would result in undue delay and prejudice to the other party.

■ **PROCEDURAL BASIS**

Decision on a motion for leave to amend an answer.

■ **FACTS**

Crompton & Knowles (D), the defendant in a products liability action, moved to amend its answer. The answer originally stated that Crompton & Knowles (D) was without sufficient information to admit or deny David's (P) allegation that it designed, manufactured, and sold the machine that injured him. Crompton & Knowles (D) moved to amend its answer to deny that it designed, sold, or manufactured the machine because it was manufactured by Hunter, a company that Crompton & Knowles (D) had purchased after the machine was manufactured. Crompton & Knowles (D) claimed that it learned after answering that the contract by which it purchased Hunter did not make it liable for claims of this nature.

■ **ISSUE**

Is Crompton & Knowles (D) entitled to amend its answer?

■ **DECISION AND RATIONALE**

(Huyett, J.) No. Leave to amend a pleading will be denied if it would result in undue delay and prejudice to the other party. Crompton & Knowles (D) brought its motion to amend long after the statute of limitations had run, so that David (P) would be barred from bringing his claim against another party. Crompton & Knowles (D) knew the essential facts for a considerable amount of time before attempting to assert the defense. The long delay between the commencement of the action and the revelation that Crompton & Knowles (P) might not be legally responsible lulled David (P) into thinking that his action had been properly brought. David (P) has been prejudiced by the long delay. Motion to amend denied.

Analysis:

The claim that Crompton & Knowles (D) learned of a possible defense only after extensive discovery and the passage of much time strains credibility. If the answer were amended and if the defense were successful, David (P) would have no one against whom to bring his claim. The possibility that the late revelation is no accident is strong enough to merit the concomitant possibility of imposing liability on a party who bears no legal responsibility. The resulting injustice, if any, would spring from Crompton & Knowles's (D) own actions.

■ CASE VOCABULARY

PREJUDICE: Damage or detriment to one's legal rights or claims.

STATUTE OF LIMITATIONS: A law that bars claims after a specified period; specifically, a statute establishing a time limit for suing in a civil case, based on the date when the claim accrued (as when the injury occurred or was discovered). The purpose of such a statute is to require diligent prosecution of known claims, thereby providing finality and predictability in legal affairs and ensuring that claims will be resolved while evidence is reasonably available and fresh.

Goodman v. Praxair, Inc.

(Manufacturer) v. *(Successor to Lobbying Firm)*

494 F.3d 458 (4th Cir. 2007 en banc)

AN AMENDMENT TO ADD A PARENT–COMPANY DEFENDANT'S SUBSIDIARY AS A PARTY RELATES BACK TO THE ORIGINAL COMPLAINT

■ **INSTANT FACTS** Goodman (P) sued a company that he believed was the successor to a lobbying company with which he had contracted, but he had actually sued the successor's parent company; the defendants moved to dismiss the complaint after Goodman (P) added the subsidiary, arguing that by then it was barred by the statute of limitations.

■ **BLACK LETTER RULE** Under Federal Rule of Procedure 15(c), an amendment that changes the party against whom a claim is asserted relates back to the date of the original pleading if (1) the claim in the amended complaint arose out of the same transaction that formed the basis of the claim in the original complaint, (2) the party to be brought in by the amendment received notice of the action such that it will not be prejudiced in maintaining a defense to the claim, and (3) it should have known that it would originally have been named a defendant were it not for a mistake concerning the identity of the proper party.

■ **PROCEDURAL BASIS**

Federal appellate court review of a federal district court decision dismissing the plaintiff's complaint on statute of limitations grounds.

■ **FACTS**

Goodman (P) contracted with Tracer Research Corp. in 1998 to lobby the EPA for exemptions from costly regulatory requirements related to Goodman's (P) products. The EPA concluded that some of Goodman's (P) products were exempt, but not others. Praxair Services, Inc. (D), a wholly owned subsidiary of Praxair, Inc. (D), acquired Tracer in 2002. Based on Tracer's failure to achieve full exemption, Goodman (P) sued Praxair, Inc. (D) for breach of contract. Praxair, Inc. (D) removed the case to federal court and moved to dismiss, because *it* had not acquired Tracer and Tracer's contractual obligations; *its subsidiary*, Praxair, Services, Inc. (D), had. Goodman (P) then amended his complaint to add Praxair Services, Inc. (D) as a defendant, as well as a claim that Praxair, Inc. (D) was the alter ego of Praxair Services (D). Once again, the defendants moved to dismiss, and once again the federal court granted the motion.

The district court dismissed Goodman's (P) amended complaint under Fed. R. Civ. P. 12(b)(6) because the face of the amended complaint, which added Praxair Services, Inc. (D) as a defendant, showed that the three-year statute of limitations had run, and, per the court, the amendment adding Praxair Services (D) did not relate back to the date of the original pleading. The court held that Goodman's (P) mistake in suing the parent rather than its subsidiary was not the type of mistake that justified relation back under Rule 15(c). Goodman (P) appealed.

■ ISSUE

Was Goodman's (P) amended complaint adding a new defendant barred by the statute of limitations, even though the original complaint was timely filed?

■ DECISION AND RATIONALE

(Niemeyer, J.) No. Under Federal Rule of Procedure 15(c), an amendment that changes the party against whom a claim is asserted relates back to the date of the original pleading if (1) the claim in the amended complaint arose out of the same transaction that formed the basis of the claim in the original complaint, (2) the party to be brought in by the amendment received notice of the action such that it will not be prejudiced in maintaining a defense to the claim, and (3) it should have known that it would originally have been named a defendant were it not for a mistake concerning the identity of the proper party. Goodman (P) asserts that Rule 15, the relation-back rule, should apply to save his pleading from the bar of the statute of limitations, but the defendants argue that the Rule does not apply when one defendant is *substituted* for another. We discern no policy that would be advanced by the application of the defendants' narrow view. Rule 15 implements the notions that a plaintiff may amend his pleadings freely for whatever reason, and that amendments should be freely allowed. Praxair Services (D) knew that it was the successor to Tracer's contractual liability, and therefore it should have known, within the limitations period, that it was the proper party to Goodman's (P) suit. Praxair Services (D) has conceded that it suffered no prejudice to its defense of Goodman's claim, so we conclude that the requirements for relation back under Rule 15 have been met.

In addition, in order to dismiss a case under Federal Rule of Civil Procedure 12(b)(6) based on the existence of an affirmative defense such as the statute of limitations, all facts necessary to the defense must clearly appear on the face of the complaint. Under Maryland law, which applies here, a breach of contract claim must be brought within three years of the time the claim accrues. The complaint in this case alleges neither a date when the contract was breached nor a date when Goodman (P) may have discovered the breach, so the complaint simply could not be dismissed under Rule 12(b)(6) on statute of limitations grounds. Since it is still possible, however, that the court may later find that the claim accrued more than three years before the amended complaint was filed, it was necessary to address the Rule 15(c) arguments. Reversed and remanded.

■ CONCURRENCE

(Gregory, J.) The majority's decision will result in more lawsuits filed against incorrect defendants, and these defendants will unjustifiably bear the costs associated with defending against lawsuits until the proper plaintiffs are found. Today's decision will unfairly allow plaintiffs to file suit against "placeholder defendants" while continuing to search for the proper party to sue.

Analysis:

The third condition imposed by Rule 15(c) is that the defendant sought to be added "knew or should have known that, but for a mistake concerning the identity of the proper party, the action would have been brought against the party." The definition of "mistake" has been the source of conflict among the courts, as it was between the parties here. Some courts hold that a mistake occurs whenever a party that may be liable was omitted. These courts take the position that the Rule covers cases in which the plaintiff may have made a mistake in selecting the original defendants, as well as cases in which a party is misnamed or misdescribed. Other courts have rejected this approach, holding that the plaintiff must in fact have been mistaken about the identity of the correct party. Under that approach, an amendment will not relate back if the plaintiff made no mistake about the defendant's identity, but simply chose the wrong party to sue. These cases reason that, in the absence of a true mistake by the plaintiff, the new defendant may assume that he or she was not originally joined for tactical reasons, or for lack of proof.

■ CASE VOCABULARY

ALTER EGO: A corporation used by an individual in conducting personal business, the result being that a court may impose liability on the individual by piercing the corporate veil when fraud has been perpetrated on someone dealing with the corporation.

EN BANC: [Law, French: "on the bench."] With all judges present and participating; in full court, as in "an en banc rehearing," or "the court heard the case en banc."

RELATION BACK: The doctrine that an act done at a later time is, under certain circumstances, treated as though it occurred at an earlier time. In federal civil procedure, an amended pleading may relate back, for purposes of the statute of limitations, to the time when the original pleading was filed.

CHAPTER FOUR

Establishing the Structure and Size of the Dispute

Southern Methodist University Association of Women Law Students v. Wynne and Jaffe

Instant Facts: Lawyers A, B, C, and D sought to remain anonymous in their suit against several law firms for sex discrimination.

Black Letter Rule: A plaintiff may use a fictitious name only when the litigation involves matters of a sensitive and highly personal nature.

Kedra v. City of Philadelphia

Instant Facts: Kedra (P) and her children brought suit against the City of Philadelphia (D) for acts of police brutality that occurred over a span of one and one-half years.

Black Letter Rule: Joinder of reasonably related claims for relief by or against different parties is allowed.

Insolia v. Philip Morris, Inc.

Instant Facts: Insolia (P) and two others sued Philip Morris (D) for health problems allegedly caused by smoking, and Philip Morris (D) sought to sever their claims.

Black Letter Rule: Joinder of parties will not be allowed if each party has a highly individualized claim.

Janney Montgomery Scott, Inc. v. Shepard Niles, Inc.

Instant Facts: Janney Montgomery Scott (P) brought an action against Shepard Niles (D) for breach of contract, and Shepard Niles (D) claimed that its parent company was required to be joined as a party.

Black Letter Rule: A party is a necessary party if complete relief could not be granted without the absent party's presence, or if the relief requested would prejudice the absent party.

Clark v. Associates Commercial Corp.

Instant Facts: Clark (P) sued Associates Commercial Corp. (D) for injuries arising out of the repossession of a tractor, and Associates (D) filed a third-party complaint against the parties hired to do the repossession.

Black Letter Rule: A third-party complaint may be brought against a party who may be liable for all or part of the original plaintiff's claim against the third-party plaintiff.

State Farm Fire & Casualty Co. v. Tashire

Instant Facts: State Farm (P) insured a truck driver who was involved in an accident with a bus, deposited the limits of its coverage, and brought an interpleader action.

Black Letter Rule: The scope of an interpleader action is limited to claims that relate to the ownership of the property deposited with the court.

Natural Resources Defense Council, Inc. v. United States Nuclear Regulatory Commission

Instant Facts: The American Mining Congress (Intervenor ("I")) and Kerr–McGee Nuclear Corp. (I) sought to intervene in a suit challenging the procedures for issuing licenses to operate uranium mines.

Black Letter Rule: A party may intervene in an action if it has a significant protectable interest that would, as a practical matter, be impaired by non-participation in the litigation and the parties to the suit would not adequately represent that interest.

Hansberry v. Lee

Instant Facts: Hansberry (D) claimed that a racially restrictive covenant never became effective, but the trial court found that Hansberry (D) was bound by a prior decision upholding the validity of that covenant.

Black Letter Rule: The judgment in a class or representative suit binds only members of the class and those whose interests were represented by the class.

Walters v. Reno

Instant Facts: Walters (P) brought suit challenging procedures used by the Immigration and Naturalization Service (D), and the INS (D) objected to certification of a class action.

Black Letter Rule: Class certification requires a showing of questions of law or fact that are common to all class members and that the claims of the class representatives are adequately representative of the class as a whole.

Castano v. The American Tobacco Co.

Instant Facts: Tobacco users brought a class action against various tobacco companies for the injury of nicotine addiction, and the district court certified some issues for class treatment; the defendants appealed.

Black Letter Rule: A district court must conduct a rigorous analysis of the Rule 23 prerequisites before certifying a class.

Southern Methodist University Association of Women Law Students v. Wynne and Jaffe

(*Law Students*) v. (*Law Firm*)
599 F.2d 707 (5th Cir. 1979)

PLAINTIFFS MAY REMAIN ANONYMOUS ONLY IN SPECIAL CIRCUMSTANCES

■ **INSTANT FACTS** Lawyers A, B, C, and D sought to remain anonymous in their suit against several law firms for sex discrimination.

■ **BLACK LETTER RULE** A plaintiff may use a fictitious name only when the litigation involves matters of a sensitive and highly personal nature.

■ **PROCEDURAL BASIS**

Appeal from pretrial orders of the district court

■ **FACTS**

The Southern Methodist University Association of Women Law Students (P) and Lawyers A, B, C, and D (P) brought suit against Wynne and Jaffe (D) for sex discrimination in hiring associates and summer law clerks. Wynne and Jaffe (D) served interrogatories that asked for the true identities of Lawyers A, B, C, and D (P). Lawyers A, B, C, and D (P) objected and asked for permission to remain anonymous. Lawyers A, B, C, and D (P) asked that they be allowed to disclose their identities only to Wynne and Jaffe's (D) attorney. They argued that disclosure of their identities would leave them vulnerable to retaliation from their employers, prospective employers, and the organized bar.

■ **ISSUE**

May Lawyers A, B, C, and D (P) remain anonymous?

■ **DECISION AND RATIONALE**

(Ainsworth, J.) No. A plaintiff will be allowed to use a fictitious name only when the litigation involves matters of a sensitive and highly personal nature. No rule or statute provides for anonymous plaintiffs; in fact, Fed. R. Civ. P. 10(a) states that the complaint must include the names of all parties in the title of the action. When plaintiffs have been allowed to use fictitious names, the lawsuit has involved matters of a highly personal and sensitive nature, such as birth control, homosexuality, welfare benefits for abandoned families, or children born out of wedlock. Those suits also have involved violations of laws or regulations or a desire to engage in proscribed activities. Plaintiffs in those suits were required to divulge personal information of great intimacy. Lawyers A, B, C, and D (P) do not need to reveal information of a personal nature and they have expressed no desire to engage in proscribed activities. They have alleged that their reputations will suffer as a result of their participation in this litigation, but their harm to reputation is no greater than that suffered by any other plaintiff in a sex discrimination action. Wynne and Jaffe (D) face damage to their reputations, as they stand accused of serious violations of federal law. Fairness dictates that Lawyers A, B, C, and D (P) be required to disclose their names as well. Affirmed.

Analysis:

Although all parties here could suffer some damage to their reputations solely by virtue of being named as a party, the court does not consider whether the damage to reputation is comparable. Law firms traditionally have been male-dominated bastions and, although the situation is changing, change has been slow. The public perception of the bar and law firms remains that both are largely male institutions. Allegations of sex discrimination could be regarded as a lawsuit over "business as usual" hiring practices. In such a situation, the damage to reputation of a plaintiff and a defendant cannot be compared.

■ CASE VOCABULARY

REPUTATION: The esteem in which a person is held by others.

SEX DISCRIMINATION: Discrimination based on gender, especially against women. The Supreme Court has established an intermediate-scrutiny standard of review for gender-based classifications, which must serve an important governmental interest and be substantially related to the achievement of that objective.

Kedra v. City of Philadelphia

(Police Misconduct Victim) v. *(Municipal Authority)*

454 F.Supp. 652 (E.D. Pa. 1978)

REASONABLY RELATED CLAIMS MAY BE JOINED

■ **INSTANT FACTS** Kedra (P) and her children brought suit against the City of Philadelphia (D) for acts of police brutality that occurred over a span of one and one-half years.

■ **BLACK LETTER RULE** Joinder of reasonably related claims for relief by or against different parties is allowed.

■ **PROCEDURAL BASIS**

Decision on a motion to sever actions.

■ **FACTS**

Kedra (P) and her children sued the City of Philadelphia (D) for acts of police brutality and civil rights violations. The actions complained of took place at various times over one and one-half years and did not all happen to the same parties. The City of Philadelphia (D) alleged that joinder was improper.

■ **ISSUE**

Was joinder of the several claims occurring over a one-and-one-half-year period improper?

■ **DECISION AND RATIONALE**

(Luongo, J.) No. Joinder of reasonably related claims for relief by or against different parties is allowed. The events here extended over a lengthy period of time, but they are reasonably related to one another as part of a systematic deprivation of rights. The extended time span does not attenuate the factual relationship between the events. The question of prejudice remains, however, particularly with regard to an incident that involved different actors. That issue will be considered after discovery has been conducted.

Analysis:

Apart from the issue of economy, it is very much to Kedra's (P) advantage to have all of the claims brought at once. A pattern of conduct, rather than one or two isolated incidents, is more likely to result in a jury's finding of liability. In other words, the isolated incidents may seem less severe than a continued course of acts. For the defendants, however, joinder creates a risk that the jury will confuse the acts of one with other, more culpable, defendants, thus creating or inflating liability by association.

■ **CASE VOCABULARY**

JOINDER: The uniting of parties or claims in a single lawsuit.

PERMISSIVE JOINDER: The optional joinder of parties if (1) their claims or the claims asserted by or against them are asserted jointly, severally, or in respect of the same transaction or occurrence, and (2) any legal or factual questions common to all of them will arise.

SEVERANCE: The separation of claims, by the court, of multiple parties either to permit separate actions on each claim or to allow certain interlocutory orders to become final.

Insolia v. Philip Morris, Inc.

(Ex–Smoker) v. *(Tobacco Company)*
186 F.R.D. 547 (E.D. Wis. 1999)

UNRELATED CLAIMS CANNOT BE JOINED

■ **INSTANT FACTS** Insolia (P) and two others sued Philip Morris (D) for health problems allegedly caused by smoking, and Philip Morris (D) sought to sever their claims.

■ **BLACK LETTER RULE** Joinder of parties will not be allowed if each party has a highly individualized claim.

■ **PROCEDURAL BASIS**

Decision on a motion to sever claims.

■ **FACTS**

Insolia (P), Mays (P), and Lovejoy (P) brought suit against Philip Morris (D) and other cigarette manufacturers. The plaintiffs claimed that each of them had been diagnosed with lung cancer, and that the cancer had been caused by cigarette smoking. Insolia (P) began smoking in 1934 and quit in 1974. Mays (P) and Lovejoy (P) began smoking in 1953 and quit around 1995. All plaintiffs alleged that Philip Morris (D) and the other defendants worked together to suppress scientific evidence that showed that smoking is harmful and addictive. This alleged conspiracy allegedly began in 1958, with the founding of the Tobacco Institute, and continued for many years after that date.

■ **ISSUE**

Should the claims of Insolia (P) and the other plaintiffs be severed?

■ **DECISION AND RATIONALE**

(Crabb, J.) Yes. Joinder of parties is not allowed if each party has a highly individualized claim. The only common thread to these three claims is the allegation of an industry-wide conspiracy to suppress the truth. The misinformation reached the three plaintiffs in different ways and at different times. Insolia (P) began smoking over twenty years before the conspiracy allegedly began. Mays (P) and Lovejoy (P) started smoking almost twenty years after Insolia (P) and quit over twenty years later. The plaintiffs smoked different brands and quit smoking under different circumstances. The cause of each plaintiff's cancer may have been different, and there is doubt as to whether Lovejoy (P) ever had cancer. Thus, many of the facts needed to prove Mays' (P) and Lovejoy's (D) claims would b different from the evidence needed to prove Insolia's (P) claims. It is unlikely that the jury would be able to keep the various claims straight. Judicial economy is not served when a jury is subjected to a welter of evidence relevant to some parties, but not to another. The trial plan proposed by the plaintiffs would only compound the difficulties. Motion to sever granted.

Analysis:

The purpose of joinder is to promote efficiency and judicial economy. The disadvantage of joinder is that, except for the absolute simplest of lawsuits, the potential for jury confusion and wasted resources

---

is always present. The risk increases as cases become more complex and as parties are added. A strict view of the desirability of economy must be tempered by the interests of the parties in keeping the issues clear, to ensure a fair trial.

■ CASE VOCABULARY

CIVIL CONSPIRACY: An agreement between two or more persons to commit an unlawful act that causes damage to a person or property.

Janney Montgomery Scott, Inc. v. Shepard Niles, Inc.

(*Investment Banker*) v. (*New York Corporation*)

11 F.3d 399 (3d Cir. 1993)

NOT ALL RELATED BUSINESS ENTITIES ARE NECESSARY PARTIES

■ **INSTANT FACTS** Janney Montgomery Scott (P) brought an action against Shepard Niles (D) for breach of contract, and Shepard Niles (D) claimed that its parent company was required to be joined as a party.

■ **BLACK LETTER RULE** A party is a necessary party if complete relief could not be granted without the absent party's presence, or if the relief requested would prejudice the absent party.

■ PROCEDURAL BASIS

Appeal from an order for judgment on the pleadings for failure to join a necessary party.

■ FACTS

Janney Montgomery Scott (P), a Pennsylvania corporation, agreed to provide financial services to Underwood, a Pennsylvania corporation, and its wholly owned subsidiary Shepard Niles (D), a New York corporation. After advising Shepard (D) and Underwood on a transaction, Janney (P) sued Shepard (D) in federal district court, alleging that Janney (P) was not paid for services rendered. Jurisdiction was based on diversity of citizenship. Shepard (D) brought a motion for judgment on the pleadings, on the ground that Janney's (P) suit did not include Underwood as a party (joinder of Underwood would have destroyed diversity). The district court granted the motion.

■ ISSUE

Was Underwood a necessary party?

■ DECISION AND RATIONALE

(Hutchinson, J.) No. A party is a necessary party only if complete relief could not be granted without the absent party's presence, or if the relief requested would prejudice the absent party. The question of complete relief is determined by looking at the underlying substantive law. Under Pennsylvania law, complete relief may be granted in a breach of contract action if only one co-obligor is named as a party. The liability of co-obligors may be joint and several, depending upon the contract, and it appears that the contract here calls for joint and several liability. Complete relief may therefore be granted without all of the co-obligors being made parties to the suit.

In order to constitute impairment or impediment of a party's interest, there must be a showing of a direct impact on a non-party's rights. The mere possibility that a federal adjudication could be persuasive authority in a state court lawsuit is not enough to show an impact. If the federal litigation would have a preclusive or collateral estoppel effect on a subsequent suit, joinder of the party would be compulsory. There must, however, be a showing that such an effect is reasonably likely, not just possible. The rights of an absent joint obligor are not subject to preclusion.

In this case, there is no risk of inconsistent adjudication. The outcome of the federal suit will be binding only on Janney (P) and Shepard (D). There is a possibility that Shepard (D) could be liable for the entire

---

claim of Janney (P), and that Underwood could escape liability altogether. This liability would not amount to a double recovery. Janney (P) would not be able to claim the same amounts from Underwood and Shepard (D). Reversed.

Analysis:

It is important to the court's holding that Underwood is not automatically liable for Shepard's (D) debt. The excerpt does not say so explicitly, but it is clear that Underwood's status as the sole owner of Shepard (D) does not necessarily make it a guarantor of Shepard's (D) obligations. If Underwood were a guarantor, the result here probably would have been different. There would have been no question of a guarantor's liability once the underlying obligation was established.

■ CASE VOCABULARY

COLLATERAL ESTOPPEL: An affirmative defense barring a party from relitigating an issue determined against that party in an earlier action, even if the second action differs significantly from the first one.

DIVERSITY JURISDICTION: A federal court's exercise of authority over a case involving parties from different states and an amount in controversy greater than a statutory maximum (now $75,000).

JUDGMENT ON THE PLEADINGS: A judgment based solely on the allegations and information contained in the pleadings, and not on any outside matters.

RES JUDICATA: [Latin, "a thing adjudicated."] An issue that has been definitively settled by judicial decision; an affirmative defense barring the same parties from litigating a second lawsuit on the same claim, or any other claim arising from the same transaction or series of transactions and that could have been—but was not—raised in the first suit. The three essential elements are (1) an earlier decision on the issue, (2) a final judgment on the merits, and (3) the involvement of the same parties, or parties in privity with the original parties.

Clark v. Associates Commercial Corp.

(Tractor Owner) v. *(Secured Creditor)*
149 F.R.D. 629 (D. Kan. 1993)

DEFENDANTS CAN SUE OTHERS WITH POTENTIAL LIABILITY

■ **INSTANT FACTS** Clark (P) sued Associates Commercial Corp. (D) for injuries arising out of the repossession of a tractor, and Associates (D) filed a third-party complaint against the parties hired to do the repossession.

■ **BLACK LETTER RULE** A third-party complaint may be brought against a party who may be liable for all or part of the original plaintiff's claim against the third-party plaintiff.

■ **PROCEDURAL BASIS**
Decision on a motion to dismiss a third-party complaint.

■ **FACTS**
Clark (P) brought an action against Associates Commercial (D) for personal injuries and property damage sustained when Associates (D) repossessed a tractor that was the collateral for a loan. Associates (D) filed a third-party complaint seeking indemnity from Howard (D), its employee, and two others hired by Howard (D) to assist in the repossession. Howard (D) and the other third-party defendants moved to dismiss the third-party complaint, claiming that Associates (D) had no valid claim for relief against them under Kansas law. Clark (P) also objected to the third-party complaint on the ground that Howard (D) and the other third-party defendants owed no duty under the contract between Clark (P) and Associates (P). In the alternative, Clark (P) asked that the suit between Associates (D) and Howard (D) be heard in a separate trial.

■ **ISSUE**
Could Associates (D) file a third-party complaint against Howard (D)?

■ **DECISION AND RATIONALE**
(Belot, J.) Yes. A third-party complaint may be brought against a party who may be liable for all or part of the original plaintiff's claim against the third-party plaintiff. It does not matter that the third-party defendant has no liability to the original plaintiff. The question is whether the third-party defendant has some liability to the third-party plaintiff. The decision whether to allow a third-party complaint rests with the discretion of the trial court. In exercising that discretion, the court should be mindful that the purpose of the rule allowing third-party complaints to adjudicate the rights of all the parties in one proceeding and prevent multiple lawsuits.

Associates (D) seeks indemnity from Howard (D) on an agency theory. This theory is viable under Kansas law. And Associates (D) may bring its third-party complaint even though Howard (D) had no duty to Clark (P). The claim against Howard (D) may be different from the claim Clark (P) has against Associates (D). The third-party claim, although derivative of the original complaint, does not have to be the type of claim that is established automatically by virtue of the success of the plaintiff's claim against the third-party plaintiff. The criterion under the rules requires that the third-party defendant "is or may be" liable. The supposed inconsistency in claiming indemnity while denying the existence of an agency relationship is the type of alternative pleading permitted by the rules. There is no merit to the argument that the multiple issues involved will prove confusing. Motion to dismiss denied.

Analysis:

In theory, it should not matter to a plaintiff that a third-party defendant is brought in, since it does nothing to the legalities of the claims against the original defendant. As a practical matter, however, the concern of many plaintiffs is that the addition of a party not necessarily liable to the plaintiff will take the focus away from the original claims. The third-party complaint is like a "lawsuit within a lawsuit," and third-party litigants may raise defenses and arguments against one another, just as in any other litigation. This "finger pointing" between the third-parties can distract the jury from the underlying claim against the original defendant.

■ CASE VOCABULARY

AGENCY: A fiduciary relationship created by express or implied contract or by law, in which one party (the *agent*) may act on behalf of another party (the *principal*) and bind that other party by words or actions.

ALTERNATIVE PLEADING: A form of pleading whereby the pleader alleges two or more independent claims or defenses that are not necessarily consistent with each other, such as alleging both intentional infliction of emotional distress and negligent infliction of emotional distress based on the same conduct.

INDEMNITY: 1. A duty to make good any loss, damage, or liability incurred by another. 2. The right of an injured party to claim reimbursement for its loss, damage, or liability from a person who has such a duty. 3. Reimbursement or compensation for loss, damage, or liability in tort; especially, the right of a party who is secondarily liable to recover from the party who is primarily liable for reimbursement of expenditures paid to a third party for injuries resulting form a violation of a common-law duty.

RESPONDEAT SUPERIOR: [Law, Latin, "let the superior make answer."] The doctrine holding an employer or principal liable for the employee's or agent's wrongful acts committed within the scope of the employment or agency.

State Farm Fire & Casualty Co. v. Tashire

(*Insurance Company*) v. (*Accident Victim*)

386 U.S. 523, 87 S.Ct. 1199 (1967)

CLAIMS AGAINST THE SAME PROPERTY MAY BE INTERPLEADED

■ **INSTANT FACTS** State Farm (P) insured a truck driver who was involved in an accident with a bus, deposited the limits of its coverage, and brought an interpleader action.

■ **BLACK LETTER RULE** The scope of an interpleader action is limited to claims that relate to the ownership of the property deposited with the court.

■ **PROCEDURAL BASIS**

Appeal from an order of the Ninth Circuit Court of Appeals dissolving an injunction and dismissing an action.

■ **FACTS**

Tashire (D) and others were injured in a collision place in northern California between a Greyhound bus and a truck. The truck was driven by Clark (D), who had an insurance policy issued by State Farm (P). Four of the injured passengers brought suit against several defendants, including Clark (D). State Farm (P) brought an interpleader action in federal district court in Oregon against Clark (D), the other defendants in the injury suit, the plaintiffs in the injury suit, and the remaining potential plaintiffs. State Farm (P) deposited $20,000, the limit of its coverage of Clark (D), in court as required by the interpleader statute. The complaint in the interpleader action asked the court to order that all claims against Clark (D) be brought in the single interpleader proceeding and that State Farm (P) be discharged from further obligations under Clark's (P) policy. Alternately, State Farm (P) asked for a determination that Clark's (D) policy did not cover Clark (D) for claims arising out of the accident.

The district court issued an order that enjoined the defendants from bringing or prosecuting any claims against Clark (D) except in the interpleader action. The injunction was broadened to provide that other potential defendants, including Greyhound, could be sued only within the confines of the interpleader action. The Ninth Circuit Court of Appeals dissolved the injunction, however, and dismissed the interpleader action. The court held that interpleader was not available to State Farm (P) under these facts, because Oregon law did not allow "direct action" suits against insurers until claims against the insureds have been reduced to judgment.

■ **ISSUE**

Could State Farm (P) bring an interpleader action under these circumstances?

■ **DECISION AND RATIONALE**

(Fortas, J.) Yes. The scope of an interpleader action is limited to claims that relate to the ownership of the property deposited with the court. The interpleader statute permits an action when adverse claimants "may claim" benefits. There is no requirement that the claimants to the proceeds of an insurance policy have their claims reduced to final judgments prior to the commencement of an interpleader action. But although the interpleader action may be brought, the injunction issued by the

---

district court was too broad. State Farm (P) was entitled to an order limiting claims against the insurance policy to the interpleader action, but that injunction could not apply to all claims that arose or might arise from the accident. The injunction should have been limited to claims against Clark's (D) insurance policy. Other potential defendants, such as Greyhound, are not entitled to the protection of an injunction, since their liability is not limited to a particular fund.

Interpleader actions are not intended to be a way to handle all types of multiparty tort litigation. The sole question to be determined is the ownership of a particular piece of property. Jurisdiction over this particular case is proper in federal courts, since the interpleader statute requires only minimal diversity of parties, not complete diversity. Remanded.

Analysis:

As the Court notes, interpleader is not intended to function as an all-purpose solution to multiparty litigation. State Farm's (P) interest in the complete litigation relating to the accident is a relatively minor one, compared to the interests of the alleged tortfeasors, and it does not seem fair to allow a comparatively minor player to determine the entire course of all of the lawsuits. If State Farm (P) had wanted to avoid coverage for the accident, it could have had its rights determined in a separate suit that would not have attempted to adjudicate the tort liabilities of the parties involved.

■ CASE VOCABULARY

BILL OF PEACE: An equitable bill filed by one who is threatened with multiple suits involving the same right, or with recurrent suits on the same right, asking the court to determine the question once and for all and to enjoin the plaintiffs from proceeding with the threatened litigation.

COMPLETE DIVERSITY: In a multiparty case, diversity between both sides to the lawsuit so that all plaintiffs have different citizenship from all defendants. Complete diversity must exist for a federal court to have diversity jurisdiction over the matter. The rule of complete diversity was first laid down by Chief Justice Marshall in *Strawbridge v. Curtiss,* 7 U.S. (3 Cranch) 267 (1806).

DIRECT ACTION: A lawsuit by an insured against his or her own insurance company rather than against the tortfeasor and the tortfeasor's insurer; a lawsuit by a person claiming against an insured but suing the insurer directly instead of pursuing compensation indirectly through the insured.

INTERPLEADER: A suit to determine a right to property held by a usu. disinterested third party (called a *stakeholder*) who is in doubt about ownership and who therefore deposits the property with the court to permit interested parties to litigate ownership. Typically, a stakeholder initiates an interpleader both to determine who should receive the property and to avoid multiple liability.

Natural Resources Defense Council, Inc. v. United States Nuclear Regulatory Commission

(*Environmental Group*) v. (*Licensing Agency*)

578 F.2d 1341 (10th Cir. 1978)

MOTIONS TO INTERVENE ALLOW NON-PARTIES TO PROTECT THEIR INTERESTS

■ **INSTANT FACTS** The American Mining Congress (Intervenor ("I")) and Kerr–McGee Nuclear Corp. (I) sought to intervene in a suit challenging the procedures for issuing licenses to operate uranium mines.

■ **BLACK LETTER RULE** A party may intervene in an action if it has a significant protectable interest that would, as a practical matter, be impaired by non-participation in the litigation and the parties to the suit would not adequately represent that interest.

■ **PROCEDURAL BASIS**

Appeal from an order denying motions to intervene.

■ **FACTS**

The National Resources Defense Council (NRDC) (P) brought an action to challenge the procedures used for granting licenses to operate uranium mills. NRDC (P) claimed that the licenses should be granted only after an environmental impact study was conducted. NRDC (P) named as defendants in the suit the U.S. Nuclear Regulatory Commission (D) and the New Mexico Environmental Improvement Agency (D). The United Nuclear Corporation (D), which had been granted a license to operate a mill, was granted permission to intervene. Kerr–McGee (I) and the American Mining Congress (I), along with other energy and mining companies, also moved to intervene. Those motions were denied. The district court held that intervention would engender delay and that filing amicus curiae briefs would be sufficient to protect the moving parties' interests.

■ **ISSUE**

Should Kerr–McGee (I) and American Mining (I) be allowed to intervene?

■ **DECISION AND RATIONALE**

(Doyle, J.) Yes. A party may intervene in an action if it has a significant protectable interest that would, as a practical matter, be impaired by non-participation in the litigation and the parties to the suit would not adequately represent that interest. Here, Kerr–McGee (I) has a significant interest in the outcome of the litigation. The interest is not necessarily a direct interest, but is a significant one. The consequence of this litigation could be the imposition of new requirements for the issuance of a license to operate a uranium mill, or the termination of the New Mexico Environmental Improvement Agency's (D) authority to issue those licenses. There is thus a substantial threat to the interests of Kerr–McGee (I), and this case presents a chance of impairing that interest. An adverse decision would not be res judicata, but there could be a precedential effect, particularly since this case is one of first impression. The rules refer to impairment "as a practical matter" and do not limit consideration to strictly legal factors.

The party moving to intervene bears the burden of showing that representation by the existing parties may be inadequate. That burden is minimal. It is enough to show that representation "may be" inadequate. United Nuclear (D) has interests similar to Kerr–McGee's (I), but those interests are not

---

identical. The possibility of divergence of interests need not be great in order to show inadequacy of representation. Reversed and remanded with instructions to grant the motions to intervene.

Analysis:

The court dismisses the argument that the addition of parties could make the case unwieldy by saying, in effect, that adding only Kerr–McGee (I) and American Mining (I) shouldn't pose much of a problem. The court states that it is not going to consider the question of whether other parties could be added, but remarks that it should not be necessary to add more parties. Query whether, under the liberal standard for intervention enunciated by the court, other parties could not show a need to intervene. Query also whether the "unwieldy" nature of a case should operate to deny a party the opportunity to intervene when the criteria for doing so are met.

■ CASE VOCABULARY

AMICUS CURIAE: [Latin, "friend of the court."] A person who is not a party to a lawsuit but who petitions the court or is requested by the court to file a brief because that person has a strong interest in the subject matter.

INTERVENOR: One who voluntarily enters a pending lawsuit because of a personal stake in it.

STARE DECISIS: [Latin, "to stand by things decided."] The doctrine of precedent, under which it is necessary for a court to follow earlier judicial decisions when the same points arise again in litigation.

Hansberry v. Lee

(Homebuyer) v. *(Homeowner)*
311 U.S. 32, 61 S.Ct. 115 (1940)

CLASS–ACTION RULINGS BIND ONLY MEMBERS OF THE CLASS

■ **INSTANT FACTS** Hansberry (D) claimed that a racially restrictive covenant never became effective, but the trial court found that Hansberry (D) was bound by a prior decision upholding the validity of that covenant.

■ **BLACK LETTER RULE** The judgment in a class or representative suit binds only members of the class and those whose interests were represented by the class.

■ **PROCEDURAL BASIS**

Appeal from a judgment of the Illinois Supreme Court.

■ **FACTS**

Hansberry (D), an African–American, purchased a home in a Chicago neighborhood. The home was subject to a restrictive covenant that prohibited sales to African–Americans. Lee (P) and other homeowners in the neighborhood brought suit to set aside the conveyance. Hansberry (D) claimed that the covenant was invalid because it had been signed by only fifty-four percent of the homeowners, rather than the ninety-five percent required by the terms of the covenant. The trial court found that Hansberry (D) was bound by the stipulations in a prior suit brought by the neighborhood property owners' association, which provided that 95% of the property owners had in fact signed the covenant. The trial court held that this judgment was binding on Hansberry's (D) grantor, who was represented by the plaintiffs in the prior suit. The Illinois Supreme Court affirmed, holding that the stipulation, though factually inaccurate, was not collusive or fraudulent.

■ **ISSUE**

Is the prior class-action decision binding on Hansberry (D)?

■ **DECISION AND RATIONALE**

(Stone, J.) No. The judgment in a class or representative suit binds only members of the class and those whose interests were represented by the class. There is a failure of due process if absent parties, whose interests were not protected, are bound by the judgment. The restrictive agreement in this case does not create a joint obligation or agreement. Those who seek to enforce the agreement are in a different class from those who challenge the agreement. These potentially conflicting interests make it impossible to say that any two parties are of the same class. Thus, it cannot be said that the parties to the earlier suit were representative of the parties here. Reversed.

Analysis:

At the time this case was decided, racially restrictive covenants in residential real estate developments were the rule rather than the exception. It would be another eight years before the Supreme Court struck down such covenants in *Shelley v. Kraemer,* 334 U.S. 1 (1948). The Court's opinion in that case found that judicial enforcement of such covenants was "state action," thus making lawsuits to enforce the covenants an unconstitutional denial of equal protection. Legislation to end racial discrimination in housing was not enacted until 1968, with the passage of the Fair Housing Act, 42 U.S.C. § 3601 *et seq.*

■ CASE VOCABULARY

CLASS ACTION: A lawsuit in which the court authorizes a single person or a small group of people to represent the interests of a larger group; specifically, a lawsuit in which the convenience either of the public or of the interested parties requires that the case be settled through litigation by or against only a part of the group of similarly situated persons and in which a person whose interests are or may be affected does not have an opportunity to protect his or her interests by appearing personally or through a personally selected representative, or through a person specially appointed to act as a trustee or guardian. Federal procedure has several prerequisites for maintaining a class action: (1) the class must be so large that individual suits would be impracticable, (2) there must be legal or factual questions common to the class, (3) the claims or defenses of the representative parties must be typical of those of the class, and (4) the representative parties must adequately protect the interests of the class.

RESTRICTIVE COVENANT: A private agreement, usually in a deed or lease, that restricts the use or occupancy of real property, especially by specifying lot sizes, building lines, architectural styles, and the uses to which the property may be put.

Walters v. Reno

(Alien) v. *(Attorney General)*
145 F.3d 1032 (9th Cir. 1998)

COMMON QUESTIONS AND ADEQUATE REPRESENTATION ARE NECESSARY FOR CERTIFICATION OF A CLASS

■ **INSTANT FACTS** Walters (P) brought suit challenging procedures used by the Immigration and Naturalization Service (D), and the INS (D) objected to certification of a class action.

■ **BLACK LETTER RULE** Class certification requires a showing of questions of law or fact that are common to all class members and that the claims of the class representatives are adequately representative of the class as a whole.

■ **PROCEDURAL BASIS**

Appeal from an order of the district court certifying a class action and granting injunctive relief.

■ **FACTS**

Walters (P) brought an action that challenged the administrative procedures used by the (former) Immigration and Naturalization Service (INS) (D) to obtain final orders under the document fraud provisions of the immigration laws. Walters (P) claimed that the notice provided to aliens accused of document fraud was insufficient to give adequate notice of the steps that must be taken to contest the charges against them and of the consequences of the failure to contest the charges. The suit asked for preliminary and permanent injunctive relief, summary judgment, and an order requiring the INS (D) to reopen class members' document fraud cases and provide hearings, if necessary. Walters (P) also moved to certify a class of 4000 aliens who had been or were subject to final orders for document fraud.

The trial court granted Walters' (P) motion and certified the class. Membership in the class was established if an alien attested that he or she did not understand either his or her rights in a document fraud proceeding or the consequences of a waiver of those rights. The trial judge also granted summary judgment, finding that the procedures and forms used by the INS (D) were unconstitutional. The court also entered injunctive relief. The INS (D) objected to the order of the district court, claiming that the procedures used were constitutional. The INS (D) also objected to the certification of a plaintiff class.

■ **ISSUE**

Was the certification of the class proper?

■ **DECISION AND RATIONALE**

(Reinhardt, J.) Yes. Class certification requires a showing of questions of law or fact that are common to all class members and that the claims of the class representatives adequately represent the class as a whole. Although the factual claims of each individual member of the class may be different here, it could be presumed that the same constitutionally deficient procedures were followed in all cases. There was no showing that the forms or procedures used were modified to any great extent. Although there may be individual differences, all of the plaintiffs suffered the same due process deprivation.

The commonality also relates to the propriety of the certification of the class as a mandatory class action under Fed. R. Civ. P. 23(b)(2). Certification under that rule is appropriate when injunctive or declaratory relief for the class as a whole is appropriate. The suit seeks injunctive, not monetary, relief. Although the injunction entered by the district court will require individualized hearings to determine the immigration status of individual class members, certification of the class eliminates the necessity of individualized hearings to determine the constitutionality of the proceedings. The policy of eliminating duplicitous litigation is served.

The class representation is adequate. Adequacy of representation depends upon the qualifications of counsel, an absence of antagonism, shared interests between representatives and absent members, and the unlikelihood of collusion. The district court found that the representation was adequate because the representatives were not antagonistic to the class interests and were interested and involved in obtaining relief. The court also noted that the attorneys for the class were well qualified. Although there may be factual differences in the claims of the parties, the differences do not relate to the ability of the class representatives to pursue those claims. The adequacy of representation is also shown by the success the representative members have had in obtaining relief for the class.

The district court was correct in determining that the forms and procedures violated due process. The forms were not only confusing, they were misleading. The individual interests at stake are high. The INS (D) has a strong interest in enforcing the immigration laws, but that interest will not be unduly burdened by modifying the forms to prevent an erroneous deprivation of rights. The existing procedures have prejudiced class members, by depriving them of adequate notice and the opportunity to raise defenses at a hearing. The injunction issued was tailored to address the constitutional violation. The inadequate notice was the constitutional violation, and the injunction was made to prevent that violation. Summary judgment was therefore appropriate in this case, because the essential facts that determine the outcome of the case were not in dispute. Affirmed, but remanded to correct one of the terms of the injunction.

Analysis:

The court's decision in this case did not put an end to the litigation nor make a final determination of rights. The court was careful to make no suggestion that the class members were entitled to any further relief beyond proper notice of their rights, except for those class members who were already deported and who were entitled to have the proceedings start over. The deportation and exclusion were not the violations, rather it was the procedures employed that violated due process.

■ CASE VOCABULARY

DEPORTATION: The act or an instance of removing a person to another country; especially, the expulsion or transfer of an alien from a country.

Castano v. The American Tobacco Co.

(Nicotine Addict) v. *(Tobacco Company)*

84 F.3d 734 (5th Cir. 1996)

NICOTINE ADDICTS WERE NOT ENTITLED TO CLASS TREATMENT

I hear you're coming into a pile of dough.

Nah, turns out smoking isn't as profitable as I thought.

stus.com

■ **INSTANT FACTS** Tobacco users brought a class action against various tobacco companies for the injury of nicotine addiction, and the district court certified some issues for class treatment; the defendants appealed.

■ **BLACK LETTER RULE** A district court must conduct a rigorous analysis of the Rule 23 prerequisites before certifying a class.

■ **PROCEDURAL BASIS**

Federal circuit court review of a federal district court decision partially certifying a class action.

■ **FACTS**

The plaintiffs filed a class action lawsuit against the defendant tobacco companies, seeking compensation for their nicotine addiction. The proposed class consisted of all nicotine-dependent individuals, including all current, former, and deceased smokers since 1943. The plaintiffs conceded that addiction would have to be proven by each class member, and the defendants argued that proving class membership would require individual mini-trials to determine whether addiction actually existed. The court organized the class action issues into (1) core liability issues; (2) injury-in-fact, proximate cause, reliance, and affirmative defenses; (3) compensatory damages; and (4) punitive damages. The court found that the predominance requirement of Rule 23 was met on the core liability issues. Holding that common issues predominated in that category, the court certified the core liability issues for class treatment, because resolution of those issues would significantly advance the individual cases. The court also found that a class action was superior to other methods to adjudicate the core liability issues, given the specter of thousands, if not millions, of similar trials on liability. The court refused to certify the second category of issues, finding that they were replete with individual circumstances. In addition, the claim for compensatory damages was so intertwined with proximate cause and affirmative defenses that class certification of that issue would not advance the individual cases either. The punitive damages issue, however, was certified for class treatment.

■ **ISSUE**

Did the court properly certify the issues for class treatment?

■ **DECISION AND RATIONALE**

(Smith, J.) No. A district court must conduct a rigorous analysis of the Rule 23 prerequisites before certifying a class. The party seeking certification has the burden of proof. Here, the court erred in two ways. First, it failed to consider the impact of variations in state law affect and how those variations affect the required predominance of common claims. Moreover, whether the specter of millions of cases outweighs any manageability problems is uncertain when the scope of those problems is unknown. In the face of such uncertainty, a comparison to millions of individual trials is meaningless. Second, the court's predominance inquiry failed because it did not include consideration of how a trial on the merits

---

HIGH COURT CASE SUMMARIES 79

would be conducted. In other words, it failed to consider how the plaintiffs' addiction claims would be tried, individually or on a class basis.

Moreover, the class in this case must be decertified because it independently fails the superiority requirement of Rule 23(b)(3). Class-action treatment is not the superior mode for resolving these disputes. Certification dramatically affects the stakes for defendants, and magnifies and strengthens the number of unmeritorious claims. Aggregation of claims also makes it more likely that a defendant will be found liable, and results in significantly higher damage awards. Judicial efficiency would not be served by certifying the class here, because any imagined savings would be overwhelmed by the procedural problems that certification of a sui generis cause of action would entail. Even assuming that certification would result in judicial efficiency, certification of an immature tort brings with it unique problems that may consume more judicial resources than certification would save. Determining whether common issues are a significant part of each individual case is too abstract when no court in the country has yet tried an injury-as-addiction claim.

The district court thus abused its discretion by ignoring variations in state law and how a trial on the alleged causes of action would be tried. Those errors cannot be remedied on remand because of the novelty of the plaintiffs' claims. Accordingly, we hold that class treatment is not superior to individual adjudication. Traditional ways of proceeding reflect far more than habit; they reflect the very culture of the jury trial. Reversed and remanded with instructions that the district court dismiss the class complaint.

Analysis:

The court here focused on that part of Rule 23 that requires the court to find "that the questions of law or fact common to class members predominate over any questions affecting only individual members, and that a class action is superior to other available methods for fairly and efficiently adjudicating the controversy." Fed. R. Civ. P. 23(b)(3). A class may also be certified if prosecuting separate actions would create a risk of inconsistent adjudications that would establish incompatible standards of conduct, or a risk of adjudications that are dispositive of interests of other potential class members who are not parties to the adjudication, or that would substantially impair their ability to protect their interests. *Id.* at R. 23(b)(1).

■ CASE VOCABULARY

SUI GENERIS: [Latin, "of its own kind."] Of its own kind or class; unique or peculiar. The term is used in intellectual-property law to describe a regime designed to protect rights that fall outside the traditional patent, trademark, copyright, and trade-secret doctrines. For example, a database may not be protected by copyright law if its content is not original, but it could be protected by a sui generis statute designed for that purpose.

CHAPTER FIVE

Obtaining Information for Trial

Hickman v. Taylor

Instant Facts: Hickman (P) brought suit against Taylor (D), and Taylor objected to certain discovery requests made by Hickman (P).

Black Letter Rule: The purpose of discovery is to narrow and clarify the basic issues between the parties and to obtain information about the facts relative to those issues.

In Re Convergent Technologies Securities Litigation

Instant Facts: Convergent Technologies (D) served over 1000 interrogatories on the plaintiffs, asking for facts supporting the allegations that the plaintiffs made.

Black Letter Rule: Discovery requests should be tailored to obtain necessary information in the most cost-effective way possible.

Davis v. Ross

Instant Facts: Davis (P) sued Ross (D) for defamation and asked for information relating to Ross's (D) income, the names of other former employees, and fees paid to her attorney; in turn, Ross (D) requested disclosure of Davis's (P) psychiatric records.

Black Letter Rule: Discovery will be allowed only of information relevant to a material issue in the case.

Kozlowski v. Sears, Roebuck & Co.

Instant Facts: Kozlowski (P) sued Sears (D) for injuries sustained when pajamas sold by the defendant caught fire and requested production of records of other complaints of burn injuries.

Black Letter Rule: A discovery request is not objectionable merely because it is costly or time-consuming if the requested material is relevant and necessary to the discovery of evidence.

McPeek v. Ashcroft

Instant Facts: McPeek (P) moved the court for an order requiring the Department of Justice (D) to search the backup systems of its computer network in order to find documents that may have been deleted from the system.

Black Letter Rule: Discovery requests must balance the likelihood that relevant information will be found with the cost of conducting a search for that information.

Hickman v. Taylor

Instant Facts: Hickman (P) sought discovery of statements taken by Taylor's (D) attorney shortly after an accident.

Black Letter Rule: Discovery of attorney work product prepared in anticipation of litigation may be had only if the material sought is not privileged and is essential to the preparation of the requesting party's case.

Upjohn Co. v. United States

Instant Facts: Upjohn (D) refused to produce documents that related to an internal investigation conducted by its general counsel, claiming that the documents were protected by the attorney-client privilege.

Black Letter Rule: A communication by a corporation's employee to the corporation's attorney is protected by the attorney-client privilege if the communication is about matters within the scope of the employee's employment and was obtained for the purpose of providing legal advice to the corporation.

In Re Shell Oil Refinery

Instant Facts: The plaintiffs requested disclosure of expert witnesses who would not be called to testify at trial.

Black Letter Rule: Experts ordinarily employed by a party will be considered retained or specially employed if their employer assigns them to work on a particular matter in anticipation of litigation or for trial.

Corley v. Rosewood Care Center, Inc.

Instant Facts: Corley (P) took statements from witnesses under oath, before a court reporter, and did not give notice of taking depositions to Rosewood Care Center (D).

Black Letter Rule: The Federal Rules of Civil Procedure do not prohibit a party from taking recorded statements without notice to the opposing party.

Cine Forty–Second Street Theatre Corp. v. Allied Artists Pictures Corp.

Instant Facts: Cine Forty–Second Street Theatre (P) failed to comply with Allied Artists' (D) discovery requests.

Black Letter Rule: A preclusion order or dismissal of a party's pleading is justified if the party is at fault when failing to respond to a discovery order.

Hickman v. Taylor

(*Crew Member*) v. (*Tugboat Owner*)
329 U.S. 495, 67 S.Ct. 385 (1947)

DISCOVERY NARROWS AND CLARIFIES THE ISSUES

■ **INSTANT FACTS** Hickman (P) brought suit against Taylor (D), and Taylor objected to certain discovery requests made by Hickman (P).

■ **BLACK LETTER RULE** The purpose of discovery is to narrow and clarify the basic issues between the parties and to obtain information about the facts relative to those issues.

■ **PROCEDURAL BASIS**

Appeal from an order of the Third Circuit Court of Appeals, reversing an order holding Taylor's (D) counsel in contempt for failure to comply with a discovery order.

■ **FACTS**

A tugboat operated by Taylor (D) sunk, causing the deaths of several crew members. Taylor's (D) counsel took statements of witnesses shortly after the incident. Hickman (P) asked to see the statements and Taylor's (D) counsel refused, claiming attorney-client privilege protected the materials from discovery.

■ **ISSUE**

What is the purpose of pretrial discovery?

■ **DECISION AND RATIONALE**

(Murphy, J.) The purpose of discovery is to narrow and clarify the basic issues between the parties and to obtain information about the facts relative to those issues. Pleadings are now restricted to general notice-giving. Discovery is therefore the process by which facts are learned and by which issues are framed. Parties now are able to obtain the fullest possible knowledge of the issues and facts before the trial. Affirmed.

Analysis:

Before the Federal Rules of Civil Procedure were adopted, discovery was a complex, formalized process. It was carried out with close involvement by the court and did not always result in complete fact-finding by either party. "Trial by ambush"—surprising adversaries with new, previously unknown evidence or witnesses at the trial—was common. The federal rules make surprises at trial less common, and relieve the courts of much of their supervisory role over the process.

■ Case Vocabulary:

DISCOVERY: The act or process of finding or learning something that was previously unknown; compulsory disclosure, at a party's request, of information that relates to the litigation.

In Re Convergent Technologies Securities Litigation

(Securities Lawsuit Defendant)

108 F.R.D. 328 (N.D. Cal. 1985)

DISCOVERY METHODS SHOULD BE COST–EFFECTIVE

■ **INSTANT FACTS** Convergent Technologies (D) served over 1000 interrogatories on the plaintiffs, asking for facts supporting the allegations that the plaintiffs made.

■ **BLACK LETTER RULE** Discovery requests should be tailored to obtain necessary information in the most cost-effective way possible.

■ **PROCEDURAL BASIS**

Decision on a discovery motion.

■ **FACTS**

Convergent Technologies (D) served over 1000 interrogatories on the plaintiffs. Many of those interrogatories asked for facts that supported the plaintiffs' contention that Convergent Technologies (D) violated securities laws. The plaintiffs agreed that the interrogatories should be answered, but they did not agree as to *when* they should be answered. Over $40,000 was spent on litigating the discovery dispute.

■ **ISSUE**

Should plaintiffs be compelled to answer extensive interrogatories?

■ **DECISION AND RATIONALE**

(Brazil, Magistrate J.) Yes. However, discovery requests should be tailored to find necessary information in the most cost-effective way possible. The large amount spent on one discovery issue in this case is a strong indication that the system of pretrial discovery has broken down. The spirit of the rules is to encourage "just, speedy, and inexpensive" resolutions of actions. The discovery rules also mandate that discovery requests not be unduly burdensome or expensive.

The requirement that discovery requests be reasonably calculated to lead to admissible evidence is a threshold determination. The next questions involve whether the information sought is of sufficient potential importance to justify the burden of the request, whether the method of discovery is the best method of obtaining the information, and whether the timing of the request is sensible. In essence, the rules require good faith and common sense, with the focus on what information a party is likely to need and what is the most cost effective way to get it. Here, the plaintiffs are required to respond to Convergent Technologies' (D) requests, but they may wait to do so until more discovery is completed.

Analysis:

Discovery motions are frustrating to many courts. The time spent hearing and deciding such motions uses up judicial resources on matters that are often relatively minor. In addition, as noted by the court in this case, discovery is supposed to be something handled by the parties on their own, without judicial intervention unless absolutely necessary. The federal rules, along with many state court rules, require the parties to a discovery dispute to confer before a motion on the dispute will be heard.

■ **Case Vocabulary:**

INTERROGATORY: A written question (usually in a set of questions) submitted to an opposing party in a lawsuit as part of discovery.

MOTION TO COMPEL DISCOVERY: A party's request that the court force the party's opponent to respond to the party's discovery request (as to answer interrogatories or produce documents). Often shortened to *motion to compel*.

Davis v. Ross

(Former Employee) v. *(Former Employer)*
107 F.R.D. 326 (S.D.N.Y. 1985)

DISCOVERY IS LIMITED TO RELEVANT MATTERS

■ **INSTANT FACTS** Davis (P) sued Ross (D) for defamation and asked for information relating to Ross's (D) income, the names of other former employees, and fees paid to her attorney; in turn, Ross (D) requested disclosure of Davis's (P) psychiatric records.

■ **BLACK LETTER RULE** Discovery will be allowed only of information relevant to a material issue in the case.

■ **PROCEDURAL BASIS**

Decision on a motion to compel discovery.

■ **FACTS**

Davis (P) sued recording star Diana Ross (D) and her former employer for defamation. Davis (P) alleged that a letter Ross (D) sent out, which stated that seven of her former employees who were listed in the letter were terminated either for unacceptable work or personal habits, was false. Davis (P) sought discovery regarding Ross's (D) net worth and annual income, claiming that this information was relevant to an action for punitive damages. Davis (P) also sought documents regarding bills and payments made to attorneys for Ross (D). Davis (D) claimed that this evidence related to a possible bias on the part of Ross's (D) attorney, who had been identified as a witness. Davis (P) also asked for the names of other employees who had complained about Ross (D), alleging that these other employees would be able to provide evidence that related to the truth of Ross's (D) claim that Davis's (P) work was unsatisfactory. Davis (P) also claimed that the information was relevant to Ross's (D) credibility.

Ross (D) brought her own motion to compel discovery. She requested discovery of information that related to Davis's (P) psychiatric treatment during the time she worked for Ross (D). Ross (D) claimed that the information was relevant and that any physician-patient privilege had been waived.

■ **ISSUE**

Should discovery motions seeking tangential information be granted?

■ **DECISION AND RATIONALE**

(Carter, J.) No. Discovery will be allowed only of information relevant to a material issue in the case. The information regarding Ross's (D) net worth and annual income is relevant to a claim for punitive damages. However, under New York law, that evidence may not be introduced until a jury returns a special verdict that finds that the plaintiff is entitled to punitive damages. Discovery of Ross's (D) net worth will be necessary only if the jury returns such a special verdict. Discovery will also be denied with regard to the amount of fees paid to Ross's (D) attorney. The bias of a witness is relevant evidence, and Davis (P) will be allowed discovery of fee arrangements and retainer agreements. But the amount of fees earned is not in itself probative of bias. It is not relevant to the inquiry here that Davis (P) signed a confidentiality agreement to prevent her disclosure of the information. The information regarding former employees of Ross (D) is also not discoverable. Davis (P) has alleged that statements made about her

---

were false, and evidence of complaints by other employees about Ross (D) has no bearing on that allegation. The former employees; testimony would also have no bearing on Ross's (D) credibility. There is no connection between Ross's (D) reputation as an employer and her capacity for telling the truth.

Ross's (D) motion to compel discovery of Davis's (P) psychiatric records will, however, be granted. Davis (P) has put her mental condition at issue by claiming emotional distress. She has therefore waived the physician-patient privilege. Even if, as Davis (P) argues, damages are to be presumed in a case for libel per se, Ross (D) still is allowed to rebut that presumption. Accordingly, Davis's (P) motions to compel discovery are denied, while Ross's (D) motion is granted.

Analysis:

Although the scope of discovery is broad, it is by no means infinite. There must be some plausible connection between the issues to be litigated and the discovery requests. The rules do not require that the information sought by discovery be "relevant," as that term is used in the rules of evidence. At the same time, the request still must be "reasonably calculated" to lead to evidence that will be admissible at trial.

■ CASE VOCABULARY:

DEFAMATION: 1. The act of harming the reputation of another by making a false statement to a third person. If the alleged statement involves a matter of public concern, the plaintiff is constitutionally required to prove both the statement's falsity and the defendant's fault. 2. A false written or oral statement that damages another's reputation.

DOCTOR–PATIENT PRIVILEGE: The right to exclude from evidence in a legal proceeding any confidential communication that a patient makes to a physician for the purpose of diagnosis or treatment, unless the patient consents to the disclosure.

LIBEL PER SE: Libel that is actionable in itself, requiring no proof of special damages; libel that is defamatory on its face, such as the statement "Frank is a thief."

PUNITIVE DAMAGES: Damages awarded in addition to actual damages when the defendant acted with recklessness, malice, or deceit.

Kozlowski v. Sears, Roebuck & Co.

(Burned Child) v. *(Pajama Maker)*
73 F.R.D. 73 (D. Mass. 1976)

A PARTY MAY NOT CREATE OBSTACLES TO DISCOVERY

■ **INSTANT FACTS** Kozlowski (P) sued Sears (D) for injuries sustained when pajamas sold by the defendant caught fire and requested production of records of other complaints of burn injuries.

■ **BLACK LETTER RULE** A discovery request is not objectionable merely because it is costly or time-consuming if the requested material is relevant and necessary to the discovery of evidence.

■ **PROCEDURAL BASIS**

Decision on a motion to remove a default judgment entered for failure to comply with discovery orders.

■ **FACTS**

The plaintiff was severely injured when pajamas manufactured and sold by Sears (D) caught on fire. Kozlowski (P) brought an action for negligence, breach of warranty, and strict liability in tort, and requested production of all complaints and communications regarding injuries or death allegedly caused by the burning of children's nightwear made or marketed by Sears (D). Sears (D) filed a motion to quash the request, but the request was denied and Sears (D) was ordered to produce the requested documents within thirty days. Sears (D) did not produce the documents, and the court entered judgment by default for Sears' (D) willful and deliberate failure to comply with the order. Sears (D) moved to remove the judgment by default, claiming that it was unable to produce the requested information because of the manner in which its records were kept. Claims were not sorted by product type, but alphabetically, by the name of the claimant. Sears (D) claimed that there was no practical way of determining whether similar claims had been made unless all of the claims were reviewed. Sears (D) did not produce any evidence to support its representation.

■ **ISSUE**

Is a time-consuming and expensive discovery request always unreasonable?

■ **DECISION AND RATIONALE**

(Julian, J.) No. A discovery request is not objectionable merely because it is costly or time-consuming if the requested material is relevant and necessary to the discovery of evidence. The existence or non-existence of complaints about injuries caused by Sears' (D) sleepwear is relevant to the issue of whether Sears (D) had notice that its product was unreasonably dangerous. Kozlowski (P) has a need for the documents about those complaints, they are in the possession of Sears (P), and Kozlowski (P) has no other access to them. Sears (D) has a duty to produce that information. Any burden imposed on Sears (D) by producing the records is of its own creation. The filing system used is inadequate, but Sears (D) cannot use the inadequacy of its own business methods to frustrate discovery. And Sears' (D) offer to transport Kozlowski's (P) attorney to the records, so that he may either locate the records or verify the impossibility of locating them, is not sufficient. The court will not shift the financial burden of

---

discovery onto the discovering party where the costliness of the procedure is something over which Kozlowski (P) had no control. Motion to remove the default judgment denied.

Analysis:

The cost-effectiveness of a discovery method is a concern, but not the only concern, when a court looks at a motion to compel discovery. There is expense involved in complying with any discovery request, and that expense will only mount as the litigation becomes more complex. In this case, there was no other way for Kozlowski (P) to obtain certain information that was important to the case. In addition, the court's decision may have been influenced by disbelief or skepticism about Sears' (D) claim: why would a manufacturer and marketer of many different products not want to keep complaints of injuries sorted according to the allegedly dangerous product?

■ CASE VOCABULARY

DEFAULT JUDGMENT: A judgment entered against a defendant who has failed to plead or otherwise defend against the plaintiff's claim, often by failing to appear at trial; a judgment entered as a penalty against a party who does not comply with an order, especially an order to comply with a discovery request.

STRICT LIABILITY: Liability that does not depend on actual negligence or intent to harm, but that is based on the breach of an absolute duty to make something safe.

McPeek v. Ashcroft

(Employee) v. *(Employer)*
202 F.R.D. 31 (D.D.C. 2001)

DISCOVERY COSTS MUST BE BALANCED AGAINST THE LIKELIHOOD OF FINDING RELEVANT INFORMATION

■ **INSTANT FACTS** McPeek (P) moved the court for an order requiring the Department of Justice (D) to search the backup systems of its computer network in order to find documents that may have been deleted from the system.

■ **BLACK LETTER RULE** Discovery requests must balance the likelihood that relevant information will be found with the cost of conducting a search for that information.

■ **PROCEDURAL BASIS**

Decision on a motion to compel discovery.

■ **FACTS**

McPeek (P) brought suit against the Department of Justice (DOJ) (D), alleging retaliation for an earlier sexual harassment claim. Pursuant to a discovery request, the DOJ (D) searched for electronic and paper documents. McPeek (P) requested an order directing the DOJ (D) to search its backup systems for its computer networks. McPeek (P) claimed that such a search might yield information such as data that was deleted but remained on the backup tape. The DOJ (D) claimed that the remote possibility that such information existed could not justify the expense of such a search. There were three different systems used by DOJ (D) at various times covered by McPeek's (P) request, and for one of those systems there never was a system-wide backup policy. The backup systems that were in place did not cover the entire period of time requested by McPeek (P) because they were not intended for archival preservation. Additionally, the backup tapes may not have contained all of the documents or emails of a particular user. The backup was merely a "snapshot" of the system as of the particular time and date the backup was run. Once the backup tapes were produced, they would have to be restored or made readable by a user. The file would then have to be reviewed to determine whether it fell within one of the document requests. A DOJ (D) employee estimated that restoring the emails from a single backup tape would take eight hours and cost no less than $93 per hour. There also was no way of knowing in advance what material was on the individual backup tapes.

■ **ISSUE**

Should McPeek's (P) discovery motion for a search of the DOJ's (D) computer backup system be at least partially granted?

■ **DECISION AND RATIONALE**

(Facciola, Magistrate J.) Yes. The request should be granted in a limited form. Discovery requests must balance the likelihood that relevant information will be found with the cost of conducting a search for that information. In this case, because it is impossible to know in advance what is on any of the backup tapes, there is a theoretical possibility that relevant information will be on the tapes. That information could advance a settlement of the case, and if the DOJ (D) has no reason to search the tapes, that

---

possibility of settlement could be lost. On the other hand, the costs and burden of performing such a search would be great. Government agencies could be tempted to forego backing up their computer systems, which could lead to disastrous consequences. Shifting the costs to the requesting party would not work, because agency employees still would, as a practical matter, perform the searches. In addition, such cost shifting is not required for other discovery methods, however burdensome or expensive they may be. A better approach is to balance the costs against the potential benefit.

In this case, in order to determine how likely it is that there is discoverable information on the tapes, the DOJ (D) is ordered to do a backup restoration of the tapes containing the emails of McPeek's (P) immediate superior, covering July 1, 1998, to July 1, 1999. The DOJ (D) will document the time and money spent doing the search and, when the search is completed, it will file a sworn certification of the time and money spent and of the results of the search. After the certification is filed, the parties may argue why the results and expense do or do not justify a further search.

Analysis:

A growing issue in civil litigation is the destruction of computer files that could contain discoverable evidence. A computer file may be easily deleted with a simple keystroke, while traditional paper files are not disposed of as easily or discreetly. In many cases, unlike paper files, computer files are not maintained permanently on a system, but are regularly purged. Courts have threatened sanctions against parties who delete relevant computer files, even if those files were deleted in the regular course of business, which in turn leads many attorneys to advise clients to delete no files if they are faced with even the possibility of litigation.

■ CASE VOCABULARY

SEXUAL HARASSMENT: A type of employment discrimination consisting of verbal or physical abuse of a sexual nature.

Hickman v. Taylor

(*Crew Member*) v. (*Tugboat Operator*)

329 U.S. 495, 67 S.Ct. 385 (1947)

ATTORNEY WORK PRODUCT IS AFFORDED PROTECTION FROM DISCOVERY

■ **INSTANT FACTS** Hickman (P) sought discovery of statements taken by Taylor's (D) attorney shortly after an accident.

■ **BLACK LETTER RULE** Discovery of attorney work product prepared in anticipation of litigation may be had only if the material sought is not privileged and is essential to the preparation of the requesting party's case.

■ **PROCEDURAL BASIS**

Appeal from an order of the Third Circuit Court of Appeals, reversing an order holding Taylor's (D) counsel in contempt for failure to comply with a discovery order.

■ **FACTS**

Taylor (D) operated a tugboat that sank; five crew members drowned. Taylor (D) employed a law firm to represent it in any possible ensuing litigation. The attorney took statements from the surviving crew members, in anticipation of litigation. The attorney also interviewed other possible witnesses. Four of the claims for the deaths of the crew were settled without litigation. Hickman (P), however, filed a claim under the Jones Act and served interrogatories on Taylor (D). Some of those interrogatories asked for copies of any written statements or the "exact provisions" of any oral statements. Taylor's (D) counsel admitted that statements had been taken, but refused to turn them over, claiming that the request asked for privileged matter obtained in anticipation of litigation and was an indirect attempt to obtain counsel's files. The trial court held that the requested matters were not privileged and directed that they be provided to Hickman (P). Counsel for Taylor (D) refused and was imprisoned for contempt. The Third Circuit Court of Appeals reversed, holding that the requested information was part of attorney work product and thus privileged from discovery.

■ **ISSUE**

Must witness statements taken in anticipation of litigation be turned over to the opposing party?

■ **DECISION AND RATIONALE**

(Murphy, J.) No. Discovery of attorney work product prepared in anticipation of litigation may be had only if the material sought is not privileged and is essential to the preparation of the requesting party's case. In order to represent a client properly, it is essential that an attorney be allowed to work without unnecessary intrusion from the opposing party. If an attorney's work product were open to discovery upon demand, the attorney's thoughts would no longer be private, and much of what is now written down would remain unwritten. The quality of legal representation would suffer, the effect on the legal profession would be demoralizing, and the interests of the clients and of justice would be poorly served. Discovery still will be allowed, however, of non-privileged material that is essential to the preparation of a party's case. The general policy against infringing on the privacy of an attorney is so strong that such discovery will not be allowed as a matter of course; rather, the party who seeks such discovery bears the burden of showing adequate reasons to justify production. That burden is necessarily implicit in the rules.

In this case, Hickman (P) has not shown the need for discovery of the written statements, so discovery will be denied. Under the circumstances of the case, there can be no showing of sufficient necessity to merit disclosure of the non-written statements. No legitimate purpose would be served by their production, and producing the statements would turn Taylor's (D) counsel into a witness, testifying as to his recollections of what the witnesses said. Hickman's (P) attorney acknowledged that he only requested the oral statements to make sure he had overlooked nothing. There is no showing of a justification for the requested discovery. Affirmed.

■ **CONCURRENCE**

(Jackson, J.) A trial remains an adversary proceeding. Counsel for Hickman (P) argues that discovery is meant to do away with the old situation in which a trial is a battle of wits, but discovery is not intended to allow a litigant to proceed to trial with no wits, or with someone else's wits. The effect of the practice advocated by Hickman (P) would be demoralizing on the legal profession. Lawyers would be turned into witnesses and would be forced to take the stand to defend their own credibility. Statements of lying or biased witnesses would likewise have to be turned over, even if the attorney would not vouch for the witness's credibility.

Analysis:

The Court's opinion reads a "necessity" requirement into the discovery rule. The language of the rule did not require a showing of necessity, but only a request for non-privileged information. In a sense, the Court's opinion represents a slight retreat from the liberal scope of discovery allowed by the rules, and creates a new exception to the broad scope of discovery. Note that the statements involved in this case were not privileged, in the evidentiary sense, because they were not communications between an attorney and a client.

■ **CASE VOCABULARY**

ATTORNEY–CLIENT PRIVILEGE: The client's right to refuse to disclose and to prevent any other person from disclosing confidential communications between the client and the attorney.

JONES ACT: A federal statute that allows a seaman injured during the course of employment to recover damages for the injuries in a negligence action against the employer. If a seaman dies from such injuries, the seaman's personal representative may maintain an action against the employer.

WORK PRODUCT: Tangible material or its intangible equivalent—in unwritten or oral form—that was either prepared by or for a lawyer or prepared for litigation, either planned or in progress. Work product is generally exempt from discovery or other compelled disclosure. The term is also used to describe the products of a party's investigation or communications concerning the subject matter of a lawsuit if made (1) to assist in the prosecution or defense of a pending suit, or (2) in reasonable anticipation of litigation.

Upjohn Co. v. United States

(Corporation) v. *(Investigating Authority)*
449 U.S. 383, 101 S.Ct. 677 (1981)

COMMUNICATIONS BETWEEN A CORPORATION'S EMPLOYEES AND ITS COUNSEL MAY BE PRIVILEGED

■ **INSTANT FACTS** Upjohn (D) refused to produce documents that related to an internal investigation conducted by its general counsel, claiming that the documents were protected by the attorney-client privilege.

■ **BLACK LETTER RULE** A communication by a corporation's employee to the corporation's attorney is protected by the attorney-client privilege if the communication is about matters within the scope of the employee's employment and was obtained for the purpose of providing legal advice to the corporation.

■ **PROCEDURAL BASIS**

Appeal from an order of the Sixth Circuit Court of Appeals affirming an order enforcing a summons.

■ **FACTS**

Corporate officers of Upjohn (D) directed the corporation's general counsel to conduct investigations into possible illegal bribes paid by Upjohn's (D) employees. In the course of his investigation, questionnaires were sent to employees of Upjohn (D) identified as "general and area managers," who were told that the questionnaires were for counsel's investigation. The questionnaire was accompanied by a policy statement, in which employees were informed that bribes or illegal payments were against corporate policy.

Upjohn (D) voluntarily submitted a report to the Securities and Exchange Commission and the Internal Revenue Service, which disclosed the possible illegal payments. The United States (P) began its own investigation of Upjohn (D) and requested production of the completed questionnaires. Upjohn (D) provided the names of the employees who answered the questionnaires, but refused to provide the completed questionnaires. Upjohn (D) claimed that the answers were protected by the attorney-client privilege. The district court disagreed, holding that the questionnaires were not privileged. The court of appeals agreed that the privilege did not apply to those employees not responsible for directing Upjohn's (D) response to legal advice, but it also noted that the chairman and president of Upjohn (D) had been interviewed by counsel, and it therefore remanded for a factual determination as to which Upjohn employees were within the "control group" whose responses would be privileged.

■ **ISSUE**

Are corporate employees' responses to an investigative questionnaire from counsel covered by the attorney-client privilege?

■ **DECISION AND RATIONALE**

(Rehnquist, J.) Yes. Communications between a corporation's employees and the corporation's attorney are protected by the attorney-client privilege if they concern matters within the scope of the employees' employment and are obtained for the purpose of providing legal advice to the corporation. The purpose of the privilege is to encourage full and frank communication between attorneys and their clients. The privilege exists not just to protect the professional advice given by an attorney to those who can act on the advice, but also the giving of information to the attorney to enable him or her to give sound and informed advice.

The court of appeals applied a test that was too narrow to advance the purpose of the privilege. In many cases, it will be middle-and lower-level employees who have the information needed by a corporation's lawyers. The actions of middle-and lower-level employees can cause serious legal difficulties for a corporation. These are the employees who would have the relevant information necessary to give counsel the information needed for adequate representation. In addition, the advice given by counsel often will be more significant to employees outside the control group of the corporation. The questionnaires here sought information that would not be available to upper management, and that information was needed to provide legal advice to the corporation. The advice of counsel often is sought to make sure that the corporation is in compliance with the law. It is important to know in advance whether particular communications will be protected. An uncertain privilege is little better than no privilege at all.

There was, however, no showing of necessity sufficient to compel disclosure of notes reflecting interviews by counsel. The notes are not necessarily *always* protected by privilege, although some courts have concluded that such material is never discoverable. But that is not an issue that needs to be decided in this case. There must be a far stronger showing of necessity than was made here before the notes must be disclosed. Reversed.

Analysis:

The attorney-client privilege is stronger than the protection against discovery afforded to attorney work-product. The Federal Rules of Civil Procedure specifically exempt privileged materials from discovery, while there is a possibility that work product will be disclosed if there is a proper showing of necessity. There is no showing of necessity that will defeat the attorney-client privilege.

■ CASE VOCABULARY

CONTROL GROUP: The persons with authority to make decisions on a corporation's behalf.

In Re Shell Oil Refinery

(Destroyed Oil Refinery)
132 F.R.D. 437 (E.D. La. 1990)

INVESTIGATIONS BY A COMPANY'S REGULAR EMPLOYEES IN THE COURSE OF THEIR EMPLOY-
MENT MAY BE PROTECTED BY PRIVILEGE

■ **INSTANT FACTS** The plaintiffs requested disclosure of expert witnesses who would not be called to testify at trial.

■ **BLACK LETTER RULE** Experts ordinarily employed by a party will be considered retained or specially employed if their employer assigns them to work on a particular matter in anticipation of litigation or for trial.

■ **PROCEDURAL BASIS**

Decision on a motion for reconsideration of a ruling denying discovery.

■ **FACTS**

Part of an oil refinery operated by Shell Oil (D) exploded. The litigation against Shell Oil (D) arising out of that explosion was filed on the same day as the explosion. The cases filed were eventually certified as a class action. The plaintiff's legal committee (PLC) (P) and Shell (D) both retained experts and investigated the accident. Two employees of Shell (D), Nordstrom and Nelson, were present during metallurgical and chemical tests on material retrieved from the site of the explosion. The court ordered the parties to turn over the preliminary reports of experts who visited the site of the explosion and who would be called to testify at trial. Shell (D) turned over the reports of Nordstrom and Nelson. The PLC (P) filed a number of motions seeking expert discovery, particularly the results of tests conducted on materials from the site of the explosion, and also asked for leave of the court to depose expert witnesses.

Shell (D) responded that it did not yet know the names of experts it would call at trial and that it did not intend to call Nordstrom or Nelson as witnesses or use their preliminary expert reports. The PLC (P) argued that the opinions of Nordstrom and Nelson were discoverable, even though they would not be called to testify at trial, because they were not experts "retained or specially employed." Nordstrom and Nelson would have performed the testing regardless of the anticipated litigation, as a part of their duties as employees of Shell (D). PLC (P) argued, alternatively, that there were exceptional circumstances that mandated discovery, in that it would require great expense to duplicate the tests performed by Shell.

■ **ISSUE**

Are expert reports prepared by regular employees, but in anticipation of litigation, discoverable?

■ **DECISION AND RATIONALE**

(Mentz, J.) No. Experts ordinarily employed by a party will be considered retained or specially employed if their employer assigns them to work on a particular matter in anticipation of litigation or for trial. Nordstrom and Nelson investigated the explosion and prepared reports at the direction of Shell's (D) attorneys. They probably would have investigated the explosion in the normal course of their duties, but their usual duties do not include litigation assistance, so they will be considered "retained or specially

---

employed." There has been no showing of exceptional circumstances that would justify discovery. Courts generally have interpreted exceptional circumstances to mean that the information sought is unavailable from other sources. The information contained in the reports of Nordstrom and Nelson cold be obtained by the PLC's (P) own experts. Although such testing may be expensive, the PLC (P) will not be allowed a free ride at the expense of Shell (D), and at the expense of revealing Shell's (D) trial strategy. Motion for reconsideration denied.

Analysis:

The litigation that related to the explosion started the same day as the explosion took place. Under the definition of an expert "retained or specially employed," virtually any employee of Shell (D) involved in the investigation or analysis of the incident could be an expert whose opinion was not discoverable. This would be particularly true if the employee were ordered to give a copy of his or her findings to counsel—something that would have, in all probability, happened.

■ CASE VOCABULARY

EXPERT WITNESS: A witness qualified by knowledge, skill, experience, training, or education to provide a scientific, technical, or other specialized opinion about the evidence or a fact issue.

Corley v. Rosewood Care Center, Inc.

(RICO Plaintiff) v. *(Nursing Home)*
142 F.3d 1041 (7th Cir. 1998)

NOTICE IS NOT REQUIRED TO TAKE A STATEMENT THAT IS NOT A DEPOSITION

■ **INSTANT FACTS** Corley (P) took statements from witnesses under oath, before a court reporter, and did not give notice of taking depositions to Rosewood Care Center (D).

■ **BLACK LETTER RULE** The Federal Rules of Civil Procedure do not prohibit a party from taking recorded statements without notice to the opposing party.

■ **PROCEDURAL BASIS**

Appeal from an order granting a protective order.

■ **FACTS**

Corley (P) brought a Racketeer Influenced and Corrupt Organizations Act (RICO) action against Rosewood Care Center (D). Corley (P) interviewed non-party witnesses, under oath, and in the presence of a court reporter. The witnesses participated voluntarily. Rosewood Care Center (D) obtained a protective order that required Corley (P) to give notice of the interviews as if they were depositions.

■ **ISSUE**

Was Corley (P) required to give notice to the opposing party before taking the non-depositional statements?

■ **DECISION AND RATIONALE**

(Rovner, J.) No. The Federal Rules of Civil Procedure do not prohibit a party from taking recorded statements without notice to the opposing party. Notice was not required because the statements were not depositions, and the statements were not depositions because the rules for taking depositions were not complied with. Since the rules were not complied with, the statements could not be used as depositions at trial. The fact that the statements were not depositions does not mean that Corley (P) was not entitled to take them. The rules are concerned only with whether the statements are discoverable, and with the uses to which the statements may be put at trial. Reversed.

Analysis:

The disadvantage to Corley (P) of taking recorded statements, rather than depositions, is that the statements may not be used in the same ways as a deposition could be used at trial. For example, a deposition may be used in lieu of live testimony by a witness. However, the advantages of such a statement may outweigh the disadvantages. Note that there is nothing that prevents Rosewood Care (D) from taking, or attempting to take, a statement from the same witnesses as Corley (P).

■ CASE VOCABULARY

DEPOSITION: A witness's out-of-court testimony that is reduced to writing (usually by a court reporter) for later use in court or for discovery purposes; the session at which such testimony is recorded.

RACKETEER INFLUENCED AND CORRUPT ORGANIZATIONS ACT: A law designed to attack organized criminal activity and preserve marketplace integrity by investigating, controlling, and prosecuting persons who participate or conspire to participate in racketeering. Enacted in 1970, the federal RICO statute applies only to activity involving interstate or foreign commerce.

Cine Forty–Second Street Theatre Corp. v. Allied Artists Pictures Corp.

(Theater Owner) v. *(Rival Theater Chain)*

602 F.2d 1062 (2d Cir. 1979)

FAILURE TO COMPLY WITH A DISCOVERY ORDER JUSTIFIES SANCTIONS

■ **INSTANT FACTS** Cine Forty–Second Street Theatre (P) failed to comply with Allied Artists' (D) discovery requests.

■ **BLACK LETTER RULE** A preclusion order or dismissal of a party's pleading is justified if the party is at fault when failing to respond to a discovery order.

■ **PROCEDURAL BASIS**

Interlocutory appeal from an order assessing costs for failure to comply with discovery orders.

■ **FACTS**

Cine Forty–Second Street Theatre (P) brought an action against Allied Artists Pictures (D), alleging a conspiracy and abuse of process to prevent Cine (P) from opening a movie theater or to drive that theater out of business. Cine (P) sought $3,000,000 in treble damages under the antitrust laws and injunctive relief. Allied Artists (D) served interrogatories on Cine (P) in November 1975. Cine (P) secured an agreement to defer discovery on the issue of damages until it could retain an expert witness. Cine (P) did not answer the remaining interrogatories until four months after the agreed-upon deadline. The answers were ambiguous and generally inadequate. Cine (P) claimed the interrogatories amounted to harassment, but did not object. Cine (P) filed supplemental responses that also were inadequate and failed to obey two subsequent orders to compel discovery. In October 1977, the magistrate found Cine's (P) responses to be inadequate and assessed $500 in costs against it. The magistrate also warned Cine (P) that further noncompliance would result in dismissal.

Cine (P) did not retain the expert it claimed necessary to answer the interrogatories that related to damages. The magistrate ordered Cine (P) to produce a plan to answer, and when Cine (P) failed to comply, the magistrate ordered that the damages interrogatories be answered. The answers were seriously deficient, and one set was filed late. In September 1978, the magistrate again ordered compliance with the discovery orders, on pain of dismissal. Cine (P) did not comply and Allied Artists (D) moved for dismissal. At a hearing on the dismissal motion in October 1978, Cine's (P) counsel claimed an "understanding "that the deposition of Cine's (P) principal officer would replace the answers. No written evidence documenting such an understanding was introduced.

The magistrate concluded that there was no basis for Cine's (P) assumption that answers would not be due on the dates set out in the orders and concluded that Cine's (P) non-compliance was willful. She recommended an order precluding Cine (P) from introducing evidence relating to damages at trial. The district court judge did not accept the finding of willfulness, saying that he could not determine whether the failure was grossly negligent or willful. The district court judge concluded that he could not enter a preclusion order if the failure to comply was grossly negligent, so he entered an order imposing sanctions of $1000. The judge certified the case for an interlocutory appeal, recognizing that he may have misperceived the controlling law of the Second Circuit.

■ ISSUE

Did Cine Forty–Second Street Theatre's (P) failure to respond to discovery requests justify entry of a preclusion order?

■ DECISION AND RATIONALE

(Kaufman, J.) Yes. A preclusion order or dismissal of a party's pleading is justified if the party is at fault when failing to respond to a discovery order. Fault may include gross negligence, willfulness, or bad faith. One of the purposes of imposing discovery sanctions on a party is to deter future conduct of the type sanctioned. If Cine's (P) counsel failed to understand the terms of the order, even that is conduct that should be deterred. Although responses ultimately were filed, the sanctions must be weighed in light of the full record in the case. The responses were very late and served to prolong discovery. Any lesser sanctions would encourage dilatory tactics and encourage compliance only when counsel was faced with sanctions. Reversed.

Analysis:

Delays in conducting discovery may occur through no fault of either party, or through the fault of the parties' counsel. The time limits set out for complying with discovery requests may not be long enough, particularly in complex cases. The court's opinion seems to recognize that all discovery delays will not merit sanctions. There is no question here, however, that Cine's (P) failures were inexcusable. The excuse that counsel did not know that it had to comply with the orders by the dates set out in those orders seems especially egregious.

■ CASE VOCABULARY

INTERLOCUTORY APPEAL: An appeal that occurs before the trial court's final ruling on the entire case. Some interlocutory appeals involve legal points necessary to the determination of the case, while others involve collateral orders that are wholly separate from the merits of the action.

PRECLUSION ORDER: An order barring a litigant from presenting or opposing certain claims or defenses for failing to comply with a discovery order.

TREBLE DAMAGES: Damages that, by statute, are three times the amount that the fact-finder determines is owed.

CHAPTER SIX

Adjudication Before Trial: Summary Judgment

Adickes v. S. H. Kress & Co.

Instant Facts: Adickes (P) was denied service at the defendant's store and was arrested when she entered the store in the company of six black students.

Black Letter Rule: The moving party bears the burden of proving an absence of a genuine issue of material fact in order to sustain a motion for summary judgment.

Celotex Corp. v. Catrett

Instant Facts: Catrett (P) sued fifteen named asbestos manufacturers, including Celotex Corp. (D), alleging that they were liable for her husband's death based on negligence, breach of warranty, and strict liability.

Black Letter Rule: Summary judgment will be granted when the moving party demonstrates the absence of a genuine issue of material fact and that, as a matter of law, it is entitled to judgment in its favor, based on the pleadings, depositions, answers to interrogatories, and admissions on file, with or without supporting affidavits.

Arnstein v. Porter

Instant Facts: Arnstein (P) sued Porter (D) for copyright infringement, although he did not know whether Porter (D) was actually involved with those allegedly stealing his songs.

Black Letter Rule: When a factual issue turns on the credibility of the witnesses, summary judgment is inappropriate.

Dyer v. MacDougall

Instant Facts: Dyer (P) sued MacDougall (D) for slander in a four-count complaint.

Black Letter Rule: A party may not rely on mere speculation that a witness may change his testimony or that his demeanor may convince the jury of his untruthfulness to escape summary judgment.

Adickes v. S. H. Kress & Co.

(White School Teacher) v. *(Store Owner)*

398 U.S. 144, 90 S.Ct. 1598, 26 L.Ed.2d 142 (1970)

QUESTIONS OF MATERIAL FACT PRECLUDE SUMMARY JUDGMENT

■ **INSTANT FACTS** Adickes (P) was denied service at the defendant's store and was arrested when she entered the store in the company of six black students.

■ **BLACK LETTER RULE** The moving party bears the burden of proving an absence of a genuine issue of material fact in order to sustain a motion for summary judgment.

■ **PROCEDURAL BASIS**

Certiorari to review a decision of the Second Circuit Court of Appeals affirming the trial court's summary judgment and directed verdict for the defendant.

■ **FACTS**

Adickes (P), a white school teacher, sued S.H. Kress & Co. (D) in federal court under 42 U.S.C. § 1983 after the defendant refused to serve her lunch in its Mississippi store and she was subsequently arrested for vagrancy. At the time, Adickes (P) was accompanied by six black students from a Mississippi school at which she was teaching for the summer. The students were offered service and were not arrested. The plaintiff alleged a conspiracy between the defendant and the local police to arrest her because she was associating with African Americans. Relying on the deposition of an employee indicating that he had no prior communications with the police regarding Adickes (P), and affidavits from the arresting officers stating that the employee had not requested Adickes' (P) arrest, Kress (D) moved for summary judgment. Adickes (P) responded with an unsworn statement from a Kress (D) employee indicating that the police had been in the store on the day she was arrested. The court granted summary judgment because Adickes (P) failed to present any facts from which a conspiracy could be inferred. On appeal, the Second Circuit Court of Appeals affirmed. Adickes (P) appealed.

■ **ISSUE**

Is summary judgment appropriate when the moving party fails to demonstrate that there are no genuine issues of material fact?

■ **DECISION AND RATIONALE**

(Harlan, J.) No. The party moving for summary judgment bears the burden of proving the absence of a genuine issue of material fact in order to sustain the motion. Under § 1983, the plaintiff must prove that the defendant and the local police entered into an understanding to deny the plaintiff service or arrest her for entering the store in the company of African Americans. In granting the defendant's motion for summary judgment on the conspiracy count, the district court held that no evidence supported a reasonable inference of a conspiracy. But as the moving party, the defendant had the burden of showing the absence of a genuine issue of material fact, viewing the evidence in a light most favorable to the plaintiff. Here, the defendant failed to carry that burden, as it offered no evidence to foreclose the possibility that the policeman was in the store when the plaintiff entered as a result of an agreement with the defendant. While the store manager testified by deposition that no such agreement existed, affidavits from third-party witnesses and the police officers involved in the arrest failed to rebut the plaintiff's claim in her complaint that the policeman was in the store by agreement with the defendant.

Because the inference of an agreement must be viewed in the light most favorable to Adickes (P), summary judgment was inappropriate. The plaintiff need not produce an affidavit in response to the defendant's motion for summary judgment to establish the existence of a material fact unless the defendant, upon whom the burden of proof initially lies, produces some evidence that would bring the material fact into question. Rule 56(e) does not shift the burden of proof from the moving party to his or her opponent. Since the defendant offered no affidavit from the policeman or otherwise that the policeman was not in the store when Adickes (P) entered, the defendant failed to meet its burden of proof. Adickes (P) need not provide any evidence in support of her position for purposes of the defendant's summary judgment motion. Reversed.

Analysis:

Adickes demonstrated the difficulty of obtaining summary judgment throughout the 1970s and early 1980s. In order to succeed on a motion for summary judgment, a party had to negate all possible material fact issues. Failure to bring forth evidence on a material fact alleged in a plaintiff's complaint, such as the police officer's presence in *Adickes*, prohibited summary judgment in this case. The *Adickes* requirement, while still good law, was reshaped by the Supreme Court's trilogy of summary judgment cases in 1986.

■ CASE VOCABULARY

GENUINE ISSUE OF MATERIAL FACT: In the law of summary judgments, a triable, substantial, or real question of fact supported by substantial evidence. An issue of this kind precludes entry of summary judgment.

MATERIAL FACT: A fact that is significant or essential to the issue or matter at hand.

SUMMARY JUDGMENT: A judgment granted on a claim about which there is no genuine issue of material fact and upon which the movant is entitled to prevail as a matter of law.

Celotex Corp. v. Catrett

(Asbestos Manufacturer) v. *(Widow)*

477 U.S. 317, 106 S.Ct. 2548, 91 L.Ed.2d 265 (1986)

AFFIDAVITS ARE NOT REQUIRED FOR SUMMARY JUDGMENT

HELLO? I CAN'T SEE THROUGH ALL OF THIS ASBESTOS DUST, BUT ARE YOU THE NEW GUY?

IT'S SOMETHING LIKE THAT.

■ **INSTANT FACTS** Catrett (P) sued fifteen named asbestos manufacturers, including Celotex Corp. (D), alleging that they were liable for her husband's death based on negligence, breach of warranty, and strict liability.

■ **BLACK LETTER RULE** Summary judgment will be granted when the moving party demonstrates the absence of a genuine issue of material fact and that, as a matter of law, it is entitled to judgment in its favor, based on the pleadings, depositions, answers to interrogatories, and admissions on file, with or without supporting affidavits.

■ PROCEDURAL BASIS

Certiorari to review a decision of the U.S. Circuit Court of Appeals for the District of Columbia, reversing summary judgment entered on the behalf of the defendant.

■ FACTS

Catrett (P) sued Celotex Corp. (D) for the wrongful death of her husband due to his exposure to asbestos products. The defendant moved for summary judgment, arguing that the plaintiff had failed to identify any of the defendant's products to which the decedent had been exposed. In response, Catrett (P) offered a transcript of the deposition of the decedent, a letter from an official of the decedent's former employers, and a letter from an insurance company to her attorney, all tending to show that the decedent had been exposed to asbestos at his job site over a two-year period. The district court granted the defendant's motion for summary judgment because the plaintiff's evidence failed to establish that any Celotex (D) product was the proximate cause of the decedent's death. The U.S. Circuit Court of Appeals for the District of Columbia reversed, because the defendant had not supported its motion with any evidence to prove the absence of a genuine issue of material fact. Celotex (D) appealed.

■ ISSUE

Must a party moving for summary judgment support its motion with evidence affirmatively proving the absence of a genuine issue of material fact?

■ DECISION AND RATIONALE

(Rehnquist, J.) No. Under Rule 56(c) of the Federal Rules of Civil Procedure, summary judgment is appropriate "if the pleadings, depositions, answers to interrogatories, and admissions on file, together with the affidavits, if any," indicate the absence of a genuine issue of material fact and that the moving party is entitled to judgment in its favor as a matter of law. A party moving for summary judgment need not affirmatively negate an essential element of an opponent's claim when the opponent bears the burden of proof and fails to prove that element. No evidence, by affidavit or otherwise, is needed to support a motion for summary judgment unless the moving party bears the burden of proof at trial.

Rule 56(a) and (b) explicitly provide that summary judgment may be requested "with or without affidavits." Without affidavits, a motion for summary judgment remains properly supported by the "pleadings, depositions, answers to interrogatories, and admissions on file." No additional evidence is required. As the Court held in *Adickes v. S.H. Kress Co.*, Rule 56 does not shift the initial burden of proof away from the moving party to demonstrate the absence of a genuine issue of material fact. *Adickes* requires, however, that the moving party direct the court's attention to an absence of evidence supporting the nonmoving party's case. Rule 56(e) was adopted not to shift the moving party's burden of proof to the nonmoving party, but to require the nonmoving party to come forward with evidence beyond the pleadings to establish a genuine issue of material fact when the moving party has met its initial burden. The court of appeals failed to address whether Catrett (P) offered such evidence and whether such evidence would be sufficient to carry her burden of proof at trial. Because the court of appeals is better suited to make such a determination, the decision of the court of appeals is reversed and the case is remanded.

■ CONCURRENCE

(White, J.) While the Court is correct that the moving party must always support its motion for summary judgment with evidence showing the absence of a genuine issue of material fact, the moving party may not support its motion by conclusory statements that the nonmoving party cannot prove her case. The nonmoving party may possess evidence to prove her case that has not been disclosed to the moving party because the moving party has failed to properly conduct discovery. Accordingly, the moving party must demonstrate with affirmative evidence that no genuine issue of material fact exists.

■ DISSENT

(Brennan, J.) The majority's decision fails to explain what is required of a moving party seeking summary judgment. The party moving for summary judgment bears both the burden of production and the burden of persuasion in establishing the absence of material issues of fact. The burden of production requires a moving party to set forth prima facie evidence supporting summary judgment. If the moving party also bears the burden of persuasion at trial, it must offer credible evidence that would entitle it to a directed verdict if not contraverted at trial. If the nonmoving party bears the burden of persuasion at trial, however, the moving party may meet its burden of production by offering evidence that negates the nonmoving party's claims or by proving to the court that the nonmoving party's evidence does not support the claims brought. Either way, the moving party must make an affirmative showing, rather than unsupported conclusory assertions, to meets its burden of production. The moving party must show credible evidence, such as the deposition testimony of the nonmoving party's witnesses or the inadequacy of documentary evidence, to meet its burden of production.

Adickes was consistent with these principles, but has often been misconstrued as requiring Kress to present affirmative evidence that there was no policeman in the store, as alleged in the plaintiff's complaint. The plaintiff, however, also provided deposition testimony alleging the policeman's presence, though the defendant offered no evidence on the issue. The defendant failed to meet its initial burden of production. Similarly, Celotex (D) provided no affirmative evidence to discount the possibility that the decedent had been exposed to its product. Catrett (P), on the other hand, offered at least one witness who would testify at trial that the decedent had been exposed to the defendant's products. The defendant has ignored this evidence, just as Kress ignored Adickes' evidence that a policeman was present. Celotex (D) has failed to meet its burden of production on summary judgment.

Analysis:

Celotex was one of three important summary judgment cases decided by the Supreme Court in 1986. Along with *Anderson v. Liberty Lobby* and *Matsushita Electric Industrial Co. v. Zenith Radio Corp.*, the three cases—known as "the trilogy cases"—reshaped summary judgment procedure and requirements. The effect of the trilogy cases has been a judicial tendency to embrace summary judgment as a means of disposing of groundless cases to promote judicial economy and the interests of the parties.

■ CASE VOCABULARY

BURDEN OF PERSUASION: A party's duty to convince the fact-finder to view the facts in a way that favors that party.

BURDEN OF PRODUCTION: A party's duty to introduce enough evidence on an issue to have that issue decided by a fact-finder, rather than decided against the party in a peremptory ruling such as a summary judgment or a directed verdict.

Arnstein v. Porter

(Songwriter) v. *(Songwriter)*

154 F.2d 464 (2d Cir. 1946)

WITNESS CREDIBILITY IS WEIGHED BY THE JURY

WE DON'T KNOW ANY COLE PORTER

■ **INSTANT FACTS** Arnstein (P) sued Porter (D) for copyright infringement, although he did not know whether Porter (D) was actually involved with those allegedly stealing his songs.

■ **BLACK LETTER RULE** When a factual issue turns on the credibility of the witnesses, summary judgment is inappropriate.

■ **PROCEDURAL BASIS**

On appeal to the Second Circuit Court of Appeals to review a grant of summary judgment for the defendant.

■ **FACTS**

Arnstein (P) sued Cole Porter (D) for copyright infringement, claiming Porter (D) had "stooges" who ransacked his apartment and stole his copyrighted songs. In his deposition, Arnstein (P) admitted that he did not know whether Porter (D) was involved, but he believed that he could have been involved. Porter (D) denied ever seeing or hearing any of the plaintiff's songs or associating with anybody who may have stolen the songs. Porter (D) moved for summary judgment, which motion was granted by the trial court. Arnstein (P) appealed.

■ **ISSUE**

Is summary judgment appropriate when the ultimate issue of fact involves a credibility determination?

■ **DECISION AND RATIONALE**

(Frank, J.) No. Although there are similarities between Arnstein's (P) copyright songs and Porter's (D) compositions, there is no evidence to demonstrate that Porter (D) copied the plaintiff's songs. However, the similarities are sufficient to permit a jury to reasonably infer that if Porter (D) had access to the compositions, the songs were copied. Summary judgment is appropriate, then, only if there is no genuine issue of material fact concerning Porter's (D) access to Arnstein's (P) copyrighted material. Here, Arnstein (P) offers that "stooges" ransacked his apartment and gave Porter (D) access to his songs. Although the account appears "fantastic," the truth of the account turns on the plaintiff's credibility, which is properly left for the jury's consideration. Similarly, Porter's (D) denials require a judgment of his credibility. Porter's (D) recordings have sold more than a million copies. If the jury questions Porter's (D) credibility and disbelieves his denial, there arises a reasonable inference of access to Arnstein's (P) songs. Because the credibility of the witnesses is at issue, Arnstein (P) must be afforded his right of cross-examination before the jury. Reversed.

■ **DISSENT**

(Clark, J.) The court places too much emphasis on the ability to cross-examine. The plaintiff has deposed the defendant and the only evidence on which access may be established is the possibility that the defendant is untruthful in his denial. The court's decision appears to rest on both its faith in the

---

jury's ability to resolve issues of plagiarism and the court's dislike of the summary judgment standards handed down by the Supreme Court. As to the first, the evidence offered, even if presented to the jury, would likely result in a proper directed verdict. As to the second, the court's reluctance to use the summary judgment procedures in a copyright infringement case finds no support in the federal rules. In order to apply such a limitation, the court must inappropriately refashion the summary judgment rules. Summary judgment is an important means of disposing of useless and unnecessary trials, especially in the age of the liberal notice pleading requirements. While it is inappropriate to grant summary judgment when there exist genuine issues of material fact, it is equally inappropriate to allow trial to go forward when such factual issues are absent.

Analysis:

The court's decision to reverse summary judgment was based on more than the possibility that the jury would disbelieve Porter's (D) denial. Instead, the court believed that the similarities between Arnstein's (P) songs and Porter's (D) songs were so substantial that they could be considered more than coincidental. From this determination, the jury could reasonably question Porter's (D) credibility. Had those similarities not existed, summary judgment would likely not have been granted.

■ CASE VOCABULARY

COPYRIGHT INFRINGEMENT: The act of violating any of a copyright owner's exclusive rights granted by the federal Copyright Act, 17 U.S.C.A. §§ 106, 602. A copyright owner has several exclusive rights in copyrighted works, including the rights (1) to reproduce the work; (2) to prepare derivative works based on the work; (3) to distribute copies of the work; (4) for certain kinds of works, to perform the work publicly; (5) for certain kinds of works, to display the work publicly; (6) for sound recordings, to perform the work publicly; and (7) to import into the United States copies acquired elsewhere.

CREDIBILITY: The quality that makes something (as a witness or some evidence) worthy of belief.

DIRECTED VERDICT: A ruling by a trial judge taking a case from the jury because the evidence will permit only one reasonable verdict.

Dyer v. MacDougall

(Slander Plaintiff) v. *(Slander Defendant)*

201 F.2d 265 (2d Cir. 1952)

SUMMARY JUDGMENT CANNOT BE BASED ON SPECULATION

■ **INSTANT FACTS** Dyer (P) sued MacDougall (D) for slander in a four-count complaint.

■ **BLACK LETTER RULE** A party may not rely on mere speculation that a witness may change his testimony or that his demeanor may convince the jury of his untruthfulness to escape summary judgment.

■ **PROCEDURAL BASIS**

On appeal to review an order of the district court summarily dismissing counts three and four of the plaintiff's complaint.

■ **FACTS**

Dyer (P) sued MacDougall (D), alleging four counts of libel and slander. In count one, Dyer (P) alleged that MacDougall (D) slandered the plaintiff when he proclaimed in a directors' meeting of a corporation, "You are stabbing me in the back." In count two, Dyer (P) alleged that MacDougall (D) wrote a letter accusing Dyer (P) of making false statements to MacDougall's (D) clients. Count three alleged that MacDougall (D) had described a letter sent by plaintiff as a "blackmailing letter." Finally, count four alleged that MacDougall (D), through an agent, accused Dyer (P) of writing and mailing a blackmailing letter. MacDougall (D) moved for a summary dismissal of counts two, three, and four, denying the slanderous comments were made and relying upon affidavits and deposition testimony of the alleged recipients of the comments, who denied hearing the slanderous utterances. After Dyer (P) declined an opportunity to depose the witnesses, the court summarily dismissed counts three and four, ruling that Dyer (P) could present no evidence at trial that the slanderous utterances were made. Dyer (P) appealed.

■ **ISSUE**

In view of affidavits and deposition testimony denying that the slanderous utterances occurred, does a genuine issue of material fact exist to preclude summary dismissal of the slander counts?

■ **DECISION AND RATIONALE**

(Hand, J.) No. While the plaintiff bears the burden of proving the slanderous utterances were made, the defendant bears the burden on summary judgment of establishing that no genuine issue of material fact exists as to their existence. Because the plaintiff declined to conduct further discovery into the statements made in the affidavit, it is presumed that the deposition testimony would confirm the statements made as true. Based on this assumption, the plaintiff would have no witness at trial who would testify that the utterances were made. Under such circumstances, a directed verdict appears appropriate. Although the witnesses' credibility must be considered to determine the veracity of their statements, a directed verdict would still be appropriate. If a directed verdict could be challenged merely because the appellant wishes to submit the evidence to a jury based on the potential that the jury will disbelieve the witness, the appellate court, being unable to consider the demeanor of any

---

witness itself, would be powerless to review the judgment. The standard should be no different for summary dismissal than for a directed verdict. It is true that if the plaintiff had the opportunity to cross-examine the witnesses at trial, the witnesses could potentially recant their denials and provide the plaintiff the evidence needed to carry his burden. The plaintiff, however, has declined to depose the witnesses to establish this possibility with more than mere speculation. Had the plaintiff taken the depositions and pointed to some behavior indicating the witnesses lacked candor, the case would be different. Because the plaintiff failed to avail himself of further discovery, his argument is without merit. Affirmed.

Analysis:

A witness's demeanor on the witness stand is a powerful means of determining the veracity of the witness's testimony. For purposes of summary judgment, however, one may not merely rely upon the possibility that the witness's demeanor will raise doubts in the minds of the jury. As suggested here, if the witness had demonstrated behavior in a deposition or otherwise that may suggest a motive or intent to be untruthful, summary judgment would generally be inappropriate. By itself, however, a witness's statement made under oath will generally be afforded a presumption of veracity on summary judgment.

■ CASE VOCABULARY

DEMEANOR: Outward appearance or behavior, such as facial expressions, tone of voice, gestures, and the hesitation or readiness to answer questions. In evaluating credibility, the jury may consider the witness's demeanor.

LIBEL: 1. A defamatory statement expressed in a fixed medium, especially writing but also a picture, sign, or electronic broadcast. Libel is classified as both a crime and a tort but is no longer prosecuted as a crime. Also termed *defamatory libel*. 2. The act of making such a statement; publication of defamatory matter by written or printed words, by its embodiment in physical form, or by any other form of communication that has the potentially harmful qualities characteristic of written or printed words.

SLANDER: A defamatory assertion expressed in a transitory form, especially speech. Damages for slander—unlike those for libel—are not presumed and thus must be proved by the plaintiff (unless the defamation is slander per se).

VERACITY: Truthfulness, as in the "witness's fraud conviction supports the defense's challenge to his veracity"; accuracy, as in "you called into question the veracity of Murphy's affidavit."

CHAPTER SEVEN

Judicial Supervision of Pre–Trial and Promotion of Settlement

G. Heileman Brewing Co. v. Joseph Oat Corp.

Instant Facts: A judge sanctioned Joseph Oat Corporation (D) for failing to have a corporate representative with the authority to settle appear at a pretrial conference, as required by the court's order.

Black Letter Rule: Under Federal Rule of Civil Procedure 16 and the court's inherent authority to manage the litigation process, a court may order represented parties to appear to further settlement discussions.

Marek v. Chesney

Instant Facts: Following judgment for the plaintiff, Chesney (P) sought recovery of costs and attorney's fees incurred after he rejected the defendants' settlement offer.

Black Letter Rule: Rule 68 of the Federal Rules of Civil Procedure permits the recovery of attorney's fees as a part of the costs of litigation if so provided by the underlying substantive statute governing the action.

G. Heileman Brewing Co. v. Joseph Oat Corp.

(Plaintiff) v. *(Violator of Court Order)*

871 F.2d 648 (7th Cir. 1989)

THE COURT CAN COMPEL ATTENDANCE AT A PRETRIAL CONFERENCE

■ **INSTANT FACTS** A judge sanctioned Joseph Oat Corporation (D) for failing to have a corporate representative with the authority to settle appear at a pretrial conference, as required by the court's order.

■ **BLACK LETTER RULE** Under Federal Rule of Civil Procedure 16 and the court's inherent authority to manage the litigation process, a court may order represented parties to appear to further settlement discussions.

■ **PROCEDURAL BASIS**

On appeal to review a district court order imposing sanctions upon the defendant for violating a court order.

■ **FACTS**

A district court judge ordered the corporate parties to appear by a representative with authority to settle at a pretrial conference to discuss the posture of the case and a possible settlement. Although counsel for Joseph Oat Corporation (D) appeared at the conference, no corporate representative appeared. The court determined that Joseph Oat (D) violated its order and issued sanctions. Joseph Oat (D) appealed, contending that the court lacked the authority to compel the appearance of represented parties at the pretrial settlement conference; if the court does possess such authority, it abused its discretion in so ordering; and it was an abuse of discretion to impose sanctions.

■ **ISSUE**

May a federal court order litigants—even those represented by counsel—to appear before it in person at a pretrial conference for the purpose of discussing the posture and settlement of the litigants' case?

■ **DECISION AND RATIONALE**

(Kanne, J.) Yes. Under Federal Rule of Civil Procedure 16 and the court's inherent authority to manage the litigation process, a court may order represented parties to appear to further settlement discussions. Under Rule 16, pretrial conferences are an important tool to narrow issues for trial and arrange for settlement to dispose of unnecessary litigation. Although Rule 16 is specifically limited in its terms to the participation of counsel and unrepresented parties, a court's powers are not confined to Rule 16. A court has the inherent authority to conduct litigation to generally achieve the goals of the pretrial conference. The Federal Rules of Civil Procedure are to be liberally construed and must be considered in connection with the court's inherent authority. Accordingly, the court had the authority to order the appearance of represented parties with authority to settle the matter.

Although the court has the authority to foster settlement discussions, it may not coerce involuntary settlements. Here, the court's requirement that the corporate representatives have "authority to settle" does not indicate coercion, but merely that the representatives need be persons of sufficient stature and authority within the corporation to be able to bind the parties should settlement discussions reach such

---

a stage. The sanctions were imposed not because Joseph Oat (D) refused to settle the case, but because the company's representatives refused to appear to engage in good-faith settlement discussions in a neutral forum. Additionally, while there may be occasions when a court's order requiring a high-ranking corporate representative to attend a pretrial conference is onerous, costly, or burdensome, this is not such a case. This matter involves a claim for $4 million and a trial that is expected to last several months, resulting in substantial legal fees and court time. Joseph Oat (D) incurred the travel expense of sending its counsel a long distance to attend, costs that would have been similarly incurred for a corporate representative. Furthermore, Joseph Oat (D) made no objection to the court's order until after the sanctions were imposed. Had Joseph Oat (D) taken exception to the terms of the order, it should have presented those objections before the pretrial conference to enable the court to consider the burden, if any, caused by its order.

Finally, Joseph Oat (D) contends that the court's instructions were ambiguous and that corporate counsel constitutes a "corporate representative." It appears that Joseph Oat (D) was well aware of what was expected by the order. The court did not abuse its discretion. Affirmed.

■ DISSENT

(Posner, J.) Although the specific language of Rule 16 allows for the negative implication that represented parties may not be compelled to appear at a pretrial conference, the court need not have determined that issue because the case can be decided on much narrower grounds. The insistence of the trial judge on corporate representatives with authority to settle places upon the parties the duty to entertain good-faith settlement discussions. Neither Rule 16 nor any other federal statute places such a duty upon federal litigants. Joseph Oat (D) had previously indicated in certain terms that it was unwilling to settle the matter in any way that resulted in its payment of money. Furthermore, there is no indication that any one Joseph Oat (D) representative possesses the sole authority to settle a lawsuit on the corporation's behalf. Joseph Oat (D), therefore, may have been required to bring its entire board of directors to the conference to satisfy the judge's demand. Because the court's order unreasonably and without authority compels the parties to engage in settlement discussions, the court abused its discretion.

■ DISSENT

(Coffey, J.) The terms of Rule 16 are clear and unambiguous. Therefore, the court has no authority under the rule to compel the attendance of represented parties at a pretrial conference.

■ DISSENT

(Easterbrook, J.) Even assuming the court possessed the authority to compel a represented party to attend the pretrial conference, such power does not encompass the authority to demand a specific corporate representative rather than his agent nor the authority to insist that the person possess full settlement authority. Corporate employees are agents of the corporation to the same extent an attorney is, and the scope of each person's agency is determined by internal corporate affairs. Clearly, an attorney with the authority to speak on the corporation's behalf suffices as well as an employee vested with the same authority. Similarly, Joseph Oat's (D) attorney was rejected by the court because he indicated that he had no authority to pay money on the corporation's behalf. This is not because the attorney lacked authority, but because Joseph Oat (D) had determined that no agent possessed such authority. Had a corporate officer appeared and declared that he lacked authority to pay money on the corporation's behalf, Joseph Oat (D) still would have violated the order. Further, given the amount of money involved, Joseph Oat (D) likely would not have authorized any one individual to settle the claims against it, instead retaining that authority in the entire board of directors. Any corporate representative would have merely appeared to listen to settlement proposals and refer them to the board of directors for consideration, just as the defendant's counsel did. While the court should promote settlement as a viable resolution to a dispute, the court may not insist that a representative appear for settlement purposes contrary to the corporate party's internal business decisions.

Analysis:

Many consider Rule 16 one of the most powerful means available to judges to manage their caseloads. With the expansive understanding of the rule stated in G. *Heileman Brewing*, the court has discretionary authority over the pretrial stages in virtually all matters involving attorneys, unrepresented parties, and represented parties. Some commentators suggest, however, that the G. *Heileman Brewing* court's construction of the rule indicates a general mistrust of attorneys in settlement matters, because what may be the best outcome for the parties may not be the best outcome for the attorney representing those parties.

■ CASE VOCABULARY

PRETRIAL CONFERENCE: An informal meeting at which opposing attorneys confer, usually with the judge, to work toward the disposition of the case by discussing matters of evidence and narrowing the issues that will be tried.

SANCTION: A penalty or coercive measure that results from failure to comply with a law, rule, or order.

Marek v. Chesny

(Police Officer) v. *(Decedent's Father)*

473 U.S. 1, 105 S.Ct. 3012, 87 L.Ed.2d 1 (1985)

THERE'S NO RECOVERY OF POST–SETTLEMENT–OFFER COSTS WHEN THE RECOVERY AT TRIAL IS LESS THAN THE OFFER

■ **INSTANT FACTS** Following judgment for the plaintiff, Chesney (P) sought recovery of costs and attorney's fees incurred after he rejected the defendants' settlement offer.

■ **BLACK LETTER RULE** Rule 68 of the Federal Rules of Civil Procedure permits the recovery of attorney's fees as a part of the costs of litigation if so provided by the underlying substantive statute governing the action.

■ **PROCEDURAL BASIS**

Certiorari to review a decision of the Seventh Circuit Court of Appeals reversing a district court order denying the plaintiff's request for post-offer costs.

■ **FACTS**

Chesney's (P) son was shot and killed by Marek (D) and two other police officers responding to a report of a domestic disturbance. Chesney (P) sued the defendants in federal court under 42 U.S.C. § 1983 and under state tort law. Before trial, the defendants offered to settle the case for $100,000, which offer Chesney (P) refused. Following trial, Chesney (P) was awarded $5000 on his wrongful death claim, $52,000 for § 1983 violations, and $3000 in punitive damages. Chesney (P) then filed a petition with the court under 42 U.S.C. § 1988 to require the defendants to pay over $170,000 in costs and attorney's fees incurred both before and after the settlement offer. The defendants opposed the request, arguing that Rule 68 of the Federal Rules of Civil Procedure requires the plaintiff to bear his own costs and fees incurred after rejecting a settlement offer that exceeds the plaintiff's recovery at trial. The district court agreed and denied the plaintiff's request for post-offer costs and fees. After the parties agreed to payment of pre-offer costs and fees, the plaintiff appealed the denial of post-offer costs and fees. The Seventh Circuit Court of Appeals reversed, holding that Rule 68 cannot be linked with the fee-shifting provisions of 42 U.S.C. § 1988 because it would deprive civil rights plaintiffs of a meaningful choice when considering the adequacy of a settlement offer. The defendants appealed.

■ **ISSUE**

Must attorney's fees incurred by a plaintiff subsequent to an offer of settlement under Rule 68 of the Federal Rules of Civil Procedure be paid by the defendant under 42 U.S.C. § 1988, when the plaintiff ultimately recovers a judgment for less than the offer?

■ **DECISION AND RATIONALE**

(Burger, C.J.) No. Under the American Rule, each party is generally required to bear his own costs of litigation, including attorney's fees. Rule 68 and 42 U.S.C. § 1988, however, shift this burden to the unsuccessful party in litigation under certain circumstances. Rule 68 is designed to encourage settlement of claims and avoid litigation, prompting both parties to evaluate the risks and costs of litigation and balance them against the likelihood of success at trial. Similarly, 42 U.S.C. § 1988,

---

permitting a court to award reasonable attorney's fees to a prevailing civil rights litigant, ensures a civil rights plaintiff will not be financially deterred from holding the defendants responsible for civil rights violations. Chesney (P) argues that Marek's (D) offer of settlement was invalid under Rule 68 because it "lumped" the amount of damages and the amount of costs together in a single offer. When that happens, Chesney (P) argues, the plaintiff is unable to determine the true value of the settlement and make an informed decision whether to accept it. A settlement offer under Rule 68, however, need not bifurcate money damages and costs. At the time of a settlement, a plaintiff knows the amount of costs and attorneys' fees accrued as of the offer and can reasonably determine what portion of the defendant's offer must be allocated to costs.

While Rule 68 permits the recovery of "costs," it does not define the term or specifically provide for an award of attorney's fees. However, at the time of its adoption, numerous federal fee-shifting statutes existed addressing both costs and attorney's fees. Because of the importance of the term "costs" to Rule 68, the reasonable inference to be drawn from the failure to distinguish attorney's fees from other costs is that the drafters intended Rule 68 to apply to all costs, including attorney's fees, that are recoverable under the underlying statutes governing the merits of the case. Here, § 1988 specifically permits a prevailing party to recover attorney's fees "as a part of the costs." Since Congress expressly provided so by statute, attorney's fees are recoverable as costs under Rule 68. This construction is the only means of giving effect to both Rule 68 and § 1988, and it does not frustrate the goal of ensuring civil rights plaintiffs' access to justice, for it merely requires a plaintiff to evaluate the risks of litigation in light of the offer, just as in any civil case. Together, Rule 68 and § 1988 combine to encourage plaintiffs to bring meritorious civil rights suits, but also settle those claims upon receipt of a reasonable settlement offer. Reversed.

■ DISSENT

(Brennan, J.) The Court's decision to include attorney's fees within the meaning of the term "costs" as used in Rule 68 creates variations in the application of the numerous federal fee-shifting statutes because of the precise language chosen in a particular statute. Congress and the Judicial Conference of the United States have launched strenuous attacks on Rule 68 in an effort to bring attorney's fees within its scope. These attacks indicate the legislative viewpoint that federal statutes speaking only in terms of attorney's fees are not to be inexplicably incorporated within Rule 68's meaning of "costs." While the plain meaning of Rule 68 addresses only costs and § 1988 specifically provides that attorney's fees are a component of costs, the Court must look beyond the implication of the statutory words to reach the legislative intent of their meaning.

"Costs," as it is used in Rule 68, must be considered only to mean those taxable costs traditionally allowed at common law. This is so because nowhere in the historical treatment of the Federal Rules is it insinuated that costs should vary in application depending on the language of the substantive statute at issue. Further, the Federal Rules provide that costs may be taxed by the court clerk, suggesting "costs" is limited to only those charges readily determinable from the records of the court. Likewise, elsewhere in the Federal Rules, attorney's fees are given separate treatment when a rule is intended to cover both costs and fees. Finally, words expressed in the Federal Rules must be construed in favor of a consistent application, as the drafters could not have intended different results from Rule 68 in the absence of qualifying language.

Using the Court's approach, Rule 68, when applied along with Rule 54(d), would require an unsuccessful civil rights plaintiff to pay the defendant's attorney's fees and costs, which directly conflicts with § 1988. The Court's decision impermissibly brings the explicit language of federal fee-shifting statutes within the requirements of Rule 68, which runs contrary to the legislative intent of those statutes and results in the inconsistent application of the rule. With specific reference to § 1988, the Court's decision conflicts with the congressional policies underlying the statute. Section 1988 requires that attorney's fees be reasonable considering various factors, such as the number of hours expended and the hourly rate charged, and permits the court to be sensitive of the complexities of the merits. Rule 68, on the other hand, contains no such provision. It strips the court of all discretion by requiring the shifting of costs incurred after a settlement is rejected. Rule 68 pressures a plaintiff to accept a low offer early in litigation for fear of bearing all the fees even if later discovery would indicate a stronger case than first contemplated. Because Rule 68 permits a defendant to make subsequent offers, the inclusion of attorney's fees within the rule encourages the defendants to gradually increase their unacceptable settlement offers in an effort to further cut off the plaintiff's right to recover fees under § 1988 should he or she prevail.

Analysis:

While Rule 68, on its face, applies to both plaintiffs and defendants, the interpretation of § 1988 has been that plaintiffs are not responsible for the costs and attorney's fees incurred by the defendant absent certain circumstances. Though a defendant may succeed entirely on the merits of the case, the policy of § 1988 of promoting civil rights plaintiffs' access to justice requires the defendant to bear its own costs in defending legitimate, though unsuccessful, claims. This conclusion is often supported by the fact that the defendant controls its own conduct and has committed at least some act that gives rise to potential liability, though none was imposed.

■ CASE VOCABULARY

AMERICAN RULE: The general policy that all litigants must bear their own attorney's fees, including the prevailing party.

CHAPTER EIGHT

Trial

Beacon Theatres, Inc. v. Westover

Instant Facts: Beacon Theatres (D) petitioned for a writ of mandamus to order a district court judge to vacate orders denying a jury trial.

Black Letter Rule: Whenever possible, a court must exercise its discretion to preserve the right to a trial by jury.

Dairy Queen v. Wood

Instant Facts: Dairy Queen's (P) motion for a jury trial in a trademark infringement case was denied.

Black Letter Rule: A claim for a money judgment is a claim wholly legal in nature, however the complaint is construed.

Ross v. Bernhard

Instant Facts: Ross (P) brought a shareholders' derivative action and the court denied a request for a jury trial.

Black Letter Rule: The right to a jury trial in a derivative action attaches to those issues that would entitle the corporation to a jury trial if the corporation were suing in its own right.

Curtis v. Loether

Instant Facts: Curtis (P) brought suit under the Fair Housing Act and Loether (D) made a demand for a jury trial.

Black Letter Rule: The Seventh Amendment applies to causes of action created by statute, and requires a jury trial if the statute creates legal rights enforceable in an action for damages.

Tull v. United States

Instant Facts: Tull's (D) request for a jury trial in an enforcement action under the Clean Water Act was denied.

Black Letter Rule: A trial by jury on the issue of liability is available in an action created by statute if the nature of the relief authorized by statute is the type traditionally available only in a court of law, but there is no right to a jury determination of the remedy.

Teamsters Local No. 391 v. Terry

Instant Facts: Terry (P) brought an action against Teamsters Local No. 391 (D) for breach of its duty of fair representation, and his request for a jury trial was granted.

Black Letter Rule: The right to a jury trial in a statutory action is determined first by comparing the action to eighteenth-century actions in England prior to the merger of he courts of law and equity, and secondly by examining the nature of the remedy sought and determining whether it is legal or equitable in nature.

Granfinanciera, S.A. v. Nordberg

Instant Facts: Nordberg (P) brought suit to recover fraudulent conveyances and the bankruptcy judge denied Granfinanciera's (D) request for a jury trial.

Black Letter Rule: Legislation that creates a right of action may not deny the right to a jury trial if the action adjudicates only private rights.

Galloway v. United States

Instant Facts: Galloway's (P) claim for disability benefits due to insanity was denied for lack of evidence.

Black Letter Rule: The Seventh Amendment was intended to preserve the basic institution of the jury trial in its most fundamental elements, not to preserve procedural forms and details.

Lavender v. Kurn

Instant Facts: The verdict finding that Lavender's (P) decedent had been killed accidentally was reversed by the Supreme Court of Missouri for a lack of substantial evidence to support the verdict.

Black Letter Rule: A jury's verdict will be overturned on appeal only if there is a complete lack of probative evidence to support the verdict.

Guenther v. Armstrong Rubber Co.

Instant Facts: Guenther (P) was injured when a tire exploded, and there was contradictory testimony regarding whether he was injured by the tire introduced into evidence at trial.

Black Letter Rule: It is not the function of the judge to resolve problems with the evidence presented.

Ahern v. Scholz

Instant Facts: The jury found for Ahern (P) in his breach of contract action against his manager Scholz (D), and Scholz's (D) motion for a new trial was denied.

Black Letter Rule: A trial court has broad discretion to grant a motion for a new trial, but a new trial should not be granted if there is a reasonable factual basis for the jury's verdict.

Dimick v. Schiedt

Instant Facts: Schiedt (P) won a verdict of $500 from Dimick (D); the court told Dimick (D) that Schiedt's (P) motion for a new trial would not be granted if he consented to an increase in the damage award to $1500.

Black Letter Rule: An inadequate verdict should not be permitted to stand, but the parties retain the right to have a jury determine the question of liability and the extent of the damages.

Whitlock v. Jackson

Instant Facts: Whitlock (P) moved for a new trial, claiming that the jury's verdict was inconsistent.

Black Letter Rule: The court must search for a reasonable way to read a verdict as expressing a coherent view of the case, and if there is any way to view a case that makes a jury's answers to special interrogatories consistent, the answers must be resolved in that way.

Sopp v. Smith

Instant Facts: Sopp (P) moved for a new trial based on a juror's affidavit stating that the juror engaged in misconduct.

Black Letter Rule: A juror's affidavit of misconduct may not be used to impeach a jury's verdict, unless that affidavit states that the verdict was arrived at by resorting to chance or that a false answer on *voir dire* concealed bias or disqualification.

People v. Hutchinson

Instant Facts: Hutchinson (D) was convicted of possession of marijuana for sale and moved for a new trial based on a juror's affidavit of coercion.

Black Letter Rule: Jurors are competent witnesses to prove objective facts to impeach a jury's verdict.

Beacon Theatres, Inc. v. Westover

(Drive–In Theater Owner) v. *(District Court Judge)*
359 U.S. 500, 79 S.Ct. 948 (1959)

WHENEVER POSSIBLE, TRIALS MUST BE BEFORE A JURY

■ **INSTANT FACTS** Beacon Theatres (D) petitioned for a writ of mandamus to order a district court judge to vacate orders denying a jury trial.

■ **BLACK LETTER RULE** Whenever possible, a court must exercise its discretion to preserve the right to a trial by jury.

■ PROCEDURAL BASIS
Appeal from an order of the Ninth Circuit Court of Appeals, refusing a petition for a writ of mandamus.

■ FACTS
Beacon Theatres (D) owned a drive-in theater near a movie theater owned by Fox West Coat Theatres (P). The Fox (P) theater had the exclusive right to show first-run movies in the area. Beacon (D) notified Fox (P) that it regarded contracts such as the one granting Fox (P) the exclusive rights to show first-run movies in an area to be overt acts in violation of the antitrust laws. Fox (P) then brought an action for declaratory relief against Beacon (D), alleging that Beacon's (D) letter, along with threats of treble damage suits against Fox (P) and its distributors, were duress and coercion that deprived Fox (P) of its right to negotiate for first-run contracts. Fox's (P) action asked for declaratory relief that the exclusive contracts it had did not violate the antitrust laws and for an injunction restraining Beacon (D) from instituting action under the antitrust laws against Fox (P). Beacon (D) filed an answer and a counterclaim. The counterclaim requested treble damages from Fox (P).

Beacon (D) requested a jury trial in the case. The district court viewed the issues raised by the complaint as equitable and directed that those issues be tried to the court, prior to a jury trial on the issues raised by the counterclaim. The court of appeals refused to reverse the district judge's order. The court held that the complaint, taken as a whole, was one for injunctive relief, which was traditionally a matter for equity. Fox (P) was entitled to have the equitable issues resolved by a judge, even though legal rights could be involved. The court also noted that equity courts are allowed to retain jurisdiction even when a legal remedy is available. The court reasoned by analogy, holding that it was not an abuse of discretion to enjoin Beacon's (D) assertion of its legal claim and try the equitable case first. The fact that trial of the equitable action first could result in a denial of a jury trial of the equitable claims, because the court's decision on the equitable action could work as res judicata or collateral estoppel, did not make the court's decision an abuse of discretion.

■ ISSUE
Was Beacon (D) entitled to a jury trial on its equitable claims?

■ DECISION AND RATIONALE
(Black, J.) Yes. Whenever possible, a court must exercise its discretion to preserve the right to a trial by jury. Injunctive relief requires a showing of irreparable harm and the inadequacy of legal remedies. The inadequacy of a legal remedy and irreparable harm must be evaluated in light of the remedies afforded

by the Declaratory Judgment Act and the Federal Rules of Civil Procedure. The federal rules allow for trial of equitable and legal claims in the same action. Any defenses Fox (P) may have to Beacon's (D) antitrust action, whether legal or equitable, could be asserted either in its suit for declaratory relief or in response to Beacon's (D) counterclaim. On a proper showing, other suits or actions could be enjoined pending the outcome of the original lawsuit. Permanent injunctive relief could be granted after the jury renders its verdict. In this manner, the issues between the parties could be resolved in one suit, without the necessity of splitting claims. Reversed.

■ **DISSENT**

(Stewart, J.) The Declaratory Judgment Act and the Federal Rules of Civil Procedure do not expand the substantive law. The Declaratory Judgment Act merely creates a new statutory remedy. That remedy is available in suits in equity and law. The availability of declaratory relief alone cannot operate to grant Beacon (D) the right to a jury trial. The right to a jury trial in this case is based solely on the assertion of the counterclaim, but the issue was primarily presented in the original claim for equitable relief. The assertion of a legal counterclaim cannot transform the equitable nature of the original complaint. It has long been established that a court of equity can retain jurisdiction even though an adequate legal remedy becomes available. The majority's opinion seems to discard this rule.

Analysis:

The rule that courts could enjoin a threatened action stems from the days when there were separate courts of equity that ordinarily did not have the jurisdiction to hear legal claims. With the merger of equity and law courts, along with the rules of procedure that provide for one form of action and liberal joinder of proceedings, there is no practical reason a court may not hear legal and equitable claims at the same time. The right to a jury trial takes precedence over the historical practices. Adherence to the former rule, as acknowledged by the court of appeal, could result in a limitation of a party's right to a jury trial, because of the preclusive effect of a decision by the court in the trial of the equitable issues.

■ **CASE VOCABULARY**

ADEQUATE REMEDY AT LAW: A legal remedy (such as an award of damages) that provides sufficient relief to the petitioning party, thus preventing the party from obtaining equitable relief.

DECLARATORY JUDGMENT: A binding adjudication that establishes the rights and other legal relations of the parties without providing for or ordering enforcement.

EQUITABLE REMEDY: A nonmonetary remedy, such as an injunction or specific performance, obtained when monetary damages cannot adequately redress the injury.

MANDAMUS: [Latin, "we command."] A writ issued by a superior court to compel a lower court or government officer to perform mandatory or purely ministerial duties correctly.

SEVENTH AMENDMENT: The constitutional amendment, ratified with the Bill of Rights in 1791, guaranteeing the right to a jury trial in federal civil cases that are traditionally considered to be suits at common law and that have an amount in controversy exceeding $20.

Dairy Queen v. Wood

(Trademark Licensee) v. *(District Court Judge)*
369 U.S. 469, 82 S.Ct. 894 (1962)

CLAIMS FOR MONEY DAMAGES MUST BE HEARD BY A JURY

■ **INSTANT FACTS** Dairy Queen's (P) motion for a jury trial in a trademark infringement case was denied.

■ **BLACK LETTER RULE** A claim for a money judgment is a claim wholly legal in nature, however the complaint is construed.

■ PROCEDURAL BASIS

Appeal from an order denying a petition for a writ of mandamus.

■ FACTS

Dairy Queen (D) was sued for trademark infringement. The complaint requested injunctive relief restraining Dairy Queen (D) from using the disputed trademark, an accounting to determine the exact amount owed and a judgment for that amount, and an in junction pending accounting preventing Dairy Queen (D) from collecting any money from "Dairy Queen" stores. Dairy Queen (D) made a motion for a jury trial, which was denied. Dairy Queen (D) brought a petition in the court of appeals for a writ of mandamus ordering a jury trial, which was denied.

■ ISSUE

Was Dairy Queen (D) entitled to a jury trial when its claims involved money damages?

■ DECISION AND RATIONALE

(Black, J.) Yes. A claim for a money judgment is a claim wholly legal in nature, however the complaint is construed. The plaintiff's complaint is cast in terms of an "accounting," rather than an action on a debt or for damages. But the right to a jury trial does not depend upon the way pleadings are drafted. A suit for an accounting is an equitable suit only if the issues are so complicated that only a court of equity can understand them. This is not such a complicated case, and a legal remedy cannot be called inadequate solely because it would require an examination of business records. In addition, the suit is not equitable because of the defenses interposed by Dairy Queen (D). The factual issues presented by the case are common to the legal and equitable claims involved. The legal claims must therefore be determined before the determination of the equitable claims. Reversed.

■ CONCURRENCE

(Harlan, J.) This case is nothing more than joinder of prayers for legal and equitable relief in the same complaint. In such circumstances, there can be no deprivation of the right to a jury trial on the legal portion of the claim.

Analysis:

The majority's opinion presents a simple rule: if there is a claim for a money judgment, the suit is a suit at law and there is a right to a trial by jury. The test focuses solely on the relief requested, not on the name given to the action or the way the issues are framed. The procedure alluded to in *Beacon Theatres, Inc. v. Westover,* 359 U.S. 500 (1959), seems to be eliminated. In that case, reference was made to the traditional practice of trying equitable claims first. In this case, the majority orders trial of the legal claims first, before the equitable claims will be heard.

■ CASE VOCABULARY

ACCOUNTING: A legal action to compel a defendant to account for and pay over money owed to the plaintiff but held by the defendant (often the plaintiff's agent).

ACCOUNTING FOR PROFITS: An action for equitable relief against a person in a fiduciary relationship to recover profits taken in a breach of the relationship.

Ross v. Bernhard

(Trustee) v. *(Corporate Director)*
396 U.S. 531, 90 S.Ct. 733 (1970)

A JURY MAY HEAR SHAREHOLDERS' DERIVATIVE SUITS

■ **INSTANT FACTS** Ross (P) brought a shareholders' derivative action and the court denied a request for a jury trial.

■ **BLACK LETTER RULE** The right to a jury trial in a derivative action attaches to those issues that would entitle the corporation to a jury trial if the corporation were suing in its own right.

■ **PROCEDURAL BASIS**

Appeal from an order of the court of appeals holding that a jury trial was not available.

■ **FACTS**

Ross (P) brought a shareholders' derivative action against Bernhard (D) and the other directors of an investment corporation and the corporation's brokers. The prayer for relief requested that the defendants "account for and pay to the Corporation for their profits and gains and its losses." The complaint also requested a jury trial. Bernhard (D) and the other defendants moved to strike the demand for a jury trial. The district court denied the motion, holding that only the shareholder's initial claim to speak for the corporation would be tried to the judge. The right to a jury trial on the remaining issues would be determined according to the corporation's own right to a trial by jury on those issues. The court of appeals reversed, holding that a jury trial is never available in a derivative action.

■ **ISSUE**

Is there a right to a jury trial in a derivative action?

■ **DECISION AND RATIONALE**

(White, J.) Yes. The right to a jury trial in a derivative action attaches to those issues that would entitle the corporation to a jury trial if the corporation were suing in its own right. At the time of the enactment of the Seventh Amendment, it was established that a corporation had the right to a jury trial in a common law action to enforce its rights. The common law did not, however, recognize actions by shareholders to enforce the rights of a corporation. Derivative suits were recognized solely as equitable actions. The reasoning was that there was the threat of an irreparable injury, and there was no adequate remedy at law for the corporation since the shareholder did not have the standing to sue. But derivative suits actually have a dual nature that is both legal and equitable. The equitable nature of the derivative suit is only in the claim of the shareholder to speak for the corporation. The legal nature is in the substance of the claims to be presented. A legal claim does not become an equitable claim by reason of being presented to a court of equity.

There is no more separation between courts of equity and courts of law. There is only one type of action, a "civil action," in which all claims may be joined and for which all types of remedies are available. After a court passes on the right of a shareholder to bring the suit, the court may hear the legal claims with the aid of a jury. The historical rules that prevented a court of law from hearing a shareholder's derivative suit are obsolete. Given the availability of both legal and equitable remedies,

---

the Seventh Amendment grants the parties to a derivative suit the same right to a jury trial as the corporation would have had. Reversed.

■ DISSENT

(Stewart, J.) The Seventh Amendment does not create new rights to a jury trial, but preserves those rights as they existed when the Amendment was adopted in 1791. Similarly, the Federal Rules of Civil Procedure do not enlarge the right to a jury trial, but preserve the right as guaranteed by the Seventh Amendment. Since the shareholder's suit could be brought only in equity, it follows that there is no constitutional right to a trial by jury in a derivative suit.

Historically, a shareholder's suit was not brought to enforce the rights of a corporation. The suit was allowed only against the corporate managers, as an equitable action to enforce the rights of a beneficiary against a trustee. Recent cases have almost unanimously held that there is no right to a jury trial in a derivative action. Cases that have expanded the scope of the right to a jury trial have involved mixed actions of law and equity, not suits that have always been regarded as equitable.

Analysis:

It is solely the nature of the substantive claim that will determine the right to a jury trial. The majority is clear that it is disregarding precedent and historical practice to reach its holding. Much of the reasoning seems to be based on a hypothesis of what early courts would have done had they been constituted as they are now. Justice Stewart's dissent, in which he comments that the majority's opinion is driven by a bias in favor of jury trials, seems accurate.

■ CASE VOCABULARY

DERIVATIVE ACTION: A suit by a beneficiary of a fiduciary to enforce a right belonging to the fiduciary; especially, a suit asserted by a shareholder on the corporation's behalf against a third party (usually a corporate officer) because of the corporation's failure to take some action against the third party.

Curtis v. Loether

(Prospective Tenant) v. *(Landlord)*

415 U.S. 189, 94 S.Ct. 1005 (1974)

A JURY CAN DECIDE FAIR HOUSING CLAIMS

■ **INSTANT FACTS** Curtis (P) brought suit under the Fair Housing Act and Loether (D) made a demand for a jury trial.

■ **BLACK LETTER RULE** The Seventh Amendment applies to causes of action created by statute, and requires a jury trial if the statute creates legal rights enforceable in an action for damages.

■ **PROCEDURAL BASIS**

Appeal from an order of the court of appeals, holding that Loether (D) was entitled to a jury trial.

■ **FACTS**

Curtis (P) brought suit against Loether (D) for violations of the Fair Housing Act, Title VIII of the Civil Rights Act of 1968 (42 U.S.C. § 3601 *et seq.*). Her complaint sought injunctive relief and punitive damages. She amended her complaint to include a claim for compensatory damages. Loether (D) demanded a jury trial, which was denied by the district court. The court of appeals reversed.

■ **ISSUE**

Is the defendant entitled to a jury trial in a civil rights case subjecting it to potential money damages?

■ **DECISION AND RATIONALE**

(Marshall, J.) Yes. The Seventh Amendment applies to causes of action created by statute and requires a jury trial if the statute creates legal rights enforceable in an action for damages. The Seventh Amendment right to a jury trial extends beyond the common law forms of action in existence in 1791. The term "common law" is used to distinguish cases from claims brought in equity and maritime or admiralty claims. The Court has long recognized the right to a jury trial in statutorily created actions.

The statute here creates a legal right analogous to an action in tort. The enactment authorizes the court to order monetary compensation for a defendant's wrongful act. More importantly, the type of relief sought is the type of relief traditionally offered in the courts of law. There is some legislative history of the Fair Housing Act indicating that the proponents of the law were concerned about the effect of racial prejudice on jury verdicts. There is also a legitimate policy concern that jury trials could delay the disposition of housing cases. These considerations are not enough to defeat the right to a jury trial. Affirmed.

Analysis:

Many rights of action created by statute do not have a precise analog in common law forms of action. In 1791, there was no right of action for discrimination in housing. The Court compares a discrimination action to a tort action, but does not rest its decision on that reasoning. The right to a jury trial in statutory actions will be determined by the nature of relief sought.

Tull v. United States

(Polluter) v. *(Environmental Law Enforcement)*

481 U.S. 412, 107 S.Ct. 1831, 95 L.Ed.2d 365 (1987)

JURIES DETERMINE LIABILITY, JUDGES DETERMINE REMEDIES

■ **INSTANT FACTS** Tull's (D) request for a jury trial in an enforcement action under the Clean Water Act was denied.

■ **BLACK LETTER RULE** A trial by jury on the issue of liability is available in an action created by statute if the nature of the relief authorized by statute is the type traditionally available only in a court of law, but there is no right to a jury determination of the remedy.

■ PROCEDURAL BASIS

Appeal from a judgment of the Fourth Circuit Court of Appeals holding that there was no right to a jury trial in an enforcement action brought under the Clean Water Act.

■ FACTS

The United States (P) brought an action against Tull (D) under the provisions of the Clean Water Act, 33 U.S.C. §§ 1311, 1344, and 1362. Tull (D) was accused of dumping fill in wetlands. Tull (D) requested a jury trial and his request was denied. The court imposed a fine of $75,000, with additional fines if Tull (D) did not undertake restoration efforts.

■ ISSUE

Was Tull (D) entitled to a jury trial in the government's environmental enforcement action, which could have resulted in monetary penalties?

■ DECISION AND RATIONALE

(Brennan, J.) Yes. A trial by jury on the issue of liability is available in an action created by statute if the nature of the relief authorized by statute is the type traditionally available only in a court of law, but there is no right to a jury determination of the remedy. The nature of the relief sought—monetary penalties— was the type of remedy that was awarded only by the common-law courts. The action here may be compared to a common-law action for debt. This leads to the conclusion that there is a right to a jury trial. The punitive nature of the relief is not analogous to an action to abate a public nuisance. Those actions traditionally were brought in equity courts, as they relied on the power of the equity court to issue injunctive relief.

There is no right to a jury trial, however, on the *amount* of the penalty. The assessment of civil penalties does not involve the "substance of a common-law right to a trial by jury," nor a fundamental element of a jury trial. Congress is free to assign that power to judges. Reversed and remanded.

■ CONCURRENCE IN PART, DISSENT IN PART

(Scalia, J.) There is a right to a trial by jury. The majority, however, creates a form of civil adjudication that is without precedent. Juries have always determined damages, as well as liability.

Analysis:

The reasoning of the majority does seem to contradict itself. The monetary penalties that could be imposed are what give rise to the right to a jury trial, but the amount of those penalties is not to be determined by a jury. In a part of the case that does not appear in the excerpt, Justice Brennan notes that the Seventh Amendment does not prohibit Congress from fixing the amount of a specific penalty, and that Congress may therefore delegate that authority to judges. However, when Congress assesses a civil penalty, it generally establishes a uniform amount, but when a judge assesses a penalty, he or she usually engages in some fact-finding, to tailor the penalty to the particular defendant. Fact-finding in individual cases would ordinarily be a matter for a jury.

■ CASE VOCABULARY

NUISANCE: 1. A condition or situation (such as a loud noise or foul odor) that interferes with the use or enjoyment of property. Liability might or might not arise from the condition or situation. 2. Loosely, an act or failure to act resulting in an interference with the use or enjoyment of property. In this sense, the term denotes the action causing the interference, rather than the resulting condition. 3. The class of torts arising from such conditions, acts, or failures to act when they occur unreasonably.

Teamsters Local No. 391 v. Terry

(Union) v. *(Union Member)*

494 U.S. 558, 110 S.Ct. 1339, 108 L.Ed.2d 519 (1990)

THE NATURE OF THE REMEDY DETERMINES WHETHER THERE IS A RIGHT TO A JURY TRIAL

■ **INSTANT FACTS** Terry (P) brought an action against Teamsters Local No. 391 (D) for breach of its duty of fair representation, and his request for a jury trial was granted.

■ **BLACK LETTER RULE** The right to a jury trial in a statutory action is determined first by comparing the action to eighteenth-century actions in England prior to the merger of he courts of law and equity, and secondly by examining the nature of the remedy sought and determining whether it is legal or equitable in nature.

■ PROCEDURAL BASIS

Appeal from an order of the Fourth Circuit Court of Appeals affirming the denial of a motion to strike a demand for a jury trial.

■ FACTS

Terry (P) was a member of Teamsters Local No. 391 (D). He filed a grievance with the union over the seniority practices of his employer, McLean Trucking (D), and Local No. 391 (D) denied the grievance. Terry (P) brought an action against McLean (D) for breach of a collective bargaining agreement and against Local No. 391 (D) for breach of its duty of fair representation. Terry (P) requested injunctive relief and compensatory damages for lost wages and health benefits.

McLean (D) filed for bankruptcy, and the suit against it was voluntarily dismissed. The claims for injunctive relief also were voluntarily dismissed. Terry (P) had requested a jury trial, and Local No. 391 (D) moved to strike the jury demand on the ground that there is no right to a jury trial in a fair representation suit. The motion was denied and the Fourth Circuit Court of Appeals affirmed the denial.

■ ISSUE

Is there a right to a jury trial in a fair representation case against a union?

■ DECISION AND RATIONALE

(Marshall, J.) Yes. The right to a jury trial in a statutory action is determined first by comparing the action to eighteenth-century actions in England prior to the merger of he courts of law and equity, and secondly by examining the nature of the remedy sought and determining whether it is legal or equitable in nature. The second part of the inquiry is the more important one. There is no historical counterpart to an action for a union's breach of a duty of fair representation. Local No. 391 (D) has compared the action to an action to set aside an arbitration award, but there has been no arbitrator's award regarding Terry's (P) claim. Local No. 391 (D) also makes a comparison to an action by a beneficiary of a trust against a trustee for breach of fiduciary duty. That analogy is closer than the attorney malpractice comparison made by Terry (P), but it overlooks the exact nature of the issues raised by Terry's (P) suit. Terry (P) must prove a breach of a collective bargaining agreement, as well as a breach of the duty of fair representation. While fair representation can be compared to an equitable issue, Terry (P) also raises a breach of contract claim, which is a legal issue. The historical inquiry does not resolve the question.

Terry's (P) suit seeks compensatory damages only, namely, backpay and benefits. The backpay is not the disgorgement of an improperly earned profit and is not restitutionary relief. The relief of backpay is not incidental to or intertwined with injunctive relief, since Terry (P) no longer claims injunctive relief. Local No. 391 (D) argues that, because the Court has labeled backpay awarded under Title VII of the Civil Rights Act of 1968, 42 U.S.C. § 2000e *et seq.*, equitable relief, Terry's (P) claim for backpay is an equitable claim. This argument fails. Congress specifically characterized backpay under Title VII as equitable relief. Although the language of the two laws is similar, Title VII and the Labor–Management Relations Act are intended to serve different purposes. The suit here seeks a legal remedy, and Terry (P) is therefore entitled to a jury trial. Affirmed.

■ CONCURRENCE

(Brennan, J.) The historical test can and should be simplified. The Court should not consider whether a claim is analogous to a form of action available in the eighteenth-century English common-law. The historical approach makes Seventh Amendment jurisprudence needlessly convoluted. The Court should focus entirely on the nature of the relief requested.

■ CONCURRENCE

(Stevens, J.) The majority opinion exaggerates the importance of finding a common-law analogue to the duty of fair representation. The suit is comparable to an attorney malpractice action. That comparison, along with a recognized duty to scrutinize any proposed curtailment of the right to a jury trial "with the utmost care," provides a sufficient basis for the result reached in this case.

■ DISSENT

(Kennedy, J.) The identification of the trust action as a model for modern duty-of-fair-representation cases is sufficient to decide the case. The Seventh Amendment requires only a determination of whether the duty of fair representation is more similar to cases tried in law courts than those tried in equity courts. The decision was made that the suit is more like an action in equity, so the inquiry should end there.

Analysis:

If the historical analysis requirement is not dead, it certainly is not at all well. The majority dismisses the results of its analysis by saying, in effect, those results are inconclusive. The majority reasons that the action is similar to an equitable action, but has as its origin a breach of contract claim (against a non-party to the suit). The majority does not explain why a purely equitable claim could not arise, as does the claim here, out of a defendant's response to a legal claim by a third-party.

■ CASE VOCABULARY

LABOR–MANAGEMENT RELATIONS ACT: A federal statute, enacted in 1947, that regulates certain union activities, permits suits against unions for proscribed acts, prohibits certain strikes and boycotts, and provides steps for settling strikes involving national emergencies. 29 U.S.C.A. §§ 141 et seq.

Granfinanciera, S.A. v. Nordberg

(Transferee of Assets) v. *(Bankruptcy Trustee)*

492 U.S. 33, 109 S.Ct. 2782, 106 L.Ed.2d 26 (1989)

JURY TRIALS MUST BE GRANTED IN SUITS INVOLVING PRIVATE RIGHTS

■ **INSTANT FACTS** Nordberg (P) brought suit to recover fraudulent conveyances and the bankruptcy judge denied Granfinanciera's (D) request for a jury trial.

■ **BLACK LETTER RULE** Legislation that creates a right of action may not deny the right to a jury trial if the action adjudicates only private rights.

■ **PROCEDURAL BASIS**

Appeal from an order of the Eleventh Circuit Court of Appeals affirming a judgment of the district court.

■ **FACTS**

Nordberg (P) was the trustee in bankruptcy for Chase & Sanborn. Nordberg (P) filed suit against Granfinanciera (D) and Medex (D) to recover fraudulent transfers made by Chase & Sanborn. The case was referred to bankruptcy court and Granfinanciera (D) and Medex (D) requested a jury trial. The judge denied the request, stating that an action to recover a fraudulent transfer was a core action that was a non-jury issue under the English common-law. After a bench trial, judgment was entered against Granfinanciera (D) and Medex (D). The district court affirmed without discussing the jury trial question. The court of appeals affirmed the district court.

■ **ISSUE**

Should a jury trial be granted in a suit to recover fraudulent conveyances?

■ **DECISION AND RATIONALE**

(Brennan, J.) Yes. Legislation that creates a right of action may not prohibit the right to a jury trial if the action adjudicates only private rights. The right to a jury trial is not automatically precluded because Congress has chosen to assign a matter to an administrative tribunal for adjudication without a jury. Adjudication of a new cause of action may be assigned to a tribunal that lacks the attributes of an Article III court only if the case involves public rights; if the cause of action is legal in nature, there is the right to a jury trial. A public right is one that involves an action by or against the United States, or in which a federal regulatory program within the legitimate authority of Congress is intertwined. But a bankruptcy trustee's right to recover a fraudulent conveyance is a private, rather than a public, right. Such suits are not part of the bankruptcy proceedings, but concern controversies that arise out of them. Actions to recover fraudulent conveyances resemble state-law contract claims more than they do normal bankruptcy claims on a portion of the bankruptcy estate. *Katchen v. Landy,* 382 U.S. 323 (1966), held that the right to a jury trial on a trustee's preference claim depended upon whether the creditor had submitted a claim against the bankruptcy estate, making the claim part of the process of allowing or disallowing claims.

An action to recover a fraudulent conveyance is not a new cause of action, but was merely reclassified as a core proceeding in bankruptcy. The reclassification cannot change the Seventh Amendment analysis. Furthermore, requiring a jury trial in fraudulent conveyance actions would not dismantle the statutory scheme of bankruptcy. There is no evidence that Congress considered the constitutional implications when it designated the actions as core proceedings, and jury trials have been mandated in certain other actions that arise out of bankruptcy proceedings. No opinion is expressed here on whether the current jury trial provisions allow fraudulent conveyance trials to be held in bankruptcy courts, or whether the trial may be conducted by bankruptcy judges. The decision is limited to the holding that Granfinanciera (D) and Medex (D) are entitled to a jury trial on the fraudulent conveyance claims. Reversed and remanded.

■ CONCURRENCE

(Scalia, J.) The public rights doctrine requires, at a minimum, that the United States be a party to the adjudication. Disputes entirely between private parties cannot be assigned to non-Article III tribunals.

■ DISSENT

(White, J.) The bankruptcy law under which *Katchen v. Landy* was decided did not include actions to set aside voidable preferences as proceedings covered by the Bankruptcy Act. The language of that case that relates to the right to a jury trial was solely a product of the statutory scheme in existence at the time. The change in the statutory language was more than a reclassification of claims. The nature of the claim is not the only consideration in determining whether a jury may hear a case. The forum in which a claim is to be heard also is important. The Seventh Amendment has been held inapplicable to civil trials in state courts, and to federal administrative proceedings. But designation of a forum cannot always take away the right to a jury trial. The right depends upon an analysis of the English practice of the eighteenth century. It is by no means certain that an English equity court in the eighteenth century would have refused to hear Nordberg's (P) claim. With the historic evidence so uncertain, it is appropriate to defer to Congress's designation of a forum.

Analysis:

Granfinanciera (P) and Medex (P) have the right to a jury trial. But the question of the court in which the trial is to be held is explicitly, if not pointedly, left unanswered. The case must be tried again, but there is no ruling in advance as to whether it should be held in bankruptcy court or in district court. The Court also raises, but ignores, the issue of whether a bankruptcy judge—who is appointed for only a limited term, and whose rulings are subject to the review of the district court—may hear the case.

■ CASE VOCABULARY

ARTICLE III COURT: A federal court that, deriving its jurisdiction from U.S. Const. art. III, § 2, hears cases arising under the Constitution and the laws and treaties of the United States, cases in which the United States is a party, and cases between the states and between citizens of different states.

Galloway v. United States

(Veteran) v. *(Insurer)*

319 U.S. 372, 63 S.Ct. 1077 (1943)

DIRECTED VERDICTS DO NOT VIOLATE THE SEVENTH AMENDMENT

■ **INSTANT FACTS** Galloway's (P) claim for disability benefits due to insanity was denied for lack of evidence.

■ **BLACK LETTER RULE** The Seventh Amendment was intended to preserve the basic institution of the jury trial in its most fundamental elements, not to preserve procedural forms and details.

■ **PROCEDURAL BASIS**

Appeal from a judgment of the circuit court of appeals affirming the district court's grant of a directed verdict.

■ **FACTS**

Galloway (P) made a claim for disability under an insurance policy issued to him by the United States (D). He claimed that he was disabled by reason of insanity that existed on May 31, 1919, the date his policy lapsed for nonpayment of premium. Veterans' Bureau physicians diagnosed Galloway (P) as insane in 1930 and 1934. Evidence was introduced regarding incidents of erratic behavior during his service in France in 1919. Galloway (P) also introduced evidence that supported his claim that he was insane after his return from France, but there were large gaps in the time covered by that evidence. In addition, one witness testified that he could not recall the person about whom he testified, and part of the time covered by that witness's testimony was a time when Galloway (P) was on active duty in the Navy, and not at the location claimed by the witness. After the close of Galloway's (P) evidence, the district court granted the motion of the United States (D) for a directed verdict. The court held that the evidence was legally insufficient to support a verdict for Galloway. The court of appeals affirmed. Galloway (P) appealed to the Supreme Court, claiming that he was deprived of his right to a trial by jury, contrary to the Seventh Amendment.

■ **ISSUE**

Was Galloway (P) deprived of his right to a trial by jury as a result of the directed verdict?

■ **DECISION AND RATIONALE**

(Rutledge, J.) No. The Seventh Amendment was intended to preserve the basic institution of the jury trial in its most fundamental elements, not to preserve procedural forms and details. In addition, the two challenges to evidence Galloway (P) says were recognized at common law were inconsistent in their effect. The party making a demurrer to evidence essentially admitted having no case, which would deny the party making the challenge the right to a jury trial. As for the motion for a new trial, there is no suggestion that the Constitution guarantees a new trial when a challenge to the evidence is sustained. The conflicting consequences demonstrate that the Seventh Amendment could not have been intended to enshrine only these two challenges to the sufficiency of evidence.

The Seventh Amendment applies to this case only because Congress has chosen to grant the right to a jury trial. There was no right to a jury trial in monetary claims against the United States (D) in 1791. The lower courts were correct in holding that Galloway (P) did not introduce sufficient evidence to make his claim of disability. There were too many gaps in the testimony to support his claim, and there is nothing to show the totality of his disability or its permanence. The inference of total disability by reason of insanity cannot be drawn. Affirmed.

■ DISSENT

(Black, J.) The common law recognized the demurrer to evidence and the motion for a new trial. The demurrer to evidence was a risky proposition, reflecting the preference for having facts examined by the jury. The directed verdict represented increased judicial control over the presentation of evidence and began the erosion of the right to a jury trial that should be stopped. The better practice would be to allow the jury to hear the case and then grant a new trial if necessary. That approach would have given Galloway (P) the opportunity to present additional evidence to satisfy his burden of proof.

Analysis:

The majority notes briefly that the extension of the Seventh Amendment right to jury trial in this case is a matter of legislative grace. There was no right to a jury trial in a claim against the sovereign in 1791, so Congress could have refused to grant the right to a jury at all. Much of what the majority says about the Seventh Amendment would seem to be irrelevant. If a jury is not constitutionally required, there can be no deprivation of the constitutional right.

■ CASE VOCABULARY

DEMURRER TO EVIDENCE: A party's objection or exception that the evidence is legally insufficient to make a case. Its effect, upon joinder in the demurrer by the opposite party, is that the jury is discharged and the demurrer is entered on the record and decided by the court. A demurrer to evidence admits the truth of all the evidence and the legal deductions from that evidence.

DIRECTED VERDICT: A ruling by a trial judge taking a case from the jury because the evidence will permit only one reasonable verdict.

Lavender v. Kurn

(*Decedent's Administrator*) v. (*Trustee of Railroad*)

327 U.S. 645, 66 S.Ct. 740 (1946)

JURY VERDICTS MUST BE UPHELD IF THERE IS ANY EVIDENCE TO SUPPORT THEM

■ **INSTANT FACTS** The verdict finding that Lavender's (P) decedent had been killed accidentally was reversed by the Supreme Court of Missouri for a lack of substantial evidence to support the verdict.

■ **BLACK LETTER RULE** A jury's verdict will be overturned on appeal only if there is a complete lack of probative evidence to support the verdict.

■ **PROCEDURAL BASIS**

Appeal from an order of the Supreme Court of Missouri, reversing a judgment for Lavender (P).

■ **FACTS**

Haney (P), Lavender's (P) decedent, was employed in a railroad switchyard. One night he was found lying unconscious near some railroad tracks. He was taken to a hospital, but was dead on arrival. The medical evidence showed that he had been struck in the back of the head, causing a fractured skull. There were no witnesses who saw what happened to Haney (P). Lavender's (P) theory was that Haney (P) had been struck in the head by a mail-hook protruding from a train. Kurn's (D) theory was that Haney (P) had been deliberately struck in the back of the head by an unknown person. One of the doctors who performed the autopsy concluded that Haney (P) was struck in the head by a small object attached to a train backing up at eight to ten miles per hour. The doctor also admitted that the injury could have been caused by a blow from a pipe or club. Lavender (P) and Kurn (D) both introduced other evidence to support their respective theories. Kurn (D) introduced evidence to show that it was impossible for Haney (P) to have been injured accidentally, and Lavender (P) introduced evidence that cast doubt on the theory that he was murdered. The jury returned a verdict for Lavender (P) and awarded damages of $30,000. On appeal, the Missouri Supreme Court reversed the judgment, holding that there was no substantial evidence of negligence to support the submission of the case to the jury.

■ **ISSUE**

Given the conflicting evidence presented by both parties, was there sufficient evidence of negligence to submit the case to the jury?

■ **DECISION AND RATIONALE**

(Murphy, J.) Yes. A jury's verdict will be overturned on appeal only if there is a complete lack of probative evidence to support the verdict. When there is an evidentiary basis, it is for the jury to discard or disbelieve whatever facts are inconsistent with its conclusion. Evidence contrary to the verdict becomes irrelevant upon appeal. It would be an undue invasion of the jury's function for an appellate court to weigh the conflicting evidence or judge the credibility of witnesses. It is immaterial that the appellate court may draw a different inference from the evidence presented. The conclusion reached by the jury in this case was not an unreasonable one in light of the evidence. Reversed and remanded.

Analysis:

Reading the recitation of evidence in this case, there does not seem to be any particular reason to prefer Lavender's (P) theory to the theory advance by Kurn (D). A jury is able to hear live testimony, however, and observe the demeanor of a witness while testifying, which is one way of judging the credibility of a witness whose testimony is not inherently lacking in believability. Juries determine a witness's credibility in many of the same ways people make such a judgment in ordinary conversations—eye contact, fidgeting, inappropriate facial expressions, etc. These observations cannot be duplicated by reading the record of the testimony.

■ **CASE VOCABULARY**

FEDERAL EMPLOYERS' LIABILITY ACT: A workers'-compensation law that provides death and disability benefits for employees of railroads engaged in interstate and foreign commerce. Abbreviated FELA.

Guenther v. Armstrong Rubber Co.

(Mechanic) v. *(Tire Manufacturer)*
406 F.2d 1315 (3d Cir. 1969)

DISCREPANCIES IN EVIDENCE MUST BE RESOLVED BY THE JURY

DON'T LISTEN TO MY CLIENT, YOUR HONOR. THIS IS THE TIRE THAT HURT HIM, WHETHER HE KNOWS IT OR NOT.

■ **INSTANT FACTS** Guenther (P) was injured when a tire exploded, and there was contradictory testimony regarding whether he was injured by the tire introduced into evidence at trial.

■ **BLACK LETTER RULE** It is not the function of the judge to resolve problems with the evidence presented.

■ **PROCEDURAL BASIS**

Appeal from a directed verdict for Armstrong Rubber (D).

■ **FACTS**

Guenther (P), an automobile mechanic, was injured when a tire he was mounting exploded. After the accident, the tire was removed and kept in the possession of the manager of the garage. The tire was later examined by experts for both Guenther (P) and Armstrong Rubber (D). At trial, Armstrong Rubber (D) admitted that it had manufactured the tire. The tire was a thirteen-inch white wall tire. Guenther (P) testified that the tire he was mounting was a fifteen-inch tire with black walls. Armstrong Rubber (D) objected to the introduction of the testimony of Guenther's (P) expert based on the difficulty in identifying the tire examined as the one that injured Guenther (P). The trial court granted Armstrong Rubber's (D) motion for a directed verdict. Guenther's (P) motion for a new trial was denied, because Guenther's (P) identification of a black wall tire as the one that injured him was in direct contradiction to the identification of the white wall tire that was examined and found defective by Guenther's (P) expert.

■ **ISSUE**

Should a directed verdict have been entered when there was conflicting evidence as to which tire injured the plaintiff?

■ **DECISION AND RATIONALE**

(McLaughlin, J.) No. It is not the function of the judge to resolve problems with the evidence presented. The jury should be able to resolve the problem posed by the conflicting testimony. Guenther's (P) case should not have gone to the jury, however, solely on the basis that the tire probably had been made by Armstrong Rubber (D). A verdict based on that probability would be at best a guess. Reversed.

Analysis:

The credibility of a party is to be evaluated in the same manner as the credibility of any other witness. Although Guenther's (P) testimony regarding the tire that injured him probably would be given much weight by the jury, the alternate testimony—that the tire introduced into evidence was in fact the one that injured him—is not inherently incredible. There is some justification for concluding that it truly was the tire, despite Guenther's (P) testimony. In most cases, careful trial and witness preparation helps litigants avoid surprise testimony, such as that presented in this case.

■ CASE VOCABULARY

CREDIBILITY: The quality that makes something (as a witness or some evidence) worthy of belief.

Ahern v. Scholz

(*Manager*) v. (*Musician*)
85 F.3d 774 (1st Cir. 1996)

NEW TRIALS SHOULD BE GRANTED ONLY WHEN THERE IS NO SUPPORT FOR A VERDICT

■ **INSTANT FACTS** The jury found for Ahern (P) in his breach of contract action against his manager Scholz (D), and Scholz's (D) motion for a new trial was denied.

■ **BLACK LETTER RULE** A trial court has broad discretion to grant a motion for a new trial, but a new trial should not be granted if there is a reasonable factual basis for the jury's verdict.

■ **PROCEDURAL BASIS**

Appeal from an order denying Scholz's (D) motion for a new trial.

■ **FACTS**

Scholz (D) entered into an agreement with Ahern (P), whereby Ahern (P) would promote and manage Scholz (D) and his band (the group "Boston"). A few years later, Ahern (P) and Scholz (D) modified their agreement and Ahern (D) ceased being Scholz's (D) manager. Ten years after the agreement between Ahern (P) and Scholz (D) was modified, Ahern (P) sued Scholz (D) for breach of the agreement. Scholz (D) asserted various defenses and counterclaims, including Ahern's (P) alleged breach of the agreement. The case was submitted to the jury solely on each party's breach of contract theory. The jury found that Scholz (D) had breached the contract and that Ahern (P) had not. The judge also found that Scholz (D) had breached the contract but also granted Ahern (P) declaratory relief and rescission. Scholz (D) moved for a new trial and to amend the court's memorandum and order and judgment, to admit new evidence. The trial court denied all of Scholz's (D) motions.

■ **ISSUE**

Should the trial court have granted Scholz's (D) motion for a new trial?

■ **DECISION AND RATIONALE**

(Torruella, J.) No. A trial court has broad discretion to grant a motion for a new trial, but a new trial should not be granted if there is a reasonable factual basis for the jury's verdict. The judge's discretion should be exercised with regard to the rights of both parties to have disputed questions resolved by a jury. The judge may not overturn a jury's verdict solely because he or she disagrees with the result, or because he or she would have reached a different result in a bench trial. On appeal, the trial court's decision will be reversed only for a clear abuse of discretion. The appellate court does not weigh testimony or assess the credibility of witnesses. As long as there is a reasonable basis for the jury's verdict, the trial court's ruling will not be reversed on appeal.

The trial court did not abuse its discretion in denying the motion for a new trial in this case. The jury's verdict was not against the weight of the evidence. There was ample evidence to support the jury's verdict. Although some of the evidence was contradictory, it cannot be said that the jury made a mistake. Affirmed on the issue of a new trial for breach of contract, reversed on the issue of violations of

---

the Massachusetts Deceptive Trade Practices Act, and remanded for a new trial on the issue of rescission of contract.

Analysis:

New trial motions are seldom successful, possibly due to an unspoken notion that an unsuccessful litigant shouldn't get a second try when he or she failed the first time. The motions are, however, a part of the appellate process in many jurisdictions. The motion is made with little expectation of seeing it granted, and an appeal is taken from the order denying the motion.

■ CASE VOCABULARY

RESCISSION: A party's unilateral unmaking of a contract for a legally sufficient reason, such as the other party's material breach, or a judgment rescinding the contract. Rescission is generally available as a remedy or defense for a nondefaulting party and is accompanied by restitution of any partial performance, thus restoring the parties to their precontractual positions.

Dimick v. Schiedt

(*Motorist*) v. (*Injured*)

293 U.S. 474, 55 S.Ct. 296 (1935)

THE COURT MAY NOT INCREASE A DAMAGE AWARD

■ **INSTANT FACTS** Schiedt (P) won a verdict of $500 from Dimick (D); the court told Dimick (D) that Schiedt's (P) motion for a new trial would not be granted if he consented to an increase in the damage award to $1500.

■ **BLACK LETTER RULE** An inadequate verdict should not be permitted to stand, but the parties retain the right to have a jury determine the question of liability and the extent of the damages.

■ **PROCEDURAL BASIS**

Appeal from an order of the court of appeals reversing the district court's denial of a motion for a new trial.

■ **FACTS**

Schiedt (P) sued Dimick (D) for personal injuries caused by a motor vehicle accident. The jury returned a verdict in favor of Schiedt (P) for $500, and Schiedt (P) moved for a new trial on the grounds that the verdict was contrary to the evidence, that it was a compromise verdict, and that the damages were inadequate. The district court granted Schiedt (P) a new trial on the ground of the inadequacy of the damages, unless Dimick (D) consented to an increase in the damage award to $1500. Schiedt's (P) consent was neither required nor given. Dimick (D) consented to the increase and the motion for a new trial was denied. Schiedt (P) appealed and the court of appeals reversed.

■ **ISSUE**

Did the district court err in refusing to grant a new trial if the defendant agreed to pay the plaintiff increased damages?

■ **DECISION AND RATIONALE**

(Sutherland, J.) Yes. An inadequate verdict should not be permitted to stand, but the parties retain the right to have a jury determine the question of liability and the extent of the damages. There is some precedential support for a judge's reducing a jury's award if it is considered excessive. The practice was not universal in the English common law, and has been often criticized, but it has been the practice for many years. The practice will not be extended by analogy, however, to increasing an inadequate verdict. Although decreasing a verdict has been done in many cases, no case can be found in which the court increased the verdict. When a verdict is excessive, the practice of eliminating the excess leaves intact part of the jury's verdict, but increasing the verdict has the effect of adding something that was not in the original verdict. The trial court's actions here deprived Schiedt (P) of the right to a trial by jury. Affirmed.

■ **DISSENT**

(Stone, J.) Trial courts have long had the power to set aside verdicts deemed either inadequate or excessive, and to grant or deny a new trial. Implicit in that power is the authority to determine the upper and lower limits within which recovery will be permitted. The Seventh Amendment is intended to preserve only the essence of the jury trial as it existed in 1791. The particular procedures to be followed are not prescribed, as long as the power of the jury to decide questions of fact is not taken away. The court retains control over the jury's verdict, in determining the issues that are for the jury to decide. The jury's function was not curtailed in this case. A denial of the motion for a new trial would not have been a denial of the right to a jury trial. It was not a denial here, because a proper recovery had been assured. Schiedt (P) suffered no denial of the right to a jury trial, and Dimick's (D) consented and so suffered no denial either.

Analysis:

Although a judge has the authority to determine whether a verdict is too large or too small, the judge's authority ordinarily is limited to just that determination. The parties then have the opportunity to try again. The judge may have some notion of a permissible range of verdicts, but that opinion generally is not voiced. Judges do not instruct a jury when it begins its deliberations as to the permissible range of damage awards, and "correcting" a verdict to make it reflect the exact sum the judge had in mind is no less an invasion of the jury's function.

■ CASE VOCABULARY

ADDITUR: [Latin, "it is added to."] A trial court's order, issued usually with the defendant's consent, that increases the damages awarded by the jury to avoid a new trial on grounds of inadequate damages. The term may also refer to the increase itself, the procedure, or the court's power to make the order.

REMITTITUR: The process by which a court reduces or proposes to reduce the damages awarded in a jury verdict; a court's order reducing an award of damages.

Whitlock v. Jackson

(Administratrix of Estate) v. *(Police Sergeant)*

754 F. Supp. 1394 (S.D. Ind. 1991)

JURY VERDICTS ARE PRESUMABLY INTERNALLY CONSISTENT

■ **INSTANT FACTS** Whitlock (P) moved for a new trial, claiming that the jury's verdict was inconsistent.

■ **BLACK LETTER RULE** The court must search for a reasonable way to read a verdict as expressing a coherent view of the case, and if there is any way to view a case that makes a jury's answers to special interrogatories consistent, the answers must be resolved in that way.

■ **PROCEDURAL BASIS**

Decision on a motion for additur or for a new trial.

■ **FACTS**

Whitlock (P) brought an action against Jackson (D) and others, alleging that Jackson (D) and the other defendants arrested her brother and inflicted serious injuries that caused her brother's death. Whitlock's (P) complaint alleged violations of the Fourth, Fifth, and Fourteenth Amendments. The complaint also included state law claims for battery and wrongful death. The jury's verdict awarded Whitlock (P) a total of $29,700 in compensatory and punitive damages. The jury did *not* find, however, that Jackson (D) or any other defendants committed constitutional violations, or that the defendants' actions were the proximate cause of the death of Whitlock's (P) brother. Whitlock (P) argued that the verdict was inconsistent because the jury found Jackson (D) and the other defendants liable for battery and punitive damages, but not for the alleged constitutional violations.

■ **ISSUE**

Was the jury verdict awarding damages but finding no constitutional violations inconsistent, so that a new trial should be ordered?

■ **DECISION AND RATIONALE**

(McKinney, J.) No. The court must search for a reasonable way to read a verdict as expressing a coherent view of the case, and if there is any way to view a case that makes a jury's answers to special interrogatories consistent, the answers must be resolved in that way. In this case, the jury found battery, but declined to find that the force used was excessive or that there was, as alleged by Whitlock (P), an unreasonable denial of medical care. It was not inconsistent for the jury to find that the arrest of Whitlock's (P) brother was lawful, but that he was battered while in police custody. A finding of battery and malice is not the same as finding that the force used was constitutionally excessive.

Whitlock (P) did not waive her right to object to the inconsistent verdict by not making her objection prior to the discharge of the jury. The jury's verdict was a special verdict, rendered pursuant to Fed. R. Civ. P. 49(a), which, unlike Rule 49(b), relating to general verdicts accompanied by written interrogatories, does not contain a specific directive to send a jury back for further deliberations in the event of an inconsistency in the jury's answers. Rule 49(a) does not require a party to object to inconsistencies in a

---

verdict in order to preserve the right to challenge the inconsistencies in a subsequent motion for a new trial. Here, however, the motion for a new trial is denied.

Analysis:

The strong policy in favor of trial by jury leads to a great deference to the findings of a jury. The court here suggests that a verdict must be read as consistent, even if it is a "strain" to do so. The possibility of inconsistency is present more in special verdicts, in which a jury must answer specific factual questions, than in general verdicts, in which a jury is limited to an answer that does not go much beyond "yes" or "no." Most courts and lawyers prefer special verdicts, which give some insight into the specific facts that are found, but there is no requirement that a special verdict be rendered.

■ CASE VOCABULARY

GENERAL VERDICT: A verdict by which the jury finds in favor of one party or the other, as opposed to resolving specific fact questions.

GENERAL VERDICT WITH INTERROGATORIES: A general verdict accompanied by answers to written interrogatories on one or more issues of fact that bear on the verdict.

SPECIAL VERDICT: A verdict in which the jury makes findings only on factual issues submitted by the judge, who then decides the legal effect of the jury's verdict.

Sopp v. Smith

(Accident Victim) v. *(Negligent Driver)*
59 Cal. 2d 12, 377 P.2d 649 (1963)

JUROR AFFIDAVITS MAY NOT IMPEACH A VERDICT

■ **INSTANT FACTS** Sopp (P) moved for a new trial based on a juror's affidavit stating that the juror engaged in misconduct.

■ **BLACK LETTER RULE** A juror's affidavit of misconduct may not be used to impeach a jury's verdict, unless that affidavit states that the verdict was arrived at by resorting to chance or that a false answer on *voir dire* concealed bias or disqualification.

■ **PROCEDURAL BASIS**

Appeal from an order denying a motion for a new trial.

■ **FACTS**

Sopp (P) moved for a new trial in an automobile negligence action. The motion was based on the affidavit of a juror that stated that the juror visited the scene of the accident and tested some of the claims of the witnesses. The trial court denied the motion on the ground that the affidavit was inadmissible.

■ **ISSUE**

Could a juror's affidavit stating that the juror visited the accident scene be used to challenge the jury's verdict?

■ **DECISION AND RATIONALE**

(Schauer, J.) No. A juror's affidavit of misconduct may not be used to impeach a jury's verdict, unless that affidavit states that the verdict was arrived at by resorting to chance or that a false answer on *voir dire* concealed bias or disqualification. The policy is based on balancing the interest a losing party has in obtaining relief from wrongful conduct by the jury against the interest in avoiding fraud, instability of verdicts, and juror harassment. Affirmed.

■ **DISSENT**

(Peters, J.) The only reasons the majority gives for following the standard rule here are *stare decisis* and public policy. Public policy is, at best, a vague and uncertain guide. Prior to 1785, jurors were free to impeach their own verdicts as to overt acts of misconduct. There is no reason to continue with the majority's rule. Many jurisdictions have abolished the rule and allow juror affidavits on extrinsic issues, such as access to improper matter or arriving at a verdict by improper means. Intrinsic matters, such as the thought processes of individual jurors, are not subject to impeachment by affidavit.

Analysis:

The process by which jurors arrive at a verdict has traditionally been shrouded in inviolate secrecy. Jurors are to be protected against any influence that might intimidate or otherwise improperly influence them. The secrecy poses an issue when one or more jurors have engaged in some kind of misconduct, however, or when jurors consider matters not admitted into evidence.

■ **CASE VOCABULARY**

AFFIDAVIT: A voluntary declaration of facts written down and sworn to by the declarant before an officer authorized to administer oaths, such as a notary public. A great deal of evidence is submitted by affidavit, especially in pretrial matters such as summary judgment motions.

IMPEACHMENT OF VERDICT: A party's attack on a verdict, alleging impropriety by a member of the jury.

VOIR DIRE: [Law, French, "to speak the truth."] 1. A preliminary examination of a prospective juror by a judge or lawyer to decide whether the prospect is qualified and suitable to serve on a jury. Loosely, the term refers to the jury-selection phase of a trial. 2. A preliminary examination to test the competence of a witness or evidence.

People v. Hutchinson

(Prosecuting Government) v. *(Drug Defendant)*

71 Cal. 2d 342, 455 P.2d 132, 78 Cal. Rptr. 196 (1969)

JURORS MAY TESTIFY TO IMPEACH A VERDICT

■ **INSTANT FACTS** Hutchinson (D) was convicted of possession of marijuana for sale and moved for a new trial based on a juror's affidavit of coercion.

■ **BLACK LETTER RULE** Jurors are competent witnesses to prove objective facts to impeach a jury's verdict.

■ **PROCEDURAL BASIS**

Appeal from an order denying a motion for a new trial.

■ **FACTS**

Hutchinson (D) was convicted of possession of marijuana for sale. He moved for a new trial, submitting an affidavit from a juror in support of his motion. The affidavit stated that the bailiff had engaged in intimidating behavior that caused the juror to hurry his verdict and agree to a compromise verdict. The affidavit contained specific statements made by the bailiff, including threats that the jury would be locked up overnight if a verdict were not reached. The trial court refused to consider the affidavit in support of Hutchinson's (D) motion for a new trial.

■ **ISSUE**

Should the juror's affidavit have been considered by the court?

■ **DECISION AND RATIONALE**

(Traynor, C.J.) Yes. Jurors are competent witnesses to prove objective facts to impeach a jury's verdict. The rule providing that such testimony will not be heard is based on the common law rule that a person may not allege his or her own turpitude. That rule has largely been abandoned in other areas of the law of evidence, and its survival with regard to a jury's verdict is simply a matter of adherence to precedent. The rationale for the rule has been to balance the interest in giving a losing party relief from wrongful juror conduct against the allegedly greater interest in avoiding fraud, instability of verdicts, and juror harassment. The wrong to the individual was considered the lesser of the two evils. It now appears that there is no conflict between the two policies, and the wrong to the individual cannot be considered lesser.

The experience of other states that allow evidence of extrinsic factors to impeach a verdict suggests that the practice does not result in widespread overturning of verdicts. Admission of evidence of acts of misconduct or improper influence would not breach the privacy of jury deliberations. It would merely ensure that such evidence is available to the courts to determine whether specific acts of misconduct are sufficient to merit the granting of a new trial. Admission of the affidavits should also help prevent misconduct, by lifting the secrecy that hides the misconduct. Reversed and remanded for consideration of Hutchinson's (D) motion for a new trial.

Analysis:

The court is careful to limit its ruling to evidence of extrinsic conduct—what a juror heard or observed happening. An affidavit that recites improper thought processes would not be admissible, unless there is an allegation of specific facts. Although the juror's affidavit in this case set out the juror's impressions and what he or she thought the other jurors were thinking, the affidavit also set out in detail the actions of the bailiff that led to those conclusions.

CHAPTER NINE

Choosing the Forum—Geographical Location

Pennoyer v. Neff

Instant Facts: Neff (P), who sued Pennoyer (D) to recover possession of land that had been transferred to Pennoyer (D) at a sheriff's sale after a default judgment was entered against Neff (P), claims that the default judgment was invalid because an Oregon state court did not have jurisdiction over him.

Black Letter Rule: A state court does not have jurisdiction over a nonresident defendant unless the defendant is personally served with process in the state or voluntarily appears in state court.

Harris v. Balk

Instant Facts: Balk (P) brought a suit against Harris (D) in North Carolina on a $180 debt, and Harris (D) claimed that the debt had already been satisfied in an earlier proceeding in Maryland.

Black Letter Rule: A state court may exercise jurisdiction over a debt that was incurred in another state, if the nonresident debtor is served with process while in the state.

Hess v. Pawloski

Instant Facts: Pawloski (P) sued Hess (D), a Pennsylvania resident who was driving in Massachusetts, for injuries incurred when Hess's (D) vehicle struck and injured Pawloski (P).

Black Letter Rule: A state does not violate a nonresident driver's due process rights by enacting legislation that subjects the driver to jurisdiction in the state for all actions arising from use of the state's public highways.

International Shoe Co. v. Washington

Instant Facts: The State of Washington (P) sought to recover unemployment compensation fund contributions from International Shoe Co. (D), and, even though it employed salespeople in Washington, International Shoe (D) argued that it was not subject to jurisdiction in Washington.

Black Letter Rule: A corporation is subject to jurisdiction in any state with which it has "minimum contacts," so that the exercise of jurisdiction is consistent with notions of "fair play and substantial justice."

McGee v. International Life Ins. Co.

Instant Facts: McGee (P) sued International Life Insurance Co. (D) in a Texas state court to enforce a judgment entered against the defendant in a California state court.

Black Letter Rule: A foreign corporation doing business with a resident of another state is subject to personal jurisdiction in courts of that person's state of residence.

World-Wide Volkswagen v. Woodson

Instant Facts: The Robinsons were injured in a motor vehicle accident in Oklahoma while driving from New York to Arizona. They brought suit in Oklahoma against the wholesaler and retail dealer of their automobile, both of which were businesses located in New York that did not do business in Oklahoma

Black Letter Rule: A party's single, fortuitous contact with a state, which was not initiated or intended by that party, does not constitute sufficient contact to subject the party to the personal jurisdiction of that state's courts.

Calder v. Jones

Instant Facts: When Calder (D) edited an allegedly libelous article about Jones (P) that was published in *The National Enquirer*, Jones (P) brought suit in California against *The National Enquirer* and others, including Calder (D), who had only two unrelated contacts with California before the suit.

Black Letter Rule: Personal jurisdiction is proper over nonresident defendants who engage in conduct that is directed at and causes harm to a resident of the forum state.

Burger King Corp. v. Rudzewicz

Instant Facts: Burger King Corp. (P), headquartered in Florida, brought suit in Florida federal court against Rudzewicz (D), a Michigan resident who held a Burger King franchise, to dissolve the franchise relationship.

Black Letter Rule: Contractual negotiations and an ongoing contractual relationship constitute sufficient minimum contacts to establish personal jurisdiction, even when the defendant was never physically present in the forum state.

Asahi Metal Industry Co. v. Superior Court of California

Instant Facts: Zurcher, the victim of a motorcycle accident, brought suit in California against a Taiwanese tire-tube maker, which brought a cross-claim against the Japanese manufacturer of the tire tube valve assembly.

Black Letter Rule: To be subject to personal jurisdiction in a forum state and satisfy traditional notions of fair play and substantial justice, a nonresident defendant must do more than simply place a product into the stream of commerce.

Pavlovich v. Superior Court

Instant Facts: A Texas resident who posted information infringing upon the licensing rights of a California business on a Web site created in Indiana was sued in California state court for misappropriation of trade secrets.

Black Letter Rule: A party purposefully avails itself of a forum state if the foreseeable effect of the out-of-state action would be to injure a person within the forum state.

Shaffer v. Heitner

Instant Facts: Heitner (P) brought a shareholders' derivative action against Shaffer (D) and other officers and directors of Greyhound, Inc., filing suit in Delaware and taking advantage of a Delaware statute allowing the court to sequester the defendants' stock shares.

Black Letter Rule: Minimum contacts are required for personal jurisdiction to exist, whether the proceeding is in personam or in rem.

Burnham v. Superior Court of California

Instant Facts: Burnham (D), a resident of New Jersey, was served with a summons and petition for divorce while on a brief visit to California.

Black Letter Rule: A state may assert personal jurisdiction over any person physically present within its boundaries, even if they are in the state only temporarily, and even if the suit is not related to the person's presence in the state.

Helicopteros Nacionales de Colombia, S.A. v. Hall

Instant Facts: Hall (P) and other surviving family members sued Helicopteros Nacionales (Helicol) (D), a Colombian corporation, in Texas for wrongful death caused by a helicopter crash in Peru.

Black Letter Rule: Mere purchases, even if they occur at regular intervals, are insufficient for a state to exercise jurisdiction over a nonresident in a cause of action unrelated to the purchases, but it does not otherwise offend due process to exercise general jurisdiction over a nonresident defendant whose contacts with a forum state are continuous and systematic.

Insurance Corp. of Ireland, Ltd. v. Compagnie des Bauxites de Guinee

Instant Facts: After losing $10 million due to a work stoppage, Compagnie des Bauxites de Guinee (P) sought to recover the money under a business interruption insurance policy with the defendants.

Black Letter Rule: A court may use a sanctions order for purposes of asserting personal jurisdiction.

Bates v. C & S Adjusters, Inc.

Instant Facts: Bates (P) sued C & S Adjusters, Inc. (D) in federal court for violations of the Fair Debt Collection Practices Act.

Black Letter Rule: Venue is appropriate in a judicial district in which a substantial part of the events or omissions giving rise to the claim took place.

Piper Aircraft Co. v. Reyno

Instant Facts: The estates of Scottish citizens brought a wrongful death suit against Piper Aircraft Co. (D) in Pennsylvania federal court as a result of an airplane crash in Scotland.

Black Letter Rule: Under the doctrine of forum non conveniens, a court may dismiss a case if there is an alternate forum with jurisdiction and if proceeding in the forum would impose a heavy burden on the parties or the court.

Pennoyer v. Neff

(Transferee of Title to Land) v. *(Nonresident Original Owner)*

95 U.S. (5 Otto) 714, 24 L.Ed. 565 (1877)

STATE COURTS HAVE JURISDICTION OVER PEOPLE AND PROPERTY IN THE STATE

■ **INSTANT FACTS** Neff (P), who sued Pennoyer (D) to recover possession of land that had been transferred to Pennoyer (D) at a sheriff's sale after a default judgment was entered against Neff (P), claims that the default judgment was invalid because an Oregon state court did not have jurisdiction over him.

■ **BLACK LETTER RULE** A state court does not have jurisdiction over a nonresident defendant unless the defendant is personally served with process in the state or voluntarily appears in state court.

■ **PROCEDURAL BASIS**

Review on a writ of error of the lower court's decision finding the Oregon state court's judgment against Neff (P) invalid.

■ **FACTS**

In a prior lawsuit, Mitchell sued Neff (P) for attorneys' fees in a state court in Oregon. Neff (P) was not an Oregon resident, was not personally served with notice of the lawsuit (which was published in a newspaper), and did not appear to defend the case. Because Neff (P) did not appear, the Oregon court entered a default judgment against him and in favor of Mitchell. Neff (P) owned land in Oregon, which was sold at a sheriff's sale in order to satisfy Mitchell's judgment against Neff (P). Pennoyer (D) bought Neff's (P) property at the sheriff's sale. Neff (P) brought a lawsuit in federal court against Pennoyer (D) to recover title to his property, arguing that the default judgment against him was invalid, so that the sale of his land to Pennoyer (D) was void. The district court ultimately voided the judgment, deeming service by publication from a newspaper editor, rather than from the printer of the newspaper, insufficient. Pennoyer sought a writ of error.

■ **ISSUE**

Is a state court's judgment against a nonresident defendant valid if the defendant is not personally served with process in the state and does not appear voluntarily?

■ **DECISION AND RATIONALE**

(Field, J.) No. Although service by publication is sufficient if coming from a newspaper editor rather than the printer, a state court may not exercise in personam jurisdiction over a nonresident defendant unless the defendant is personally served with process in the state or appears voluntarily. If a state court does not have in personam jurisdiction over a nonresident, any judgment rendered against that defendant is invalid and violates the party's due process rights under the Fourteenth Amendment. However, a state court may properly exercise jurisdiction over property owned by a nonresident for purposes of an in rem proceeding, even if service is by publication, because a defendant in an in rem proceeding is not personally bound by the judgment beyond the property in question. In such an in rem proceeding, substituted service by publication is appropriate service upon a nonresident defendant because the property owned lies within the state. The law presumes property to always be in its owner's possession. Accordingly, unlike with in personam jurisdiction, the court's authority does not extend beyond its state's borders to reach the nonresident defendant. In this case, the judgment against Neff (P) was a

---

money judgment, requiring the Oregon court to have in personam jurisdiction. The Oregon proceedings were not in rem because the court did not attach the property; rather, the court disposed of the property only to execute on a money judgment against Neff (P). Because Neff (P) was not personally served in Oregon and did not voluntarily appear, the Oregon court lacked jurisdiction over him, and the judgment and subsequent land sale were invalid. Affirmed.

Analysis:

Neff's (P) suit in federal court to challenge the Oregon court's jurisdiction over him was a "collateral attack" because it was a separate proceeding from the original suit brought by Mitchell. A defendant may also challenge a court's personal jurisdiction directly by bringing a motion to dismiss under Fed. R. Civ. P. 12(b)(2). By filing such a motion, the defendant is not voluntarily appearing or consenting to suit, and thus preserves the right to challenge personal jurisdiction. Although *Pennoyer* is no longer the law of the land, it is the background for all subsequent cases addressing personal jurisdiction.

■ CASE VOCABULARY

EX PARTE: Done or made at the instance and for the benefit of one party only, and without notice to, or argument by, any party adversely interested.

IN PERSONAM JURISDICTION: A court's power to bring a person into its adjudicative process; jurisdiction over a defendant's personal rights, rather than merely over property interests.

IN REM JURISDICTION: A court's power to adjudicate the rights to a given piece of property, including the power to seize and hold it.

WRIT OF ERROR: A writ issued by an appellate court directing a lower court to deliver the record in the case for review.

Harris v. Balk

(*Debtor*) v. (*Creditor*)

198 U.S. 215, 25 S.Ct. 625, 49 L Ed. 1023 (1905)

A NONRESIDENT DEBTOR MAY BE SERVED WHILE TEMPORARILY IN THE STATE

■ **INSTANT FACTS** Balk (P) brought a suit against Harris (D) in North Carolina on a $180 debt, and Harris (D) claimed that the debt had already been satisfied in an earlier proceeding in Maryland.

■ **BLACK LETTER RULE** A state court may exercise jurisdiction over a debt that was incurred in another state, if the nonresident debtor is served with process while in the state.

■ **PROCEDURAL BASIS**

Certiorari to review the Supreme Court of North Carolina's affirmance of a judgment against Harris (D) for the collection of a debt.

■ **FACTS**

Harris (D), a North Carolina resident, owed $180 to Balk (P), also a North Carolina resident. In turn, Balk (P) owed Epstein, a Maryland resident, more than $300. While Harris (D) was in Maryland, Epstein had a Maryland court issue a writ of attachment to attach the debt Harris (D) owed to Balk (P) and served the writ on Harris (D) while he was still in Maryland. Harris (D) did not challenge the garnishment and judgment was later rendered in favor of Epstein for $180. Harris (D) paid the $180 to Epstein's attorney. Later, Balk (P) sued Harris (D) for the $180 in a North Carolina court. Harris (D) argued that the Maryland judgment in favor of Epstein and his payment to Epstein barred Balk's (P) suit. The trial court entered judgment in favor of Balk (P), reasoning that the Maryland judgment was invalid because the Maryland court did not have jurisdiction to garnish the debt. On appeal, the North Carolina Supreme Court affirmed.

■ **ISSUE**

May a state court garnish a debt owed by a nonresident to a nonresident third party, if the nonresident is served while temporarily in the state, even though the debt was incurred out of state?

■ **DECISION AND RATIONALE**

(Peckham, J.) Yes. The Maryland judgment in favor of Epstein was valid because Harris (D) was served with process while temporarily in Maryland. In addition, Balk (P) had notice of the garnishment because Harris (D) raised the Maryland judgment as a defense to Balk's (P) suit. Jurisdiction over a debt is appropriate when state law permits attachment of the debt, the garnishee is present in the state for personal service of process, and the garnishee's creditor could have brought suit against the garnishee in the state. Maryland law allows a debt to be garnished as long as Maryland courts have jurisdiction over the debtor. Here, the Maryland court had jurisdiction over Harris (D) because he was served within the state. Moreover, Balk (P) could have sued Harris (D) in Maryland to recover the debt while Harris (D) was temporarily in Maryland. A creditor must, however, be given fair notice of the garnishment of a debt owed to him to give the creditor an opportunity to defend the debt allegedly owed to another. Here, Balk's (P) interests were adequately protected by the Maryland court. At the time of the attachment,

Epstein was required to post bond and provide adequate security for restitution should Balk (P) appear before the court and contest the validity of the debt allegedly owed by him. Likewise, Balk (P) had notice of the attachment within a few days, prompting his immediate suit against Harris (D) to recover the debt. Had Balk (P) disputed the debt owed to Epstein, he had ample opportunity to assert a defense. Thus, the Maryland judgment was valid. Reversed.

Analysis:

The decision in *Harris* turned on the notion that a debt is property, the location of which is determined by the location of the debtor. Therefore, Epstein was able to assert jurisdiction over Balk (P) in Maryland by garnishing Balk's (P) debtor, Harris (D), while Harris (D) was in Maryland. *Harris* has been criticized because it permits jurisdiction over a defendant in a forum with which the defendant has no real connection. The Supreme Court later overruled *Harris. See Shaffer v. Heitner*, 433 U.S. 186 (1977).

■ CASE VOCABULARY

ATTACHMENT: The seizing of a person's property to secure a judgment or to be sold in satisfaction of a judgment.

CREDITOR: One to whom a debt is owed; one who gives credit for money or goods.

DEBTOR: One who owes an obligation to another, especially an obligation to pay money.

GARNISHEE: A person or institution (such as a bank) that is indebted to or is bailee for another whose property has been subjected to garnishment.

GARNISHMENT: A judicial proceeding in which a creditor (or potential creditor) asks the court to order a third party who is indebted to or is bailee for the debtor to turn over to the creditor any of the debtor's property (such as wages or bank accounts) held by that third party.

Hess v. Pawloski

(Nonresident Driver) v. *(Car Accident Victim)*
274 U.S. 352, 47 S.Ct. 632, 71 L.Ed. 1091 (1927)

STATES HAVE JURISDICTION OVER NONRESIDENT DRIVERS BY APPOINTING A STATE REGISTRAR AS AGENT FOR SERVICE OF PROCESS

■ **INSTANT FACTS** Pawloski (P) sued Hess (D), a Pennsylvania resident who was driving in Massachusetts, for injuries incurred when Hess's (D) vehicle struck and injured Pawloski (P).

■ **BLACK LETTER RULE** A state does not violate a nonresident driver's due process rights by enacting legislation that subjects the driver to jurisdiction in the state for all actions arising from use of the state's public highways.

■ **PROCEDURAL BASIS**

Certiorari to review the decision of a Massachusetts state court finding jurisdiction over Hess (D).

■ **FACTS**

Hess (D), a Pennsylvania resident, was driving in Massachusetts when his car struck and injured Pawloski (P). Pawloski (P) sued Hess (D) in Massachusetts to recover damages for personal injury. No personal service was made on Hess (D), and none of his property was attached. Hess (D) moved the court to dismiss the complaint for a lack of jurisdiction. The trial court denied Hess's (D) motion based on a Massachusetts jurisdictional statute, which provided that operating a motor vehicle in the state amounts to an agreement by nonresidents to appoint the registrar as agent for service of process in suits arising from accidents or collisions on Massachusetts highways, as long as the nonresident received actual notice of the service from the registrar.

■ **ISSUE**

Does a state statute conferring jurisdiction over nonresident drivers violate due process by regarding such drivers as having consented to the appointment of a state registrar as an agent for service of process?

■ **DECISION AND RATIONALE**

(Butler, J.) No. In order to confer jurisdiction upon a state court, service must be made on a defendant personally while in the state or on an authorized agent in the state. States may make and enforce laws that are designed to promote care on the part of both residents and nonresidents who use the public highways in the state. Motor vehicles are dangerous machines that can cause serious harm to persons and property. The Massachusetts statute limits nonresidents' implied consent to proceedings arising out of accidents or collisions involving the use of motor vehicles on a highway in an effort to ensure the safe use of its highways for both residents and nonresidents alike. The Massachusetts statute does not discriminate against nonresidents, but merely places them on equal footing with residents. Affirmed.

Analysis:

As society became increasingly complex and mobile, the rigid rule set forth in *Pennoyer v. Neff*, 95 U.S. 714 (1877), was no longer adequate, requiring courts to establish a broader basis for asserting

---

jurisdiction over nonresidents. Problems arose when nonresident drivers returned home after causing an accident and injuring state residents. If the state in which the accident occurred could not exercise jurisdiction over the out-of-state driver, its injured residents would be left without an adequate remedy unless the state had expanded its jurisdiction by providing for consent to submit to the state's jurisdiction if an accident occurred. This precedent for "implied consent" jurisdiction in *Hess* led states to enact statutes addressing other activities, such as operating airplanes and watercraft, hazardous construction work, and selling securities.

■ **CASE VOCABULARY**

IMPLIED CONSENT: Consent inferred from one's conduct rather than from one's direct expression.

International Shoe Co. v. Washington

(*Delaware Corporation*) v. (*State Taxing Authority*)

326 U.S. 310, 66 S.Ct. 154, 90 L.Ed. 95 (1945)

CONTINUOUS, SYSTEMATIC CONTACTS WITH A STATE SUBJECT A DEFENDANT TO JURISDICTION

■ **INSTANT FACTS** The State of Washington (P) sought to recover unemployment compensation fund contributions from International Shoe Co. (D), and, even though it employed salespeople in Washington, International Shoe (D) argued that it was not subject to jurisdiction in Washington.

■ **BLACK LETTER RULE** A corporation is subject to jurisdiction in any state with which it has "minimum contacts," so that the exercise of jurisdiction is consistent with notions of "fair play and substantial justice."

■ PROCEDURAL BASIS

Certiorari to review a decision of the Washington Supreme Court upholding jurisdiction over International Shoe (D).

■ FACTS

International Shoe (D), a manufacturer and seller of shoes, was a Delaware corporation with its principal place of business in St. Louis, Missouri. International Shoe (D) had no office in Washington and made no contracts for sale or purchase of merchandise there. At one point, International Shoe (D) employed eleven to thirteen salesmen who resided in Washington (P) but reported to sales managers in St. Louis. The salesmen solicited orders from prospective buyers, which orders were transmitted to St. Louis, where they were processed and the products were shipped. The State of Washington (P) required employers to contribute a certain percentage of wages to its unemployment compensation fund. Because International Shoe (D) did not pay into the fund, the State (P) issued a notice of assessment, serving the notice personally on one of the salesmen and mailing a copy to International Shoe (D) at its St. Louis address. International Shoe (D) moved to set aside the notice of assessment because it was not a Washington corporation. The workers' compensation appeal tribunal denied the motion and ruled that the Commissioner was entitled to recover unpaid workers' compensation contributions. After subsequent appeals, the decision was affirmed by the Washington Supreme Court, which held that the continuous solicitation of orders in Washington by the defendant's in-state salesmen sufficiently demonstrated that International Shoe (D) did business in the state.

■ ISSUE

Is it consistent with due process to subject a nonresident defendant to jurisdiction in a state where the defendant is not present, but with which it has minimum contacts?

■ DECISION AND RATIONALE

(Stone, C.J.) Yes. No longer is a party's physical presence in a state necessary to establish in personam jurisdiction. Instead, a defendant may be subject to in personam jurisdiction, even if it is not physically present in a particular state, if it has certain "minimum contacts" with the state, so that maintaining the suit does not offend traditional notions of fair play and substantial justice. Determining whether jurisdiction is proper depends on the nature and quality of the defendant's contacts with the forum state. A defendant's single or isolated activity in a state is not enough to subject it to suits that are not connected with those activities. Conversely, if a defendant's conduct in a state is continuous and systematic, the defendant is subject to suits that are not related to those activities. To the extent a defendant exercises the privilege of conducting activities within a state, the defendant enjoys the benefits and protections of the law of that state and must accept the potential for suits to arise against them. In this case, International Shoe's (D) activities in Washington (P) were neither irregular nor casual. They were systematic, continuous, and gave rise to a large volume of interstate business. The obligation to pay into the unemployment compensation fund arose directly from International Shoe's (D) activities in the state. These activities created sufficient ties with Washington (P) so as to make it reasonable to subject International Shoe (D) to jurisdiction there. Affirmed.

■ SEPARATE OPINION

(Black, J.) The federal Constitution confers upon the states the power to tax corporations that do business in the state, and to subject those corporations to suits in the state. Nothing in the Due Process Clause can realistically be read to prevent the states from invoking these powers. Although the words "fair play," "justice," and "reasonable" have emotional appeal, the constitutional power of the states to afford judicial protection to their residents does not hinge upon these notions.

Analysis:

International Shoe departed from the rule in *Pennoyer v. Neff*, 95 U.S. 714 (1877), which required actual presence in the forum state for purposes of in personam jurisdiction. After *International Shoe*, many states enacted "long-arm" statutes authorizing state courts to exert jurisdiction over nonresidents engaging in certain types of conduct. To determine if a state court has personal jurisdiction, the long-arm statute must apply and the exercise of jurisdiction must not violate the constitutional principles embodied in the "minimum contacts" analysis.

■ CASE VOCABULARY

LONG–ARM STATUTE: A statute providing for jurisdiction over a nonresident defendant who has had contacts with the territory in which the statute is in effect.

MINIMUM CONTACTS: A nonresident defendant's forum-state connections, such as business activity or actions foreseeably leading to business activity, that are substantial enough to bring the defendant within the forum-state court's personal jurisdiction without offending traditional notions of fair play and substantial justice.

McGee v. International Life Ins. Co.

(*Life Insurance Beneficiary*) v. (*Insurance Company*)

355 U.S. 220, 78 S.Ct. 199, 2 L.Ed.2d 223 (1957)

A TEXAS INSURER ISSUING A POLICY TO A CALIFORNIA RESIDENT MAY BE SUED IN CALIFORNIA

■ **INSTANT FACTS** McGee (P) sued International Life Insurance Co. (D) in a Texas state court to enforce a judgment entered against the defendant in a California state court.

■ **BLACK LETTER RULE** A foreign corporation doing business with a resident of another state is subject to personal jurisdiction in courts of that person's state of residence.

■ PROCEDURAL BASIS

Certiorari to review decisions of Texas state courts refusing to honor a California judgment for lack of jurisdiction in California.

■ FACTS

Franklin, a California resident, entered into a life insurance contract with Empire Mutual Insurance Co., an Arizona corporation. When International Life Insurance Co. (D) assumed Empire's obligations under the contract, it delivered a reinsurance letter to Franklin in California, which Franklin accepted and made payments on from his California residence. After Franklin passed away, McGee (P) made a claim as beneficiary under the policy. International Life (D) refused to pay the claim, contending the cause of death was suicide, which was not covered under the contract. Neither Empire nor International Life (D) had ever employed any agents, maintained an office, nor solicited any other business in California. Nonetheless, McGee (P) sued International Life (D) in California state court for damages pursuant to the insurance contract, serving International Life (D) with process by registered mail at its principal place of business in Texas. The California court based jurisdiction over International Life (D) on a state statute providing that any foreign corporation entering into a contract with a California resident is subject to the court's jurisdiction, even though service of process cannot be made within the state's borders. Judgment was entered for McGee (P). Unable to collect on the judgment in California, McGee (P) filed suit on the judgment in Texas state court. The Texas courts refused to honor the judgment because it claimed jurisdiction was improper under the Fourteenth Amendment.

■ ISSUE

Does a state statute conferring personal jurisdiction over a foreign insurance corporation entering into an insurance contract with a state resident violate the Due Process Clause of the Fourteenth Amendment?

■ DECISION AND RATIONALE

(Black, J.) No. Due in large part to the expanding interstate nature of the national economy, the scope of personal jurisdiction has similarly expanded over the years from requiring a physical presence in the forum state for service of process to requiring merely sufficient minimum contacts with the forum state so as to comport with traditional notions of fair play and substantial justice. With the increased mobilization and enhanced modes of communication, commercial transactions often reach out beyond the borders of one state to touch one or more others. Just as these advancements have fostered commercial activity, so too have they minimized the burden of defending oneself in a foreign state in which such activity is conducted. Here, although International Life (D) has no physical presence in California, its contract had a substantial connection with California. The policy was delivered in California, the payments were mailed from California, and the insured resided in California. Clearly, California has significant interests at stake in protecting its insured against nonpayment of viable insurance claims. Small claims would likely go unpursued because of the expense and burden of resorting to a foreign state's courts, requiring the plaintiff and all material witnesses to be removed to the foreign jurisdiction for trial. Any burden on the defendant does not arise to a due process violation, particularly when the defendant received actual notice of the suit. Reversed.

Analysis:

The Court seems to suggest that when both the plaintiff and the forum state have an interest in the outcome of litigation, any burden on the defendant in defending itself in the forum state must be substantial in order for jurisdiction to be improper. By enacting a statute regulating foreign insurance companies, California has affirmatively stated it maintains a high interest. Likewise, a plaintiff clearly has an interest in pursuing claims in her home state. Under such circumstances, the burden on the defendant who in some manner enters a state for business reasons appears unlikely to be substantial enough to defeat jurisdiction.

■ CASE VOCABULARY

FOREIGN CORPORATION: A corporation that was organized and chartered under the laws of another state, government, or country.

World-Wide Volkswagen v. Woodson

(Automobile Distributor) v. *(District Judge Exercising Jurisdiction)*

444 U.S. 286, 100 S.Ct. 559, 62 L.Ed.2d 490 (1980)

A SINGLE, FORTUITOUS CONTACT WITH A STATE IS NOT SUFFICIENT TO CONFER JURISDICTION

■ **INSTANT FACTS** The Robinsons were injured in a motor vehicle accident in Oklahoma while driving from New York to Arizona. They brought suit in Oklahoma against the wholesaler and retail dealer of their automobile, both of which were businesses located in New York that did not do business in Oklahoma

■ **BLACK LETTER RULE** A party's single, fortuitous contact with a state, which was not initiated or intended by that party, does not constitute sufficient contact to subject the party to the personal jurisdiction of that state's courts.

■ **PROCEDURAL BASIS**

Certiorari to review a decision of the Oklahoma Supreme Court denying a writ of prohibition to restrain the trial court judge from exercising personal jurisdiction over the petitioners.

■ **FACTS**

While driving their car through Oklahoma on their way to Arizona, the Robinsons were injured in a motor vehicle collision. The Robinsons, residents of New York who were moving to Arizona, had purchased their vehicle from World–Wide Volkswagen (P), through a dealer located in New York that obtained the vehicle from a wholesaler located in New York that did business in New York, New Jersey, and Connecticut. World–Wide Volkswagen (P) did not advertise or solicit business in Oklahoma, and there was no evidence that any vehicle sold or distributed by World–Wide Volkswagen (P), other than the one driven by the Robinsons, ever entered Oklahoma. The Robinsons brought suit against World–Wide Volkswagen (P), alleging defective design and construction of the vehicle's gas tank. World–Wide Volkswagen (P) moved to dismiss for lack of jurisdiction and, when its motion was denied, requested a writ of prohibition against the trial court from the Oklahoma Supreme Court. The writ was denied based on the state's long-arm statute.

■ **ISSUE**

Can a state court exercise in personam jurisdiction over a nonresident automobile retailer and its wholesale distributor in a products-liability action, when the defendants' only connection with the state is the fact that an automobile sold in another state to residents of another state became involved in an accident in the forum state?

■ **DECISION AND RATIONALE**

(White, J.) No. Jurisdiction is not proper if a defendant's only contact with the forum state is a single, isolated occurrence. Rather, a defendant's connections with the forum state must be sufficient enough that the defendant should reasonably anticipate being brought into court in that state. When a defendant purposefully avails itself of the privilege of conducting business in a forum state, the defendant has clear notice that it is subject to suit in the state. However, a plaintiff's unilateral claim of some relationship with a nonresident defendant does not satisfy the contact requirement in a forum state. Here, World–Wide Volkswagen (P) and its wholesaler conducted no business targeted at Oklahoma, directly or indirectly, and did not avail themselves of the privileges of Oklahoma law. While it is foreseeable that the automobile, which is mobile by its nature, may be brought within the borders of

---

Oklahoma, jurisdiction over the defendants does not arise when the Robinsons fortuitously drove their vehicle into the state. Reversed.

■ **DISSENT**

(Marshall, J.) Contrary to the majority's view, World–Wide Volkswagen (P) deliberately and purposefully became part of a nationwide network for marketing and servicing automobiles. It knew that its automobiles would likely travel outside its sales territory, and it derived significant revenue from servicing cars that come from other states. As an economic entity, World–Wide Volkswagen (P) knowingly reaches out from New York, causes certain effects, and derives revenues from other states.

■ **DISSENT**

(Brennan, J.) It is neither unreasonable nor unfair to subject World–Wide Volkswagen (P) to jurisdiction in Oklahoma because of the substantial connection between the Robinsons and the forum state, and the forum state's interest in the maintaining the safety of its intrastate highways. Moreover, automobiles are not stationary items, and a dealer who intends that purchasers will use its products for interstate travel deliberately places its products in the stream of interstate commerce. In this sense, the dealer indirectly seeks the benefits of state highway systems intended for use by its end-users whether its goods reach a state through a chain of distribution or by a consumer using the product for its intended use. The mobile state of American society places manufacturers that their goods may very well find themselves in a foreign state within a matter of days. Unless jurisdiction in a sister state would significantly inconvenience a manufacturer or distributor, due process does not permit a defendant to escape injuries caused by its products in another state.

Analysis:

Note that part of the Court's decision in *World-Wide Volkswagen* hinged on notions of state sovereignty and the limitations on states' powers to reach beyond their borders. However, two years later, in *Insurance Corp. of Ireland, Ltd. v. Compagnie des Bauxites de Guinée*, 456 U.S. 694 (1982), the Court rejected the state-sovereignty rationale in favor of emphasizing that jurisdictional requirements are matters of individual liberty under the Fourteenth Amendment. The Supreme Court in *World-Wide Volkswagen* was deeply divided, showing a split concerning whether the defendant's due process rights or the forum state's interests in litigation should control the outcome.

■ **CASE VOCABULARY**

LONG ARM STATUTE: A statute providing for jurisdiction over a nonresident defendant who has had contacts with the territory where the statute is in effect.

WRIT OF PROHIBITION: An extraordinary writ issued by an appellate court to prevent a lower court from exceeding its jurisdiction.

Calder v. Jones

(Magazine Editor) v. *(Celebrity)*

465 U.S. 783, 104 S.Ct. 1482, 79 L.Ed.2d 804 (1984)

PERSONAL JURISDICTION IS PROPER OVER A DEFENDANT WHO INTENTIONALLY CAUSES HARM IN THE STATE

■ **INSTANT FACTS** When Calder (D) edited an allegedly libelous article about Jones (P) that was published in *The National Enquirer*, Jones (P) brought suit in California against *The National Enquirer* and others, including Calder (D), who had only two unrelated contacts with California before the suit.

■ **BLACK LETTER RULE** Personal jurisdiction is proper over nonresident defendants who engage in conduct that is directed at and causes harm to a resident of the forum state.

■ PROCEDURAL BASIS

Certiorari to review a decision of a California court finding jurisdiction over the defendant.

■ FACTS

Defendant South was a reporter employed by *The National Enquirer*, a Florida corporation that publishes and distributes a national magazine. South wrote an article about Shirley Jones (P), a California resident and entertainer, alleging that Jones (P) drank so heavily that she was unable to fulfill her professional obligations. The article was published in *The National Enquirer*, which has its largest circulation in California. Jones (P) sued the magazine; its distributor; South; and Calder (D), a Florida resident employed as an editor with *The National Enquirer* in California. South and Calder (D) challenged personal jurisdiction in California, claiming that they did not have sufficient minimum contacts with California for proper jurisdiction. South did most of his research for the article in Florida, but relied on phone calls to sources in California, as well as a phone call to Jones' (P) husband. Before publication of the article, Calder (D) had been to California only twice, for purposes unrelated to the article. Calder (D) reviewed and approved the subject of South's article and edited it in its final form.

■ ISSUE

May a state court exercise personal jurisdiction over a nonresident whose actions are directed at and cause harm to a resident of the forum state?

■ DECISION AND RATIONALE

(Rehnquist, J.) Yes. If a defendant engages in conduct that is directed at and causes harm to a resident of a state, that state may exercise personal jurisdiction over the defendant. The focus of a "minimum contacts" analysis for personal jurisdiction is the relationship among the defendant, the forum, and the litigation. South and Calder (D) are not charged with mere untargeted negligence. Rather, their intentional conduct was expressly aimed at a California resident when they published an article that harmed Jones (P) in California. South and Calder (D) knew both that the article would have a potentially devastating effect on Jones (P) and that Jones (P) would feel this effect in California, where she lives and works and where *The National Enquirer* has its largest circulation. Under these facts, South and Calder (D) could reasonably anticipate being brought into a California court to answer for the truth of the published statements, and Jones (P) should not be required to vindicate the intentional injuries sustained in California through the Florida court system for the convenience of the defendants. Affirmed.

Analysis:

The Supreme Court decided a similar case, *Keeton v. Hustler Magazine, Inc.*, 465 U.S. 770 (1984), on the same day as *Calder*. In *Keeton*, the Court found that *Hustler*, an Ohio corporation, was subject to personal jurisdiction in New Hampshire because the thousands of copies sold in the state amounted to sufficient purposeful contacts with the forum state. The plaintiff chose New Hampshire because of its lengthy statute of limitations for defamation suits. Some commentators have argued that *Calder* and *Keeton* expanded the ability of plaintiffs to "forum shop" in suits against media defendants by allowing plaintiffs to assert jurisdiction in multiple states where the defendant circulates its product.

■ CASE VOCABULARY

FORUM–SHOPPING: The practice of choosing the most favorable jurisdiction or court in which a claim might be heard. A plaintiff might engage in forum-shopping, for example, by filing suit in a jurisdiction with a reputation for high jury awards or by filing several similar suits and keeping the one with the preferred judge.

LIBEL: A defamatory statement expressed in a fixed medium, especially a writing, but also a picture, sign, or electronic broadcast.

Burger King Corp. v. Rudzewicz

(Florida Corporation) v. *(Michigan Franchisee)*

471 U.S. 462, 105 S.Ct. 2174, 85 L.Ed.2d 528 (1985)

SUFFICIENT JURISDICTIONAL CONTACTS MAY EXIST EVEN WITHOUT PHYSICAL PRESENCE

■ **INSTANT FACTS** Burger King Corp. (P), headquartered in Florida, brought suit in Florida federal court against Rudzewicz (D), a Michigan resident who held a Burger King franchise, to dissolve the franchise relationship.

■ **BLACK LETTER RULE** Contractual negotiations and an ongoing contractual relationship constitute sufficient minimum contacts to establish personal jurisdiction, even when the defendant was never physically present in the forum state.

■ **PROCEDURAL BASIS**

Certiorari to review a decision of the Eleventh Circuit Court of Appeals reversing the federal district court judgment against the defendant.

■ **FACTS**

Burger King Corp. (P) and Rudzewicz (D) negotiated and entered into a franchise agreement whereby Rudzewicz (D) would operate one of Burger King's (P) restaurants in Michigan for a period of twenty years. Operation of the restaurant would be according to the regulations of Burger King Corp. (P), under the supervision of Burger King's (P) representative in Michigan, and Rudzewicz (D) was to pay a monthly royalty to Burger King (P). The agreement also contained a choice-of-law provision that provided that Florida law would govern the contractual relationship of the parties. Rudzewicz (D) never traveled to Florida as a part of this franchise transaction. After a few months, Rudzewicz (D) fell behind in the monthly payments to Burger King Corp. (P). When resolution attempts proved unsuccessful, Burger King (P) brought an action in the U.S. District Court for the Southern District of Florida to terminate the franchise relationship. Rudzewicz (D) claimed that the court in Florida did not have jurisdiction to hear the case. After the court exercised personal jurisdiction over Rudzewicz (D), a judgment was entered for Burger King (P). On appeal to the Eleventh Circuit Court of Appeals, the judgment was reversed, finding that the court had no personal jurisdiction over Rudzewicz (D).

■ **ISSUE**

Is personal jurisdiction proper over a nonresident defendant who has established an ongoing business relationship with a resident of the forum state but maintains no physical presence in that state?

■ **DECISION AND RATIONALE**

(Brennan, J.) Yes. Although a contractual relationship alone is not enough to confer personal jurisdiction, if a nonresident establishes an ongoing business relationship with another party, the nonresident may be subject to jurisdiction in the other party's home state. If a defendant deliberately engages in significant activities in the state and creates continuing obligations between himself and residents of the forum state, he is subject to jurisdiction in that state even if he has never been physically present in the state. A substantial amount of business is transacted by telephone and mail, which negates the need for physical presence. As long as a commercial actor's efforts are purposefully directed towards a resident of a state, he is subject to jurisdiction in that state.

Whether a defendant in a business relationship is subject to jurisdiction in a particular state depends on the parties' prior negotiations, contemplated future obligations, the contract's terms, and the parties' actual course of dealing. Here, Rudzewicz (D) negotiated with Burger King (P) in Florida and had a regular course of dealing with the headquarters there. He understood his franchise to be operated according to the requirements established by Burger King (P) and envisioned substantial contacts with the Florida headquarters through the twenty-year franchise period. The choice-of-law provision in the parties' contract, while not controlling on the issue of jurisdiction, gave Rudzewicz (D) notice that a lawsuit in Florida was possible and established his agreement to purposefully avail himself of the rights and benefits of Florida laws. Although Michigan may have substantial interests in the litigation, these interests do not establish that Florida has no similar interests that would support personal jurisdiction in Florida courts. Moreover, Rudzewicz's (D) alleged conduct caused foreseeable injuries to a Florida corporation and personal jurisdiction over the defendant in Florida is reasonable. Reversed and remanded.

■ **DISSENT**

(Stevens, J.) Contrary to the majority's assertion, it is unfair to require a franchisee to defend a case such as this in a forum chosen by the franchisor. Rudzewicz (D) did not maintain an office, have employees, or sell any products in Florida. His only business activities were conducted exclusively within the state of Michigan. Likewise, most of the negotiations were conducted in Michigan with representatives of Burger King's (D) Michigan regional office. Nothing in the record suggests that Rudzewicz (D) purposefully availed himself of the benefits and protections of Florida law.

Analysis:

In this case, the majority stressed the forum state's interest in the litigation, whereas the dissent focused on the due process concerns of the defendant. The majority also emphasized that determining whether personal jurisdiction is proper in a particular forum depends on the facts and circumstances of each case. Although Burger King wanted the Court to announce a categorical rule relating to the franchise relationship, the Court declined to do so. As Justice Brennan stated, "We ... reject any talismanic jurisdictional formulas."

■ **CASE VOCABULARY**

CHOICE–OF–LAW CLAUSE: A contractual provision by which the parties designate the jurisdiction whose law will govern any disputes that may arise between the parties.

DIVERSITY JURISDICTION: A federal court's exercise of authority over a case involving parties from different states and an amount in controversy greater than a statutory minimum (now $75,000).

Asahi Metal Industry Co. v. Superior Court of California

(*Japanese Tire Valve Manufacturer*) v. (*California Court Exercising Jurisdiction*)
480 U.S. 102, 107 S.Ct. 1026, 94 L.Ed.2d 92 (1987)

THE SALE OF MANUFACTURED PARTS FROM JAPAN TO TAIWAN DOES NOT CONFER JURISDICTION IN CALIFORNIA COURTS

■ **INSTANT FACTS** Zurcher, the victim of a motorcycle accident, brought suit in California against a Taiwanese tire-tube maker, which brought a cross-claim against the Japanese manufacturer of the tire tube valve assembly.

■ **BLACK LETTER RULE** To be subject to personal jurisdiction in a forum state and satisfy traditional notions of fair play and substantial justice, a nonresident defendant must do more than simply place a product into the stream of commerce.

■ **PROCEDURAL BASIS**

Certiorari to review a decision of the California Supreme Court upholding personal jurisdiction over Asahi Metal Industry (D).

■ **FACTS**

Zurcher was injured in California when the rear tire of his motorcycle burst. Zurcher brought a products-liability suit in California state court against, among others, Cheng Shin Rubber Industrial Co., Ltd., the Taiwanese manufacturer of the motorcycle's tire tube. Cheng Shin Rubber filed a cross-complaint for indemnification against Asahi Metal Industry Co. (D), a Japanese company that manufactured the valve assembly in Japan and sold and shipped it to Cheng Shin Rubber in Taiwan. Sales to Cheng Shin Rubber amounted to approximately one percent of Asahi Metal's (D) income. Asahi Metal (D) denied that it had manufactured the valve at issue. Zurcher ultimately settled his claims with Cheng Shin Rubber and the other defendants, leaving only Cheng Shin Rubber's indemnity action against Asahi Metal (D). Ultimately, the California Supreme Court ruled that Asahi Metal (D) was subject to personal jurisdiction in California.

■ **ISSUE**

Is a nonresident defendant that places its product into the stream of commerce subject to personal jurisdiction in the forum state in which the product ultimately arrives?

■ **DECISION AND RATIONALE**

(O'Connor, J.) No. Merely placing a product into the stream of commerce, without more, is insufficient to confer personal jurisdiction over a nonresident defendant. If a defendant places a product into the stream of commerce and that product eventually ends up in the forum state, the defendant has done nothing to purposefully avail itself of the forum state market. Similarly, awareness that a product may end up in the forum state is not enough. Rather, fairness requires that there must be some purposeful action by the defendant to infuse its products into the forum state market. Examples include designing a product for the forum market, advertising in the forum market, or marketing a product in the forum state through a distributor. Here, Asahi Metal (D) did not purposefully avail itself of the California market. It does no business in California, does not advertise in California, and did not design its product in anticipation of California sales.

The Due Process Clause requires that the exercise of personal jurisdiction comply with traditional notions of fair play and substantial justice. Consistent with this requirement, the court must weigh the burden on the defendant, the interests of the forum state, and the plaintiff's interests in obtaining relief. Here, the burden on Asahi Metal (D) is substantial. By requiring Asahi Metal (D) to defend itself in the California court, the court compels it to travel a long way from its headquarters in Japan and defend its claim against a Taiwanese citizen, not a California resident. Although this burden can be easily overcome when minimum contacts are found, the interests of the plaintiff and the forum state do not justify jurisdiction. The dispute arises from a transaction occurring in Taiwan, and it is no more convenient to adjudicate that dispute in California than in Taiwan. Likewise, California has no significant interests given that the plaintiff is not a California resident. The issue presented does not affect California safety standards and may be judged according to Taiwanese law rather than California law. Jurisdiction was improper. Reversed.

■ CONCURRENCE IN PART

(Brennan, J.) When a defendant places its product in the stream of commerce with the knowledge that its product, as part of a manufactured whole, is marketed in the forum state, it cannot claim surprise by a lawsuit brought in the forum state. A defendant who places its product in the stream of commerce reaps economic benefit from the sale of the final product in the forum state and indirectly benefits from laws regulating commercial activity. Unlike in *World-Wide Volkswagen v. Woodson*, in which a consumer brought a single product into the forum state, Asahi Metal (D) knowingly participated in a larger marketing scheme specifically directed at California consumers. Here, Asahi Metal (D) had minimum contacts with California; it was aware of the manner in which the final product was marketed and regularly sold its components to a manufacturer it knew was making regular sales of the final product in California. However, the Court is correct in analyzing the fairness aspect of the jurisdiction test, and it would be fundamentally unfair and unreasonable to require Asahi Metal (D) to defend the suit in California.

■ CONCURRENCE IN PART

(Stevens, J.) Because jurisdiction over Asahi Metal (D) in this case would be unreasonable, there is no need to analyze minimum contacts between the defendant and California or to articulate "purposeful direction" as necessary to the minimum contacts analysis. Even assuming that the test set forth in the Court's decision is necessary, the Court misapplied it to the facts of the case. Asahi Metal's (D) dealings with Cheng Shin Rubber amount to more than merely placing its product into the stream of commerce. Whether Asahi Metal's (D) conduct rises to the level of purposeful availment depends on the volume, value, and hazardous nature of the components at issue. A regular course of delivering over 100,000 units over a period of years amounts to purposeful availment, even though the final product was marketed worldwide.

Analysis:

Although the Court unanimously held that the California state court did not have jurisdiction over Asahi Metal (D), the Justices arrived at the conclusion in different ways. Justice O'Connor applied the two-part test, analyzing first whether the California contacts were sufficient and then determining whether subjecting Asahi Metal to jurisdiction in California would be unfair and unreasonable because the parties to the indemnification action were residents of Taiwan and Japan. Both of the concurring justices agreed only with the plurality's conclusion regarding the unfairness of jurisdiction in California. Note that, as Justice Steven points out, even when a defendant has sufficient minimum contacts with a forum state, personal jurisdiction may not be reasonable.

■ CASE VOCABULARY

CROSS–COMPLAINT: A claim asserted by a defendant against another party to the action; a claim asserted by a defendant against a person not a party to the action for a matter relating to the subject of the action.

INDEMNITY: Reimbursement or compensation for loss, damage, or liability in tort; especially the right of a party who is secondarily liable to the recover from the party who is primarily liable for reimbursement of expenditures paid to a third party for injuries resulting from a violation of a common-law duty.

PLURALITY OPINION: An opinion lacking enough judges' votes to constitute a majority, but receiving more votes than any other opinion.

Pavlovich v. Superior Court

(Web Site Creator) v. *(State Court)*

58 P.3d 2 (Cal. 2002)

POSTING INFORMATION ON A WEB SITE DOES NOT ESTABLISH PERSONAL JURISDICTION IN ALL STATES

■ **INSTANT FACTS** A Texas resident who posted information infringing upon the licensing rights of a California business on a Web site created in Indiana was sued in California state court for misappropriation of trade secrets.

■ **BLACK LETTER RULE** A party purposefully avails itself of a forum state if the foreseeable effect of the out-of-state action would be to injure a person within the forum state.

■ **PROCEDURAL BASIS**

On appeal to consider the trial court's decision denying the plaintiff's motion to quash service of process.

■ **FACTS**

Pavlovich (D) was a Texas resident and the president of Media Driver, LLC. Before moving to Texas, Pavlovich (D) studied at Purdue University in Indiana and was employed in Indiana. He never lived in California, owned property in California, maintained a place of business in California, or otherwise had any business contact with California. While in Indiana, Pavlovich (D) created a Web site containing text and links to other Web sites. The Web site was informational only and neither solicited nor transacted any business. The Web site was designed to provide information to those interested in improving "video and DVD support for Linux" by defeating technology used to encrypt DVDs and prevent the unauthorized duplication of copyrighted material. The Web site provided its end users with a code that could be used to circumvent encrypted data on copyrighted DVDs. DVD Copy Control Association, Inc. (DVD CCA) (P), a Delaware corporation with its principal place of business in California, owned the licensing rights to the encryption technology. Although Pavlovich (D) was aware that circumventing the encryption technology was probably illegal and suspected that a license was required to access the encryption technology, he was unaware that DVD CCA (P) owned the licensing rights. DVD CCA (P) sued Pavlovich (D) in California state court for misappropriating trade secrets through his Web site. Pavlovich (D) filed a motion to quash service of process, contending that the California court lacked personal jurisdiction. After the motion was denied, the California Supreme Court heard the appeal.

■ **ISSUE**

Does the court have personal jurisdiction over a nonresident defendant who injures a California resident by posting information on a Web site?

■ **DECISION AND RATIONALE**

(Brown, J.) No. A court may exercise personal jurisdiction over a nonresident defendant only if the defendant has purposefully availed himself of the benefits of the forum state. Generally, the United States Supreme Court has established that a party purposefully avails itself of a forum state if the foreseeable effects of the out-of-state action would be to injure a person within the forum state. Here,

Pavlovich's (D) only contact with California is through the publication of material on the Internet that can be accessed by any Internet user in any state, including California. Although other courts have found that reaching out to a foreign state through the Internet may be a proper basis for personal jurisdiction, jurisdiction is generally based on the business advantage obtained by the Web site or the interactive exchange between the defendant and residents of the foreign state. The mere creation of an informational Web site, however, is insufficient to establish personal jurisdiction.

Here, there is no evidence that Pavlovich (D) specifically targeted California residents nor that any California residents ever accessed the Web site. To find personal jurisdiction on such facts would support minimum contacts in every state for all Internet-related claims. Such a notion would violate longstanding and well-established principles of personal jurisdiction. Although Pavlovich (D) was aware that his Web site may injure some entity that owned the licensing rights to the encryption technology, he did not know the identity of that entity nor that the entity maintained its principal place of business in California. The general knowledge that his actions may injure the motion picture industry in California is insufficient to establish that Pavlovich (D) purposefully availed himself to that jurisdiction. To hold that Pavlovich (D) purposefully availed himself to California because he should have known that his actions may harm certain California interests, though not the plaintiff's, would destroy the concept of purposeful availment. While a defendant's knowledge that his actions may affect California interests may help support personal jurisdiction, it is insufficient, by itself, to establish jurisdiction. The plaintiff may still pursue an action against the defendant, but must do so in either Indiana or Texas. Reversed and remanded.

■ DISSENT

(Baxter, J.) By posting information to be used to defeat the encryption technology used to protect DVDs from unauthorized misappropriation of copyrighted material, the defendant's intent was to damage not DVD CSS (P), but the entire motion picture and computer industries. He specifically knew that these industries were either established in or maintained a substantial presence in California. It matters not whether he specifically knew the exact identity of the party to be injured or its exact location. By specifically targeting the motion picture and computer industries in California, the defendant established minimum contacts with that state and reasonably should expect to be sued in California for injuries arising out of his conduct.

Analysis:

Most critics of the court's holding believe the California Supreme Court set the bar too high by requiring proof of the specific intended target of Internet conduct, rather than mere knowledge of the situs of the harm to be caused. This exacting knowledge requirement, it is argued, fosters intentional ignorance of a true copyright or trademark owner in order to avoid exposing oneself to jurisdiction. The opposing view, however, points out that such ignorance does not insulate a person from liability, but merely requires stronger ties to establish jurisdiction.

■ CASE VOCABULARY

MINIMUM CONTACTS: A nonresident defendant's forum-state connections, such as business activity or actions foreseeably leading to business activity, that are substantial enough to bring the defendant within the forum-state court's personal jurisdiction without offending traditional notions of fair play and substantial justice.

MOTION TO QUASH: A party's request that the court nullify process or an act instituted by the other party, as in seeking to nullify a subpoena.

SPECIFIC JURISDICTION: Jurisdiction that stems from the defendant's having certain minimum contacts with the forum state so that the court may hear a case whose issues arise from those minimum contacts.

Shaffer v. Heitner

(Officer/Director of Company) v. (Shareholder)
433 U.S. 186, 97 S.Ct. 2569, 53 L.Ed.2d 683 (1977)

PERSONAL JURISDICTION IS ALWAYS SUBJECT TO THE MINIMUM–CONTACTS TEST

■ **INSTANT FACTS** Heitner (P) brought a shareholders' derivative action against Shaffer (D) and other officers and directors of Greyhound, Inc., filing suit in Delaware and taking advantage of a Delaware statute allowing the court to sequester the defendants' stock shares.

■ **BLACK LETTER RULE** Minimum contacts are required for personal jurisdiction to exist, whether the proceeding is in personam or in rem.

■ PROCEDURAL BASIS

Certiorari to review a decision of the Delaware Supreme Court affirming a district court finding of personal jurisdiction over nonresidents with property interests in the state.

■ FACTS

Heitner (P), who was not a resident of Delaware, owned one share of stock in Greyhound, Inc., which was incorporated in Delaware but had its headquarters in Arizona. Heitner (P) brought a shareholders' derivative suit in Delaware state court against Greyhound, as well as Shaffer (D) and other individual officers and directors of the company, and requested a sequestration order under a Delaware statute that allowed a court to seize property in the state in order to compel the property owner to appear in state court and defend against a suit brought there. The court granted the request and seized shares of Greyhound stock and options belonging to the defendants. Shaffer (D) and other defendants made a special appearance to challenge personal jurisdiction in the Delaware court, arguing that they had no minimum contacts with Delaware. The Delaware court denied the challenge, holding that sequestration is merely a temporary retention of one's property interests in the state until the owner submits to the court's jurisdiction, relieving any due process concerns. On appeal, the Delaware Supreme Court affirmed.

■ ISSUE

Is the presence of the property of a defendant in a state sufficient ground for the exercise of personal jurisdiction over that defendant in a suit unrelated to the property?

■ DECISION AND RATIONALE

(Marshall, J.) No. Since *Pennoyer v. Neff*, the focus for purposes of personal jurisdiction over a nonresident in a *quasi in rem* proceeding has been on the attachment or seizure of property physically located in the state, rendering the defendant's contacts with the state immaterial. Unlike *in rem* proceedings, however, *in personam* jurisprudence has developed beyond the rule established in *Pennoyer* to require sufficient minimum contacts with a forum state to establish jurisdiction. Many lower courts have recognized that an action against one's property located within a state, effectively divesting the owner of his possessory rights, is in actuality an action against the owner directly, calling for re-examination of the *Pennoyer* rule. Seen in this light, an action against one's property is an action

---

against them personally, beckoning the application of *International Shoe*'s minimum contacts analysis to establish personal jurisdiction.

Although application of the *International Shoe* standards would have little affect on *in rem* proceedings given the forum state's strong interest in the litigation, it would markedly change the analysis in *quasi in rem* proceedings. It is those cases that would likely fall within the court's jurisdiction under *Pennoyer*, but potentially violate due process under *International Shoe*. Applying the minimum-contacts test to *quasi in rem* proceedings, a state would not be deprived of jurisdiction in matters directly related to property located in the state, rendering the proceeding *in rem* rather than *quasi in rem*, but rather would require the plaintiff to establish more than property ownership as a basis for personal jurisdiction in a suit unrelated to the property. Property owners would not be able to escape jurisdiction by placing their property in a state in which jurisdiction would otherwise be improper because property ownership would be but one consideration in exercising jurisdiction. Property ownership aside, a defendant would be subject to jurisdiction only if he has sufficient contacts with the state. If attachment of the property is later needed to enforce a judgment, a state could properly do so by honoring a valid judgment from another state through the Full Faith and Credit Clause.

Although personal jurisdiction based on property ownership is a longstanding tradition of American law, traditional notions of fair play and substantial justice can be offended by blindly honoring outdated legal requirements solely on the basis of tradition. An exercise of personal jurisdiction exclusively because of one's property ownership rights offends the fairness required of *International Shoe* and the Due Process Clause. Accordingly, all exercises of personal jurisdiction must be based on the defendant's minimum contacts with the forum state. Here, the Delaware court found jurisdiction solely on a state statute allowing jurisdiction based on a defendant's property located in the state, although the lawsuit is entirely unrelated to that property interest. Because there is no nexus between the property and the substance of the action, there must be another basis for determining the defendants' minimum contacts. The defendants' status as officers and directors of a Delaware corporation does not provide such contacts. The statute conferring jurisdiction does not do so because the defendants are officers and directors, but rather because they own some property within the state. The Delaware legislature's emphasis on property ownership in the sequestration statute diminishes its state interest in supervising the management of corporations organized under its laws, for only those directors and officers who also own stock are subject to jurisdiction. Similarly, by serving as directors and officers of the Delaware corporation, the defendants have not purposefully availed themselves of jurisdiction in the state, but rather merely agreed to be governed by its corporate laws. While the defendants have accepted the benefits and protections of Delaware laws, the most that can be said is that they have consented to the application of Delaware law, though not necessarily in a Delaware court. Because the defendants have no minimum contacts with Delaware, jurisdiction was improper. Reversed.

■ **CONCURRENCE**

(Powell, J.) *International Shoe* should be correctly applied to assertions of both *in rem* and *in personam* jurisdiction in state courts. Under that standard, the presence of defendants' stock in Delaware and the fact that they are officers and directors of a Delaware corporation are insufficient to confer jurisdiction over them in Delaware. However, it should remain open as to whether the ownership of some forms of property that may be permanently located in a particular state is sufficient to subject the defendant to jurisdiction in that state to the extent of the property's value.

■ **CONCURRENCE**

(Stevens, J.) The Due Process Clause protects defendants against judgment without notice. Some activities, such as purchasing real estate or opening a checking account, alert the individual of the possibility of future litigation in the state with proper notice of the action. Just how the Court's decision will be enforced in other circumstances, however, is uncertain.

■ **CONCURRENCE IN PART, DISSENT IN PART**

(Brennan, J.) The *International Shoe* test should apply to all questions of jurisdiction. The facts as developed in the record for this case, however, are not sufficiently clear to determine whether the defendants had sufficient minimum contacts. Because of the uncertainties in the record, the Court's decision is an impermissible advisory opinion. Nonetheless, under the appropriate standard, jurisdiction may be proper in this instance. The plaintiff's action was not a direct action against Greyhound's officers and directors, but rather was a shareholder derivative suit that inures to the benefit of the corporation and all shareholders. Seen in this light, Delaware maintains a powerful public interest in ensuring that its corporate entities have a forum to vindicate fiduciary misconduct, although it may occur outside the state. Likewise, Delaware possesses a significant regulatory interest in the governance of corporations that owe their creation solely to the benefits conferred by its laws. In a derivative suit brought in the state of incorporation, the relation between the parties, the state, and the controversy is strong. The defendants engaged in activities that foreseeably affect the forum state and they knowingly accepted the benefits and protections of the state's laws by entering into a long-term relationship with Greyhound and assuming the powers and responsibilities mandated by Delaware law. It is not unreasonable to subject them to jurisdiction in Delaware for violations of these duties.

Analysis:

Shaffer's landmark ruling saw the majority overturn the traditional approach to *in rem* jurisdiction by equating the *in rem* test with the minimum-contacts test for personal jurisdiction. After *Shaffer*, *in rem* jurisdiction was appropriate only if the defendant purposefully availed himself of the benefits and protections of the forum state or the action was sufficiently related to the forum state. In response to *Shaffer*, Delaware amended its long-arm statute to include nonresidents who become officers and directors of a Delaware corporation. The statute functioned similarly to the statute in *Hess v. Pawloski*, 274 U.S. 352 (1927), by deeming the officers to have appointed an in-state agent for service of process.

■ CASE VOCABULARY

ATTACH: To take or seize under legal authority.

DERIVATIVE ACTION: A suit by a beneficiary of a fiduciary to enforce a right belonging to the fiduciary, especially a suit asserted by a shareholder on the corporation's behalf against a third party (usually a corporate officer) because of the corporation's failure to take some action against the third party.

IN REM JURISDICTION: A court's power to adjudicate the rights to a given piece of property, including the power to seize and hold it.

QUASI IN REM JURISDICTION: Jurisdiction over a person but based on that person's interest in property located within the court's territory.

Burnham v. Superior Court of California

(Nonresident Husband) v. *(Court Exercising Jurisdiction)*
495 U.S. 604, 110 S.Ct. 2105, 109 L.Ed.2d 631 (1990)

PHYSICAL PRESENCE IN A STATE SUPPORTS JURISDICTION

■ **INSTANT FACTS** Burnham (D), a resident of New Jersey, was served with a summons and petition for divorce while on a brief visit to California.

■ **BLACK LETTER RULE** A state may assert personal jurisdiction over any person physically present within its boundaries, even if they are in the state only temporarily, and even if the suit is not related to the person's presence in the state.

■ **PROCEDURAL BASIS**

Certiorari to review state court's denial of mandamus relief following its denial of defendant's motion to quash service of process in the action.

■ **FACTS**

Burnham (D) and his wife were residents of New Jersey. They agreed to separate and Mrs. Burnham moved to California. Although Burnham (D) filed for divorce in New Jersey, he never had his wife served with process. Consequently, Mrs. Burnham filed for divorce in California. While Burnham (D) was in California on a business trip and to visit his children, he was served with the summons and petition for divorce. Burnham (D) made a special appearance to move to quash the service for lack of personal jurisdiction. Both the California Superior Court and Court of Appeals denied Burnham's (D) request, finding proper personal jurisdiction based on his physical presence in the state.

■ **ISSUE**

Is the physical presence of a defendant within a state sufficient to confer jurisdiction in that state's courts to hear a suit unrelated to the defendant's presence in the state?

■ **DECISION AND RATIONALE**

(Scalia, J.) Yes. Since *Pennoyer v. Neff*, personal jurisdiction based on a defendant's physical presence in the forum state has been a valid exercise of the court's authority over the defendant. Although jurisdictional jurisprudence has progressed beyond physical presence to encompass minimum contacts and traditional notions of fair play and substantial justice, it is well-settled in most, if not all, state and federal court systems that jurisdiction over one who is physically present in the forum state is proper. The continuous and systematic contact required to assert jurisdiction over a nonresident is used as an analogy to establish sufficient minimum contacts that equate to physical presence. Physical presence is within the traditional reach of a court's jurisdictional powers and need not be continuous nor systematic.

Neither must one's physical presence in the state be related to the subject matter of the litigation. While *Shaffer v. Heitner* suggested that all jurisdiction must be evaluated according to *International Shoe's* traditional notions of fair play and substantial justice, which leads to the argument that physical presence must be related to the subject matter of the litigation, *Shaffer* dealt with nonresidents who were absent from the forum state. It does not require that nonresidents who are physically present in the forum state be treated similarly. Affirmed.

■ CONCURRENCE IN PART

(White, J.) Personal jurisdiction based on one's physical presence in the forum state is so well accepted in jurisprudence that it cannot be said to be too arbitrary or over-reaching to require its elimination. Although personal jurisdiction often requires an examination of the particular circumstances on a case-by-case basis, when jurisdiction is based on personal service in the forum state, any factual examination would lead to substantial meaningless litigation over the validity of jurisdiction.

■ CONCURRENCE

(Brennan, J.) The majority's reliance upon traditional and historical significance as the proper basis for personal jurisdiction has been foreclosed by the decisions in *International Shoe* and *Shaffer*. International-al Shoe proclaimed that personal jurisdiction must be consistent with traditional notions of fair play and substantial justice. *Shaffer*, taking this notion further, decided that *all* exercises of personal jurisdiction, even those traditionally accepted as valid, must be guided by *International Shoe*. While tradition serves as a guide for modern jurisprudence, tradition and history alone to do not establish constitutional practices. When a defendant physically enters a state, he avails himself of the benefits of police and fire protection, travel on the roadways, and the fruits of the state's economy. Likewise, the burden on the defendant is minimal given that his presence in the state indicates an ability to travel there to defend himself. While physical presence will often be sufficient for personal jurisdiction, it must be because the test established by *International Shoe* and its progeny has been satisfied, not because of some antiquated traditional concept. Here, jurisdiction was appropriate.

■ CONCURRENCE

(Stevens, J.) The majority opinion is broader than necessary to reach the correct result that in-state service of process is sufficient to confer jurisdiction over a nonresident. However, the issues raised by Justices Scalia, Brennan, and White demonstrate that the lower court's judgment should be affirmed.

Analysis:

Burnham clarified that the traditional idea of jurisdiction based on physical presence can survive even if sufficient minimum contacts do not otherwise exist between the defendant and the forum state. Note, however, that in footnote 1 of *Burnham*, Justice Scalia excepted corporations from the analysis. Other courts have held that serving a corporate agent temporarily in the forum state is not enough to subject the corporation to jurisdiction in that state. Also, jurisdiction will not lie if a nonresident is served as a result of being tricked into visiting the state.

■ CASE VOCABULARY

MOTION TO QUASH: A party's request that the court nullify process or an act instituted by the other party, as in seeking to nullify a subpoena.

SPECIAL APPEARANCE: A defendant's pleading that either claims that the court lacks personal jurisdiction over the defendant or objects to improper service of process; a defendant's showing up in court for the sole purpose of contesting a court's assertion of personal jurisdiction over the defendant.

TRANSIENT JURISDICTION: Personal jurisdiction based on a person's temporary presence in a state.

Helicopteros Nacionales de Colombia, S.A. v. Hall

(Helicopter Company) v. *(Wrongful Death Survivors)*
466 U.S. 408, 104 S.Ct. 1868, 80 L.Ed.2d 404 (1984)

PURCHASES ALONE ARE INSUFFICIENT TO CONFER JURISDICTION IN AN UNRELATED LAWSUIT

■ **INSTANT FACTS** Hall (P) and other surviving family members sued Helicopteros Nacionales (Helicol) (D), a Colombian corporation, in Texas for wrongful death caused by a helicopter crash in Peru.

■ **BLACK LETTER RULE** Mere purchases, even if they occur at regular intervals, are insufficient for a state to exercise jurisdiction over a nonresident in a cause of action unrelated to the purchases, but it does not otherwise offend due process to exercise general jurisdiction over a nonresident defendant whose contacts with a forum state are continuous and systematic.

■ **PROCEDURAL BASIS**

Certiorari to review a decision of the Texas Supreme Court reversing judgment for the plaintiffs.

■ **FACTS**

Consorcio, a Texas-based joint venture, contracted with Helicol (D), a Colombian corporation, to provide helicopter transportation of personnel and supplies to and from a Consorcio pipeline project in Peru. Helicol (D) negotiated the contract in Texas, purchased helicopters in Texas, and sent prospective pilots to Texas for training. While working on the pipeline, four Americans were killed in a helicopter crash. Hall (P) and other survivors of the pipeline project employees sued Helicol (D) and others for wrongful death in Texas state court.

■ **ISSUE**

May a state court exercise jurisdiction over a nonresident defendant if the cause of action does not arise from the nonresident's minimal activities in the forum state?

■ **DECISION AND RATIONALE**

(Blackmun, J.) No. If a lawsuit does not arise from a nonresident corporate defendant's activities in the forum state, a state court may exercise jurisdiction only if the defendant's contacts with the state are systematic and continuous. Mere purchases, even if they occur at regular intervals, are insufficient for a state to exercise jurisdiction over a nonresident in a cause of action unrelated to the purchases. It does not offend due process to exercise general jurisdiction over a nonresident defendant whose contacts with a forum state are continuous and systematic. However, Helicol's (D) single negotiation session in Texas, acceptance of checks drawn on Texas banks, and helicopter purchases in Texas do not amount to such continuous and systematic contact.

■ **DISSENT**

(Brennan, J.) There is a substantial difference between contacts "related to" the cause of action and those that "give rise" to the cause of action. While the deaths did not arise out of the defendant's contacts with Texas, those contacts are sufficiently related to the deaths to establish specific jurisdiction. The negotiations that gave rise to the contract occurred in Texas, without which the events resulting in the deaths would not have occurred. Likewise, the helicopters used by the defendant were purchased in Texas, and the pilot whose negligence is alleged to have caused the crash was trained in

Texas. These contacts combine to establish the basis for the plaintiff's allegations of Helicol's (D) negligence. Limiting jurisdiction to those cases that specifically arise out of a defendant's specific contacts with the forum state will create a legal anomaly in which jurisdiction over a bare negligence action would be improper, but an action for negligent training would confer jurisdiction solely because it more closely "arises from" the same contacts to the forum state. It is sufficient when, as here, the cause of action relates to the defendant's contacts with the forum state.

Analysis:

Helicopteros highlights the distinction between general and specific jurisdiction and the type of contacts a nonresident defendant must have for each type of jurisdiction to be proper. Specific jurisdiction would apply if the cause of action arises out of or relates to the defendant's contacts with the forum state. When a nonresident's contacts with the forum state are systematic and continuous, the state courts may exert general jurisdiction over the nonresident, even in cases unrelated to those contacts.

■ CASE VOCABULARY

DECEDENT: A dead person, especially a person who has died recently.

GENERAL JURISDICTION: A court's authority to hear all claims against a defendant, at the place of the defendant's domicile or the place of service, without any showing that a connection exists between the claims and the forum state.

SPECIFIC JURISDICTION: Jurisdiction that stems from the defendant's having certain minimum contacts with the forum state so that the court may hear a case involving issues arising from those minimum contacts.

Insurance Corp. of Ireland, Ltd. v. Compagnie des Bauxites de Guinee

(Foreign Insurer) v. *(Bauxite Mining Company)*

456 U.S. 694, 102 S.Ct. 2099, 72 L.Ed.2d 492 (1982)

FAILURE TO COMPLY WITH DISCOVERY ORDERS PERMITS A PRESUMPTION OF PERSONAL JURISDICTION

■ **INSTANT FACTS** After losing $10 million due to a work stoppage, Compagnie des Bauxites de Guinee (P) sought to recover the money under a business interruption insurance policy with the defendants.

■ **BLACK LETTER RULE** A court may use a sanctions order for purposes of asserting personal jurisdiction.

■ **PROCEDURAL BASIS**

Certiorari to consider the court's exercise of personal jurisdiction over the foreign defendants.

■ **FACTS**

Compagnie des Bauxites de Guinee (P) was a Delaware corporation jointly owned by a Pennsylvania company and the Republic of Guinee that mined bauxite in Guinee. As part of its business operations, it obtained $10 million worth of business interruption insurance from an American insurer and an additional $10 million worth of insurance from Insurance Corp. of Ireland (D), among other foreign insurers. After the plaintiff lost $10 million due to a work stoppage, it submitted a claim to the American and foreign insurers on the policies. After the defendants denied the claim, the plaintiff sued all insurers in Pennsylvania federal court. The foreign insurers answered, but later claimed the court lacked personal jurisdiction over them and moved for summary judgment. The defendants' motion was denied. During discovery (in order to attempt to determine facts that could establish jurisdiction), the defendants agreed to disclose four million business interruption insurance files in London. The court, however, ordered them to provide the files in Pennsylvania. When the defendants refused, the court imposed discovery sanctions against the defendants and presumed jurisdiction. On appeal, the defendants challenged the sanctions order and contended that the court could not create jurisdiction by imposing sanctions when no personal jurisdiction previously existed.

■ **ISSUE**

May a sanctions order be used to establish personal jurisdiction over a defendant?

■ **DECISION AND RATIONALE**

(White, J.) Yes. Personal jurisdiction is a matter of individual rights and liberties, restricting the court's power to adjudicate matters outside its authority. Because personal jurisdiction involves individual rights, a party may waive its rights and voluntarily consent to a court's jurisdiction. For instance, a party failing to assert a challenge of the court's personal jurisdiction in its answer or responsive pleading under Rule 12 waives its affirmative defense. Although a party need not comply with an order of a court that has no personal jurisdiction, when that party appears in court for the purpose of challenging jurisdiction it is bound by the court's determination on the jurisdictional issue. A sanctions order establishing personal jurisdiction over a defendant operates in like manner.

Here, the defendants had the opportunity to comply with discovery orders to demonstrate that the court had no personal jurisdiction. By refusing to comply, the defendant waived its right to a defense of lack of jurisdiction. Defendants could have refused to submit to the court's jurisdiction entirely, permitted a default judgment to be entered, and challenged jurisdiction as a collateral attack. By presenting the issue to the court, however, its determination binds the defendants. Affirmed.

Analysis:

The Court's decision suggests the classic chicken-or-egg dilemma. If the court has no personal jurisdiction over the defendant, how can it issue discovery orders, much less sanctions for discovery violations? But if the defendant doesn't comply with the discovery orders, the court will assume jurisdiction. It is difficult to understand why the *failure* to comply with a court's order creates jurisdiction, when full compliance with the order may establish a lack of jurisdiction in the first place.

■ CASE VOCABULARY

COLLATERAL ATTACK: An attack on a judgment entered in a different proceeding.

RES JUDICATA: An issue that has been definitively settled by judicial decision.

SANCTIONS: A penalty or coercive measure that results from failure to comply with a rule, law, or order.

SPECIAL APPEARANCE: A defendant's pleading that either claims that the court lacks personal jurisdiction over the defendant or objects to improper service of process; a defendant's showing up in court for the sole purpose of contesting a court's assertion of personal jurisdiction over the defendant.

Bates v. C & S Adjusters, Inc.

(Defaulting Debtor) v. *(Collection Agency)*
980 F.2d 865 (2d Cir. 1992)

VENUE IS DIFFERENT ISSUE THAN JURISDICTION

■ **INSTANT FACTS** Bates (P) sued C & S Adjusters, Inc. (D) in federal court for violations of the Fair Debt Collection Practices Act.

■ **BLACK LETTER RULE** Venue is appropriate in a judicial district in which a substantial part of the events or omissions giving rise to the claim took place.

■ **PROCEDURAL BASIS**

On appeal from a judgment of the U.S. District Court for the Western District of New York, dismissing the plaintiff's complaint for improper venue.

■ **FACTS**

Bates (P) incurred a debt while living in Pennsylvania. When Bates (P) defaulted on the debt, the Pennsylvania creditor assigned the debt to C & S Adjusters, Inc. (D), a New York-based collection agency. After Bates (P) moved to New York, C & S Adjusters (D) mailed a collection letter to Bates's (P) Pennsylvania address and the postal service forwarded the letter to his address in New York. Alleging violations of the federal Fair Debt Collection Practices Act, Bates (P) sued C & S Adjusters (D) in New York federal court. C & S Adjusters (D) moved to dismiss for improper venue, which motion was granted by the court.

■ **ISSUE**

Does venue exist in a district in which the debtor resides and to which a bill collector's demand for payment was forwarded?

■ **DECISION AND RATIONALE**

(Newman, J.) Yes. Under the 1990 amendments to 28 U.S.C. § 1391(b)(2), venue is proper in "a judicial district in which a substantial part of the events or omissions giving rise to the claim occurred." Under this language, venue may be proper in more than one location after considering such factors as the convenience of the defendants and location of evidence and witnesses. The court need not choose the best available venue so long as the statute is met. Because the defendant mailed its collection letter with the intent that the plaintiff would receive it not necessarily in Pennsylvania but wherever he may live, actual receipt of the letter in New York constituted a substantial part of the events giving rise to the claim. Venue in New York was appropriate. Reversed and remanded.

Analysis:

Although the court construed the 1990 amendments to 28 U.S.C. § 1391(b)(2), legal principles preceding the amendments continue to be relevant to venue determinations. Among the principles to be considered in determining proper venue are the convenience of defendants, the location of evidence

---

and witnesses, and local familiarity with the laws at issue. The defendant's deliberate contact with a judicial district is a factor for personal jurisdiction, not venue.

■ **CASE VOCABULARY**

VENUE: The proper or a possible place for the trial of a case, usually because the place has some connection with the events that gave rise to the case.

Piper Aircraft Co. v. Reyno

(Airplane Manufacturer) v. *(Victims' Administratrix)*
454 U.S. 235, 102 S.Ct. 252, 70 L.Ed.2d 419 (1981)

FORUM NON CONVENIENS DETERMINATIONS ARE BASED ON PRIVATE AND PUBLIC INTERESTS

■ **INSTANT FACTS** The estates of Scottish citizens brought a wrongful death suit against Piper Aircraft Co. (D) in Pennsylvania federal court as a result of an airplane crash in Scotland.

■ **BLACK LETTER RULE** Under the doctrine of forum non conveniens, a court may dismiss a case if there is an alternate forum with jurisdiction and if proceeding in the forum would impose a heavy burden on the parties or the court.

■ **PROCEDURAL BASIS**

Certiorari to review a decision of the Third Circuit Court of Appeals reversing the district court's dismissal of the case on forum non conveniens grounds.

■ **FACTS**

A commercial airplane manufactured in Pennsylvania by Piper Aircraft Co. (D), a Pennsylvania corporation, crashed in Scotland, killing the pilot and five Scottish passengers. Parts of the airplane were manufactured by Hartzell Propeller, Inc., (D), an Ohio corporation; the airplane was owned and maintained by a British company; and a Scottish corporation operated the airplane. The airplane wreckage was located in England. Reyno (P), a California resident, was appointed the administrator of the estates of the crash victims and filed a wrongful death action against Piper (D) and others in California state court. After the case was removed to California federal court, it was transferred to a Pennsylvania federal court and Piper Aircraft (D) moved to dismiss the case based on forum non conveniens. The Pennsylvania federal court granted the defendants' motion, ruling that although Pennsylvania was a proper forum, various private interest factors, including the convenience of the parties, and public interest factors, such as the convenience of the forum, established that a Scottish court would be a more appropriate forum. The Third Circuit Court of Appeals reversed.

■ **ISSUE**

May a court dismiss a case if an alternate forum has jurisdiction to hear the case and litigating in the present forum would be overly burdensome to the defendant and the court system, even though the law of the alternate forum is less favorable to the plaintiff?

■ **DECISION AND RATIONALE**

(Marshall, J.) Yes. Although a plaintiff's chosen forum must be afforded significant consideration, a court may not deny a motion to dismiss merely because the substantive law of an alternate forum would be less favorable to the plaintiffs than the law of the forum state. Dismissal must ordinarily be granted when trial in the plaintiff's chosen forum places an undue burden on the court or the defendant and the plaintiff can provide no compelling reason that the chosen forum is more convenient. If dismissal can be defeated because the law of an alternate forum is less favorable to the plaintiff, actions would be allowed to proceed in an otherwise inconvenient forum.

In exercising its discretion to dismiss for forum non conveniens, a court must consider various "private interest factors" and "public interest factors," in addition to the plaintiff's choice of venue. Among the private interest factors are the parties' access to evidence and key witnesses, the ability to compel unwilling witnesses to testify, and other issues making litigation more convenient or less burdensome on the parties. The public interest factors include the convenience of the court and the alternate forum's interest in the litigation.

In this case, the private interests of the parties weigh in favor of trial in Scotland because most of the evidence and witnesses are located in Scotland and the defendants could more easily add third parties and claims to the lawsuit, which would not be feasible in Pennsylvania. Similarly, public interest factors also point to suit in Scotland because the claims in Pennsylvania would involve application of Scottish law to Piper Aircraft (D) and Pennsylvania law to Hartzell (D), which would confuse to the jury. Additionally, Scotland had a strong interest in the outcome of the litigation, as the real parties in interest were Scottish and the events occurred within its airspace. Because these private and public interests establish the Scottish courts as the more convenient forum, the district court did not abuse its discretion in granting the dismissal. Reversed.

Analysis:

The underlying basis of *Piper* is that the forum non conveniens doctrine applies only when venue is proper in the initial forum and there is an alternate forum available. Therefore, the common law doctrine of forum non conveniens is closely related to the concept of venue, which, for federal courts, is determined by statute. Generally, venue is proper in a judicial district where a defendant resides or where a substantial part of the events giving rise to the claim occurred. If the plaintiff files suit in a district where venue is not proper, the court may either dismiss the suit or transfer it to a venue that is proper.

■ CASE VOCABULARY

FORUM NON CONVENIENS: The doctrine that an appropriate forum—even though competent under the law—may divest itself of jurisdiction for the convenience of the litigants and the witnesses, when it appears that the action should proceed in another forum in which the action might originally have been brought.

CHAPTER TEN

Choosing the Forum—State v. Federal Court

Mas v. Perry

Instant Facts: Mr. Mas (P), a French citizen, and Mrs. Mas (P), a Mississippi citizen, sued Perry (D), a Louisiana citizen, in Louisiana federal court for invasion of their privacy while the plaintiffs rented an apartment from the defendant in Louisiana.

Black Letter Rule: A change of citizenship is established only by taking up a true, fixed, and permanent residence in a different state with an intent to remain there.

Louisville & Nashville Railroad Co. v. Mottley

Instant Facts: The Mottleys (P) sued the Louisville & Nashville Railroad Co. (D) for breach of contract for refusing to honor a previous settlement granting the plaintiffs' lifetime passes on its trains, based on later restrictions imposed by federal statute.

Black Letter Rule: Subject matter jurisdiction must be determined from the allegations contained in a well-pleaded complaint.

Grable & Sons Metal Products, Inc. v. Darue Engineering & Manufacturing

Instant Facts: After the IRS seized Grable's (D) property and sold it to Darue (D), Grable (P) brought a quiet title action, claiming that the notice it received was defective, and Darue (D) removed the case to federal court.

Black Letter Rule: The national interest in providing a federal forum for federal tax litigation is sufficiently substantial to support the exercise of federal question jurisdiction over questions presented under federal title law, and would not distort any division of labor between the state and federal courts provided or assumed by Congress.

United Mine Workers v. Gibbs

Instant Facts: Gibbs (P), a mine superintendent, sued the United Mine Workers (D) in federal court for blocking the opening of a new mine he was managing, claiming violations of both state and federal law.

Black Letter Rule: The exercise of pendent jurisdiction is within the sound discretion of the trial court.

Owen Equipment and Erection Company v. Kroger

Instant Facts: Kroger was electrocuted when a crane operated by Owen Equipment came too close to a power line owned by Omaha Public Power District (D).

Black Letter Rule: A plaintiff in a diversity case cannot rely on ancillary jurisdiction to permit an amendment to a complaint to bring a claim against a non-diverse third-party defendant.

Exxon Mobil Corp. v. Allapattah Services

Rosario Ortega v. Star–Kist Foods, Inc.

Instant Facts: In *Exxon*, a group of Exxon dealers sued Exxon for overcharging them for fuel, but not all of the dealers' claims met the minimum amount-in-controversy requirement for the exercise of federal court diversity jurisdiction. In *Ortega*, a child and her parents sued Star–Kist, but only the child's damages met the minimum amount-in-controversy requirement.

Black Letter Rule: Where other elements of jurisdiction are present and at least one named plaintiff in the action satisfies the amount-in-controversy requirement, a court may exercise supplemental jurisdiction over the claims of other plaintiffs in the same case or controversy, even if those claims are for less than the jurisdictional amount specified in the statute setting forth the requirements for diversity jurisdiction.

Mas v. Perry

(Married Students) v. *(Landlord)*
489 F.2d 1396 (5th Cir. 1974)

TAKING UP RESIDENCE IN A DOMICILE WITH AN INTENT TO REMAIN THERE ESTABLISHES CITIZENSHIP

■ **INSTANT FACTS** Mr. Mas (P), a French citizen, and Mrs. Mas (P), a Mississippi citizen, sued Perry (D), a Louisiana citizen, in Louisiana federal court for invasion of their privacy while the plaintiffs rented an apartment from the defendant in Louisiana.

■ **BLACK LETTER RULE** A change of citizenship is established only by taking up a true, fixed, and permanent residence in a different state with an intent to remain there.

■ **PROCEDURAL BASIS**

Appeal on jurisdictional grounds from a jury verdict for the plaintiff.

■ **FACTS**

The plaintiffs, a French citizen and a Mississippi citizen, were graduate assistants at Louisiana State University in Baton Rouge. Mr. and Mrs. Mas (P) were married at Mrs. Mas' (P) family home in Jackson, Mississippi. After the marriage, Mr. and Mrs. Mas (P) returned to Louisiana to resume their studies and rented an apartment from Perry (D). The plaintiffs learned that the apartment had been equipped with two-way mirrors in the bedroom and bathroom through which the defendant had watched them for several months. They filed suit against Perry (D) in Louisiana federal court and then moved to Illinois, intending to return to Louisiana to continue their studies. The plaintiffs were uncertain where they would move upon completion of their studies.

■ **ISSUE**

Had plaintiffs established citizenship in Louisiana such that the court lacked diversity jurisdiction over the matter?

■ **DECISION AND RATIONALE**

(Ainsworth, J.) No. A party changes his or her citizenship only by taking up residence in another state with an intention to remain there. Since Mr. Mas (P), a foreign citizen, and Mrs. Mas (P), a Mississippi citizen, resided in Louisiana solely for educational purposes, they lacked the requisite intent to remain there and their citizenship was unaffected. Thus, the court's diversity jurisdiction was appropriate both because it involved a suit brought by a foreign citizen against and American citizen and because Mrs. Mas (P) and Perry (D) were citizens of different states. Jurisdiction is similarly proper over Mrs. Mas' (P) claims because the court already possesses jurisdiction over Mr. Mas' (P) claims. When the claims of a wife share the same operative facts as a claim of her husband, judicial economy strongly urges federal jurisdiction.

Further, although the plaintiffs recovered only $5,000, which is below the $10,000 amount in controversy requirement for diversity jurisdiction, the plaintiffs claimed damages of $100,000 in their complaint. Federal jurisdiction is not destroyed because the plaintiffs ultimately recover damages below the jurisdictional amount. Instead, the face of the complaint demonstrates that $100,000 was claimed in good faith and was "in controversy," satisfying the requirement. Affirmed.

Analysis:

A party's citizenship for jurisdictional purposes is established by federal law, not the law of any individual state. The burden of proving citizenship lies with the party asserting jurisdiction, with the burden shifting to a party challenging proper jurisdiction. It is also important to note with regard to this case in particular that the plaintiffs' move to Illinois after suit was brought had no effect on the court's jurisdiction.

■ CASE VOCABULARY

AMOUNT IN CONTROVERSY: The damages claimed or relief demanded by the injured party in a lawsuit.

DIVERSITY JURISDICTION: A federal court's exercise of authority over a case involving parties from different states and an amount in controversy greater than a statutory minimum.

DOMICILE: The place at which a person is physically present and that the person regards as home; a person's true, fixed, principal, and permanent home, to which that person intends to return and remain even though currently residing elsewhere.

RESIDENCE: The act or fact of living in a given place for some time; the place where one actually lives, as distinguished from domicile.

Louisville & Nashville Railroad Co. v. Mottley

(Railroad Company) v. *(Passengers)*

211 U.S. 149, 29 S.Ct. 42, 53 L.Ed. 126 (1908)

SUBJECT MATTER JURISDICTION IS DETERMINED FROM THE COMPLAINT

■ **INSTANT FACTS** The Mottleys (P) sued the Louisville & Nashville Railroad Co. (D) for breach of contract for refusing to honor a previous settlement granting the plaintiffs' lifetime passes on its trains, based on later restrictions imposed by federal statute.

■ **BLACK LETTER RULE** Subject matter jurisdiction must be determined from the allegations contained in a well-pleaded complaint.

■ **PROCEDURAL BASIS**

Appeal from a judgment of the trial court finding jurisdiction.

■ **FACTS**

In settlement of a prior lawsuit against the Louisville & Nashville Railroad Co. (D), the Mottleys (P) accepted lifetime passes to ride the defendant's trains free of charge. After enactment of a federal statute prohibiting railroads from extending such passes, however, the defendant refused to honor the settlement. The Mottleys (P) sued Louisville & Nashville Railroad Co. (D) in federal court for breach of contract, anticipating that the defendant would raise the federal statute as a defense and arguing that the court had federal question jurisdiction. After the court denied the defendant's demurrer for lack of jurisdiction, the defendant appealed directly to the Supreme Court.

■ **ISSUE**

Does a federal court have federal question jurisdiction when the complaint does not arise out of federal law, but the defendant's anticipated defense raises issues of federal law?

■ **DECISION AND RATIONALE**

(Moody, J.) No. Despite the fact that a federal question may very likely be involved in the litigation of a suit, jurisdiction must be determined by the allegations presented in the plaintiff's complaint in order for jurisdiction to arise under the Constitution or federal law. Here, the Mottleys (P) sued for breach of contract under state common law. As the plaintiffs' cause of action arises out of state law, there is no federal question jurisdiction. Reversed.

Analysis:

This case represents the creation of the well-pleaded complaint rule, which requires a plaintiff to specify in his or her complaint the grounds for jurisdiction, the basis for the suit, and a demand for relief. Note that this suit did not involve diversity of citizenship. If the parties had been diverse, the court would have had subject matter jurisdiction despite the absence of a federal question.

■ CASE VOCABULARY

FEDERAL–QUESTION JURISDICTION: The exercise of a federal-court power over claims arising under the U.S. Constitution, an act of Congress, or a treaty.

WELL–PLEADED COMPLAINT: An original or initial pleading that sufficiently sets forth a claim for relief— by including the grounds for the court's jurisdiction, the basis for relief claimed, and a demand for judgment—so that a defendant may draft an answer that is responsive to the issues presented. A well-pleaded complaint must raise a controlling issue of federal law for a federal court to have federal question jurisdiction over the lawsuit.

Grable & Sons Metal Products, Inc. v. Darue Engineering & Manufacturing

(Original Owner of Seized Property) v. *(Purchaser of Seized Property)*

545 U.S. 308, 125 S.Ct. 2363, 162 L.Ed.2d 257 (2005)

EVEN CASES THAT *IMPLICATE* FEDERAL LAW MAY JUSTIFY THE EXERCISE OF FEDERAL COURT JURISDICTION

"Federal question or not federal question, that is the question."

Federal question.

stus.com

■ **INSTANT FACTS** After the IRS seized Grable's (D) property and sold it to Darue (D), Grable (P) brought a quiet title action, claiming that the notice it received was defective, and Darue (D) removed the case to federal court.

■ **BLACK LETTER RULE** The national interest in providing a federal forum for federal tax litigation is sufficiently substantial to support the exercise of federal question jurisdiction over questions presented under federal title law, and would not distort any division of labor between the state and federal courts provided or assumed by Congress.

■ **PROCEDURAL BASIS**

Supreme Court consideration of the question of federal jurisdiction only, after affirmance of the exercise of jurisdiction by the Sixth Circuit.

■ **FACTS**

In 1994 the IRS seized real property belonging to Grable & Sons (P) in order to satisfy Grable's (P) tax delinquency. Grable (P) was thereafter notified, by certified mail, that the IRS was selling the seized property to Darue Engineering (D). Grable (P) did not exercise its right to redeem the property, so, after the statutory redemption period had expired, the government gave Darue (D) a quitclaim deed to the property. Five years later, Grable (P) tried to get the property back in a state-court quiet title action, alleging that the notice it had received was deficient because the relevant statute requires personal service, not service by certified mail. Darue (D) removed the case to federal court. Grable (P) tried to get the case remanded back to state court, arguing that it did not raise a federal question, but the district court found that a federal question did exist and granted summary judgment in Darue's (D) favor. The Sixth Circuit affirmed. The Supreme Court granted certiorari on the issue of federal question jurisdiction alone in order to resolve a split in the circuits as to whether the existence of a federal cause of action is a required condition for the exercise of federal question jurisdiction.

■ **ISSUE**

Does want of a federal cause of action to try claims of title to land obtained at a federal tax sale preclude removal to federal court of a state action with non-diverse parties raising a disputed issue of federal title law?

■ **DECISION AND RATIONALE**

(Souter, J.) No. The national interest in providing a federal forum for federal tax litigation is sufficiently substantial to support the exercise of federal question jurisdiction over questions presented under federal title law, and would not distort any division of labor between the state and federal courts

---

provided or assumed by Congress. Darue (D) was entitled to remove the quiet title action to federal court if it could have been brought there originally as a civil action arising under the Constitution, laws, or treaties of the United States. The "arising under" language is sometimes read narrowly, but there is another longstanding variety of federal jurisdiction. Federal court jurisdiction lies over state law claims that *implicate* significant federal issues. That is, a state law claim can give rise to federal question jurisdiction if it appears from the complaint that the right to relief depends on the construction or application of federal law. The relevant concern is, does the state law claim necessarily raise a stated federal issue, actually disputed and substantial, that a federal forum may entertain without disturbing any congressionally approved balance of federal and state judicial responsibilities? The answer here is yes. Quiet title actions were the subject of some of the earliest exercises of federal question jurisdiction over state law claims. Although federal law does not provide for quiet title actions, the Government, its buyers, and its delinquents have a clear interest in the availability of a federal forum in tax delinquency cases like this. Moreover, it is the rare quiet title action that actually implicates federal law, so the exercise of jurisdiction here would not threaten the normal currents of litigation. The judgment of the court of appeals upholding the exercise of jurisdiction over Grable's (P) quiet title action is therefore affirmed.

■ CONCURRENCE

(Thomas, J.) I would be willing, in an appropriate case, to consider limiting 28 U.S.C. § 1331 jurisdiction to cases in which federal law *creates* the cause of action pleaded on the face of the plaintiff's complaint.

Analysis:

Justice Thomas's concurrence focuses on, and he seems to prefer, the rule announced decades earlier in *American Well Works Co. v. Layne & Bowler Co.*, 241 U.S. 257 (1916). In that case, the Court held that a suit for damages to a business caused by a threat to sue under the patent law was not itself a suit under the patent law. Whether the defendant's act was wrong or not depended on the law of the state where the act was done, the Court explained, not on the patent law, and therefore the suit arose under the law of the state. A suit arises under the law that creates the cause of action, and the fact that the justification for the wrongful acts in that case may have involved the validity and infringement of a patent was no more material to the question of under what law the suit was brought than it would have been in an action of contract.

■ CASE VOCABULARY

FEDERAL QUESTION: In litigation, a legal issue involving the interpretation and application of the U.S. Constitution, an act of Congress, or a treaty. Jurisdiction over federal questions rests with the federal courts.

FEDERAL QUESTION JURISDICTION: The exercise of federal-court power over claims arising under the U.S. Constitution, an act of Congress, or a treaty.

PERSONAL SERVICE: Actual delivery of the notice or process to the person to whom it is directed.

QUIET TITLE ACTION: A proceeding to establish a plaintiff's title to land by compelling the adverse claimant to establish a claim or be forever estopped from asserting it.

QUITCLAIM DEED: A deed that conveys a grantor's complete interest or claim in certain real property but that neither warrants nor professes that the title is valid.

REDEEM: The act or an instance of reclaiming or regaining possession by paying a specific price.

REMAND: The act or an instance of sending something (such as a case, claim, or person) back for further action.

REMOVAL: The transfer of an action from state to federal court. In removing a case to federal court, a litigant must timely file the removal papers and must show a valid basis for federal court jurisdiction.

United Mine Workers v. Gibbs

(*Union*) v. (*Mine Superintendent*)
383 U.S. 715, 86 S.Ct. 1130, 16 L.Ed.2d 218 (1966)

FEDERAL COURTS MAY HEAR STATE LAW CLAIMS JOINED TO FEDERAL CLAIMS WITH A COMMON SET OF FACTS

Is this legal?
Or is that not
the point?

UNION
YES

stus.com

■ **INSTANT FACTS** Gibbs (P), a mine superintendent, sued the United Mine Workers (D) in federal court for blocking the opening of a new mine he was managing, claiming violations of both state and federal law.

■ **BLACK LETTER RULE** The exercise of pendent jurisdiction is within the sound discretion of the trial court.

■ **PROCEDURAL BASIS**

Certiorari to review a judgment granting damages on state law claims and dismissing federal claims.

■ **FACTS**

This case grew out of the rivalry between the United Mine Workers (D) and the Southern Labor Union over representation of mine workers in the southern Appalachians. Tennessee Consolidated Coal Company laid off 100 miners represented by Local 5881 of the United Mine Workers (D) when it closed a mine. A few months later, its wholly owned subsidiary hired Gibbs (P) as mine superintendent to open a new mine using labor provided by members of the Southern Labor Union. Gibbs (P) also had a contract to haul coal from the new mine to the nearest railroad loading point. Armed members of Local 5881 prevented the new mine from opening, threatening Gibbs (P) and injuring an organizer for the Southern Labor Union. Officials of the United Mine Workers (D) were not present; when they learned of the violence, they came to the mine with instructions to establish a limited picket line, quell the violence, and keep the strike from spreading. A peaceful picket line was established and maintained for nine months; no further attempts were made to open the mine. Gibbs (P) lost his job and performed no services under the haulage contract. He claimed that he began to lose other haulage contracts and business as a result of alleged concerted union plan against him. Gibbs (P) brought suit against the United Mine Workers (D) in federal court. Jurisdiction was premised on violation of § 303 of the Labor Management Relations Act of 1947, which permits recovery of compensatory damages for unlawful secondary boycotts. He also brought state common law claims for alleged conspiracy to interfere with his employment contract and his haulage contract. The Union's (D) pressure to have Gibbs (P) discharged from employment was found to be a primary boycott, not cognizable under § 303. However, the state law claims of unlawful interference with the employment contract were sustained and judgment was entered for Gibbs (P). This judgment was affirmed on appeal.

■ **ISSUE**

Did the trial court abuse its discretion in exercising pendent jurisdiction over state law claims, even though the federal claims were ultimately dismissed?

■ **DECISION AND RATIONALE**

(Brennan, J.) No. The exercise of pendent jurisdiction is within the sound discretion of the trial court. That is, pendent jurisdiction is a doctrine of discretion, not a plaintiff's right. Pendent jurisdiction exists

---

whenever there is a claim arising under federal law and the relationship between that claim and the state claims permits the conclusion that the entire action is but one case or controversy. The federal question must have sufficient substance to confer subject matter jurisdiction. If both the state and federal claims are such that a plaintiff would ordinarily be expected to try them all in one judicial proceeding, there is power in the federal courts to hear the whole. Justification for pendent jurisdiction lies in considerations of judicial economy, convenience, and fairness to litigants. But absent these considerations, the federal court should not exercise jurisdiction over the state law claims.

Ordinarily, if the federal claims are dismissed before trial, the state claims should be dismissed as well. If it appears that the state issues will substantially predominate, then the state claims may be dismissed without prejudice and left for a state proceeding. Whenever it appears that the state claim constitutes the real body of the case, and the federal claim is only an appendage, then the state claim may be dismissed. Here, however, it does not appear that the trial court abused its discretion in proceeding to judgment on the state claim. Even though the federal § 303 claim was ultimately dismissed, that claim was substantial. Although the state and federal claims provided different remedies, the claims arose from the "same nucleus of operative facts" and reflected alternative remedies. The federal issues were not so remote nor did they play such a minor role that in effect only the state claim was tried. It was only on post-verdict motions that all the federal claims were denied, and then some only for lack of proof of damages, not for lack of liability. Finally, the issue of whether the scope of state claims was limited by federal preemption was an additional reason for exercising pendent jurisdiction, because this issue is particularly appropriate for resolution by federal courts. Under the circumstances, although the trial court *could have* refused to exercise pendent jurisdiction, it was not error to do so.

Analysis:

The U.S. Constitution contains no express grant of pendent jurisdiction. The Court here reasons that pendent jurisdiction is based on its authority to hear cases "arising under . . . the Laws of the United States." The state law claim must be so closely related to the federal claim that the two cases actually constitute only one "constitutional case." The authority of a court to hear state law claims is held to be discretionary with the trial court. Congress explicitly ratified *Gibbs* when it adopted 28 U.S.C. § 1367 in 1990. The issues raised in *Gibbs* were before the Supreme Court again in *Owen Equipment & Erection Co. v. Kroger*, 437 U.S. 365 (1978), and *Finley v. United States*, 490 U.S. 545 (1989). As these two cases and the passage of § 1367 demonstrate, the courts and Congress have continued to struggle with the exact scope of ancillary and pendent jurisdiction.

■ CASE VOCABULARY

PENDENT JURISDICTION: A court's jurisdiction to hear and determine a claim over which it would not otherwise have jurisdiction, based on the claim's arising from the same transaction or occurrence as another claim that is properly before the court. Pendent jurisdiction has now been codified as supplemental jurisdiction. 28 U.S.C.A. § 1367.

PRIMARY BOYCOTT: A boycott [a concerted refusal to do business with a party to express disapproval of that party's practices] by union members who stop dealing with a former employer.

SECONDARY BOYCOTT: A boycott [a concerted refusal to do business with a party to express disapproval of that party's practices] of the customers or suppliers of a business so that they will withhold their patronage from that business.

SUPPLEMENTAL JURISDICTION: Jurisdiction over a claim that is part of the same case or controversy as another claim over which the court has original jurisdiction. 28 U.S.C.A. § 1367.

Owen Equipment and Erection Company v. Kroger

(Crane Operator) v. *(Widow of Electrocuted Construction Worker)*

437 U.S. 365, 98 S.Ct. 2396, 57 L.Ed.2d 274 (1978)

ANCILLARY JURISDICTION DOES NOT PERMIT A CLAIM AGAINST A THIRD PARTY WHO DOES NOT HAVE COMPLETE DIVERSITY

By "complete diversity", what percentage are we talking? 51%?

100%. Total. None the same. The whole enchilada.

stus.com

■ **INSTANT FACTS** Kroger was electrocuted when a crane operated by Owen Equipment came too close to a power line owned by Omaha Public Power District (D).

■ **BLACK LETTER RULE** A plaintiff in a diversity case cannot rely on ancillary jurisdiction to permit an amendment to a complaint to bring a claim against a non-diverse third-party defendant.

■ **PROCEDURAL BASIS**

On writ of certiorari from a judgment for the plaintiff.

■ **FACTS**

Kroger was electrocuted when a crane he was walking near came in contact with a power line owned by Omaha Public Power District (OPPD) (D). The Kroger's widow (P), a citizen of Iowa, brought a wrongful death action against OPPD (D), a citizen of Nebraska, in federal district court in Nebraska, alleging that its construction, maintenance and operation of the power line caused Kroger's death. Federal jurisdiction was based on diversity of citizenship; there was no federal question. OPPD (D) filed a third-party complaint against Owen Equipment and Erection Company (D), alleging that Owen (D) owned and operated the crane and that Owen's (D) negligence caused Kroger's death. OPPD (D) moved for summary judgment. While this motion was pending, Kroger (P) was granted leave to amend her complaint naming Owen (D) as an additional defendant. OPPD's (D) motion for summary judgment was granted and trial between Kroger (P) and Owen (D) followed. At trial, it was disclosed that Owen's (D) principal place of business was in Iowa, which meant that it was also a citizen of Iowa. Owen (D) moved to dismiss for lack of jurisdiction because both Kroger (P) and Owen (D) were citizens of Iowa. The trial court deferred ruling on the motion, and the jury returned a verdict in favor of Kroger (P). The trial court then denied the motion to dismiss. The judgment for Kroger (P) was affirmed on appeal.

■ **ISSUE**

Using a court's ancillary jurisdiction in a case based on diversity of citizenship, can a plaintiff assert a claim against a third-party defendant who does not have complete diversity of citizenship from the plaintiff?

■ **DECISION AND RATIONALE**

(Stewart, J.) No. The relevant statute, 28 U.S.C. § 1332(a)(1), creates diversity jurisdiction. This statute has been consistently held to require complete diversity of citizenship: each defendant must be a citizen of a different state from each plaintiff. Kroger (P) could not have originally brought suit against both OPPD (D) and Owen (D) because citizens of Iowa would have been on both sides. Her amendment resulted in the same effect; complete diversity was destroyed just as surely as if she had sued Owen (D) initially. The court of appeals, relying on *United Mine Workers v. Gibbs*, held that the district court had discretion to adjudicate Kroger's (P) claim against Owen (D) because the claim arose from the same core of operative facts as Kroger's (P) claim against OPPD (D). But *Gibbs* involved pendent jurisdiction, the resolution of state and federal law claims against a single defendant in one action. In contrast, here there is no federal law claim; there are state law claims against two different defendants. Here, the statutory limits on diversity jurisdiction require complete diversity. If the reasoning of the court of appeals were accepted, a plaintiff could defeat the statutory requirement of complete diversity simply by suing only those defendants who were diverse and waiting for those defendants to implead the non-diverse defendants. Similarly, if a common nucleus of operative facts were the only basis for ancillary jurisdiction, there would be no principled basis for not permitting the plaintiff to join her cause of action against Owen (D) in her original complaint. The statutory requirement of complete diversity would be eviscerated.

Permitting the exercise of ancillary jurisdiction in situations involving impleader, cross-claims, or counterclaims is not inconsistent with this decision. Ancillary jurisdiction typically involves claims by a defending party brought into court against its will or by another person whose rights might be lost unless he or she could assert them in an ongoing action in federal court. Here, the plaintiff voluntarily chose to bring suit upon state law in federal court. Reversed.

Analysis:

The Court in this case raised, but did not answer, the question of whether the third-party complaint was properly permitted in the first place. The third-party complaint did not allege the basis of Owen's (D) liability to OPPD (D); it only alleged that Owen's (D) negligence caused Kroger's death, a problematic basis for a third-party complaint. Even so, the Court explains in *Owen Equipment* that ancillary jurisdiction permits a court to grant the impleading of a third-party defendant even if the addition of that party defeats complete diversity. Congress specifically preserved *Owen Equipment* when it adopted 28 U.S.C. § 1367(b) in 1990.

■ CASE VOCABULARY

ANCILLARY JURISDICTION: A court's jurisdiction to adjudicate claims and proceedings that arise out of a claim that is properly before the court. The concept of ancillary jurisdiction has now been codified, along with the concept of pendent jurisdiction, in the supplemental-jurisdiction statute. 28 U.S.C.A. § 1367.

COMPLETE DIVERSITY: In a multiparty case, diversity between both sides to the lawsuit so that all plaintiffs have different citizenship from all defendants.

DIVERSITY JURISDICTION: A federal court's exercise of authority over a case involving parties from different states and an amount in controversy greater than a statutory minimum (now $75,000). 28 U.S.C.A. § 1332.

Exxon Mobil Corp. v. Allapattah Services
(*Petroleum Dealers*) v. (*Oil Company*)

Rosario Ortega v. Star–Kist Foods, Inc.
(*Injured Child*) v. (*Tuna Company*)
545 U.S. 546, 125 S.Ct. 2611, 162 L.Ed.2d 502 (2005)

NOT ALL PLAINTIFFS IN A MULTI–PARTY SUIT MUST INDIVIDUALLY MEET THE AMOUNT–IN–CONTROVERSY REQUIREMENT

■ **INSTANT FACTS** In *Exxon*, a group of Exxon dealers sued Exxon for overcharging them for fuel, but not all of the dealers' claims met the minimum amount-in-controversy requirement for the exercise of federal court diversity jurisdiction. In *Ortega*, a child and her parents sued Star–Kist, but only the child's damages met the minimum amount-in-controversy requirement.

■ **BLACK LETTER RULE** Where other elements of jurisdiction are present and at least one named plaintiff in the action satisfies the amount-in-controversy requirement, a court may exercise supplemental jurisdiction over the claims of other plaintiffs in the same case or controversy, even if those claims are for less than the jurisdictional amount specified in the statute setting forth the requirements for diversity jurisdiction.

■ **PROCEDURAL BASIS**

On certiorari to the Supreme Court to resolve a conflict among the circuit courts of appeals regarding the proper interpretation of 28 U.S.C. § 1367.

■ **FACTS**

In the *Exxon* case, a group of Exxon dealers filed a class action lawsuit alleging that Exxon overcharged them for fuel. Not all class members met the minimum amount-in-controversy requirement for the court's exercise of federal diversity jurisdiction. The federal district court held that 28 U.S.C. § 1367, the supplemental jurisdiction statute, could be extended to include all of the plaintiffs, and the Eleventh Circuit agreed. The Supreme Court granted certiorari to resolve a conflict among the federal circuits as to whether the exercise of such supplemental jurisdiction was proper.

In the *Ortega* case, which was consolidated with *Exxon*, a child sued Star–Kist for serious injuries she received when she sliced her finger on a tuna can. Her family joined in the suit, seeking damages for emotional distress and medical expenses. The district court granted summary judgment to Star–Kist, finding that none of the plaintiffs met the minimum amount-in-controversy requirement. The First Circuit reversed in part, ruling that the girl had made allegations of damages in the requisite amount, but that the parents had not, and that jurisdiction is lacking in a diversity case if *any* plaintiff fails to satisfy the amount-in-controversy requirement. The court declined to state whether the result would be different in a class action.

■ **ISSUE**

May a federal court in a diversity case exercise supplemental jurisdiction over additional plaintiffs whose claims do not satisfy the minimum amount-in-controversy requirement, if their claims are part of the same case or controversy as the claims of the plaintiffs who do allege a sufficient amount in controversy?

■ DECISION AND RATIONALE

(Kennedy, J.) Yes. Where other elements of jurisdiction are present and at least one named plaintiff in the action satisfies the amount-in-controversy requirement, a court may exercise supplemental jurisdiction over the claims of other plaintiffs in the same case or controversy, even if those claims are for less than the jurisdictional amount specified in the statute setting forth the requirements for diversity jurisdiction. Federal district courts may not exercise jurisdiction in the absence of a statutory basis. The statute that applies in this case is 28 U.S.C. § 1367, which contains a broad grant of supplemental jurisdiction over other claims within the same case or controversy, as long as the action is one in which the district courts would have original jurisdiction. The single question before us, then, is whether a diversity case in which the claims of some plaintiffs satisfy the amount-in-controversy requirement, but the claims of other plaintiffs do not, presents a civil action over which the district courts have original jurisdiction. We conclude that the answer must be yes.

We cannot accept the view that each and every claim must individually meet the jurisdictional requirement. This "indivisibility theory" requires that all claims must stand or fall as a single action. The indivisibility theory is easily dismissed as inconsistent with the whole notion of supplemental jurisdiction. Nor is the "contamination theory" viable, because, although it may make sense to apply it in the diversity of citizenship context, it makes no sense with respect to the amount-in-controversy requirement, which is meant to ensure that a dispute is sufficiently important to warrant federal court attention. Moreover, it is the language of the statute itself that controls, not statements from its legislative history. Accordingly, we hold that § 1367 authorizes supplemental jurisdiction over all claims by diverse parties arising out of the same Article III case or controversy. Affirmed.

■ DISSENT

(Stevens, J.) Our cases have never recognized a presumption in favor of expansive diversity jurisdiction. Given the legislative history of § 1367, the federal court's exercise of jurisdiction in this case was improper.

■ DISSENT

(Ginsburg, J.) The Court reads § 1367 as enlarging federal diversity jurisdiction, allowing access to federal courts by co-plaintiffs or class members who do not meet the in-excess-of-$75,000 amount-in-controversy requirement, as long as at least one plaintiff or the named class representative has a jurisdictionally sufficient claim. I disagree with the majority and largely adopt the argument discussed by them as the indivisibility theory.

Analysis:

Section 1367, enacted in 1990, provides federal courts with jurisdiction over claims that are part of the same case or controversy as other claims over which the court has original jurisdiction. Supplemental jurisdiction includes jurisdiction over both ancillary and pendent claims, which were, prior to 1990, treated separately. Ancillary jurisdiction involved a court's jurisdiction to adjudicate claims and proceedings related to a claim that was properly before the court. For example, if a plaintiff brought a lawsuit in federal court based on a federal question (such as a claim under Title VII), the defendant could assert a counterclaim over which the court would not otherwise have jurisdiction (such as a state-law claim for stealing company property). Pendent jurisdiction involved a court's jurisdiction to hear and determine a claim over which it would not otherwise have jurisdiction, where the claim arose from the same transaction or occurrence as another claim that was properly before the court. For example, if a plaintiff brought suit in federal court claiming that the defendant, in one transaction, violated both a federal and a state law, the federal court had jurisdiction over the federal claim (under federal-question jurisdiction), and also over the state claim that was pendent to the federal claim. Pendent jurisdiction and ancillary jurisdiction have now both been codified as supplemental jurisdiction.

■ **CASE VOCABULARY**

AMOUNT–IN–CONTROVERSY: The damages claimed or relief demanded by the injured party in a lawsuit. For a federal court to have diversity jurisdiction, the amount-in-controversy must exceed $75,000.

ARTICLE III CASE OR CONTROVERSY: The constitutional requirement that, for a federal court to hear a case, the case must involve an actual dispute.

CLASS ACTION: A lawsuit in which the court authorizes a single person or a small group of people to represent the interests of a larger group; specifically, a lawsuit in which the convenience either of the public or of the interested parties requires that the case be settled through litigation by or against only a part of the group of similarly situated persons and in which a person whose interests are or may be affected does not have an opportunity to protect his or her interests by appearing personally or through a personally selected representative, or through a person specially appointed to act as a trustee or guardian. Federal procedure has several prerequisites for maintaining a class action: (1) the class must be so large that individual suits would be impracticable, (2) there must be legal or factual questions common to the class, (3) the claims or defenses of the representative parties must be typical of those of the class, and (4) the representative parties must adequately protect the interests of the class.

DIVERSITY JURISDICTION: A basis for federal-court jurisdiction that exists when (1) a case is between citizens of different states, or between a citizen of a state and an alien, and (2) the matter in controversy exceeds a specific value (now $75,000).

LEGISLATIVE HISTORY: The background and events leading to the enactment of a statute, including hearings, committee reports, and floor debates. Legislative history is sometimes recorded so that it can later be used to aid in interpreting the statute.

CHAPTER ELEVEN

Choosing the Law to Be Applied in Federal Court

Swift v. Tyson

Instant Facts: The plaintiff sought to apply New York common law in a contract action filed in federal court.

Black Letter Rule: Federal courts sitting in diversity must enforce state statutes governing the action, but not judicial decisions of the state's courts.

Erie Railroad Co. v. Tompkins

Instant Facts: Tompkins (P), a Pennsylvania citizen, was injured in Pennsylvania when he was struck by a passing train owned and operated by the Erie Railroad Co. (D), a New York corporation.

Black Letter Rule: A federal court with diversity jurisdiction must apply the law of the state in which the claim arose.

Guaranty Trust Co. v. York

Instant Facts: York (P) sued Guaranty Trust (D) in federal court in order to avoid the application of the state's statute of limitations, which would have barred the claim.

Black Letter Rule: Federal courts with diversity jurisdiction must apply the state's statute of limitations or other procedural rules if they have a significant effect on the outcome of the case.

Byrd v. Blue Ridge Rural Electric Cooperative, Inc.

Instant Facts: Byrd (P) sued Blue Ridge Rural Electrical Cooperative (D) in South Carolina federal court for injuries allegedly caused by the defendant's negligence.

Black Letter Rule: When federal law is not substantially likely to affect the outcome of a case, federal law applies.

Hanna v. Plumer

Instant Facts: Hanna (P), an Ohio citizen, sued Plumer (D), the executor of a deceased Massachusetts citizen, in Massachusetts federal court for injuries sustained as a result of an automobile accident in South Carolina.

Black Letter Rule: A federal court exercising diversity jurisdiction must apply state substantive law and federal procedural law.

Burlington Northern Railroad Co. v. Woods

Instant Facts: After a trial court judgment for Woods (P) was affirmed, the federal appeals court applied a mandatory affirmance penalty as required by a state statute.

Black Letter Rule: When a state procedural statute and a federal procedural statute conflict, a federal court sitting in diversity must apply the federal standard.

Walker v. Armco Steel Corp.

Instant Facts: Walker's (P) federal diversity action was dismissed for failure to serve the defendant within the statute of limitations as required by state law.

Black Letter Rule: When federal rules do not directly conflict with state rules, the state rules will be enforced.

Gasperini v. Center for Humanities, Inc.

Instant Facts: Gasperini (P) obtained a jury verdict in New York federal court against the Center for Humanities, Inc. (D) for breach of contract, conversion, and negligence after the defendant lost 300 photographs lent to it by the plaintiff.

Black Letter Rule: When state law interests relating to the division of the judge-jury function can be furthered in a federal diversity action without frustrating federal interests, state law will apply.

Mason v. American Emery Wheel Works

Instant Facts: Mason (P) was injured in Mississippi by an emery wheel manufactured by American Emery Wheel Works (D), a Rhode Island corporation.

Black Letter Rule: A federal court sitting in diversity need not strictly enforce the substantive state law if there is sufficient indication that a state court, given the opportunity to consider the case, would not enforce the law as stated.

Dice v. Akron, Canton & Youngstown R.R.

Instant Facts: Dice (P) sued Akron, Canton & Youngstown R.R. (D) in Ohio state court for negligence under the Federal Employers' Liability Act.

Black Letter Rule: When a substantive right is created by federal statute, states may not fashion state-law defenses to defeat the federal right.

Swift v. Tyson

(Note Holder) v. *(Endorser)*
41 U.S. (16 Pet.) 1, 10 L.Ed. 865 (1842)

FEDERAL COURTS WERE NOT BOUND BY STATE JUDICIAL DECISIONS

■ **INSTANT FACTS** The plaintiff sought to apply New York common law in a contract action filed in federal court.

■ **BLACK LETTER RULE** Federal courts sitting in diversity must enforce state statutes governing the action, but not judicial decisions of the state's courts.

■ PROCEDURAL BASIS

Certiorari to determine the appropriate substantive law to apply in a federal diversity action.

■ FACTS

The plaintiff sued the defendant in New York federal court, asserting diversity jurisdiction, to enforce a bill of exchange. At issue was whether a pre-existing debt constituted sufficient consideration for the bill. Under New York common law, the pre-existing debt was presumed not to constitute adequate consideration, while federal common law would support the debt as consideration.

■ ISSUE

Does section 34 of the Federal Judiciary Act of 1789 require federal courts sitting in diversity to apply the substantive common law of the state in which the claim arose?

■ DECISION AND RATIONALE

(Story, J.) No. Under section 34 of the Federal Judiciary Act of 1789, "the laws of the several states ... shall be regarded as the rules of decision in trials at common law in the courts of the United States in cases where they apply." Section 34, however, requires enforcement only of state statutes, not judicial decisions of the state courts. Under ordinary usage, laws include legislative rules and enactments and the state constructions of that statutory authority. They do not include common law decisions of the court, not based on statutory construction, which may be reconsidered, reversed, or modified at any time. Because the New York decisions under consideration do not involve local statutes or interests, the federal court is not bound to enforce them by the Federal Judiciary Act.

Analysis:

Underscoring Justice Story's reasoning is the perceived need for a nationally uniform body of commercial law by which all commercial transactions are governed. By vesting the federal court with the power to determine the commercial common law, however, there was no assurance that one federal court would determine the common law the same as another federal court. The result was more regional uniformity than national uniformity. As foreign as the *Swift* rule appears today, it survived as the law of the land for over one hundred years.

■ **CASE VOCABULARY**

COMMON LAW: The body of law derived from judicial decisions, rather than from statutes or constitutions.

Erie Railroad Co. v. Tompkins

(Railroad) v. *(Injured Plaintiff)*

304 U.S. 64, 58 S.Ct. 817, 82 L.Ed. 1188 (1938)

THE COURT DISAVOWS *SWIFT v. TYSON*

■ INSTANT FACTS Tompkins (P), a Pennsylvania citizen, was injured in Pennsylvania when he was struck by a passing train owned and operated by the Erie Railroad Co. (D), a New York corporation.

■ BLACK LETTER RULE A federal court with diversity jurisdiction must apply the law of the state in which the claim arose.

■ PROCEDURAL BASIS

Certiorari to review decision of a federal appeals court affirming a federal district court judgment.

■ FACTS

Tompkins (P) was a Pennsylvania citizen walking along a well-worn path in Pennsylvania when he was struck by an object protruding from a passing train owned and operated by the Erie Railroad Co. (D), a New York corporation. Tompkins (P) filed suit in New York federal court. Erie Railroad (D) argued that despite proper diversity jurisdiction in New York, the court must apply Pennsylvania law, which considered Tompkins (P) a trespasser and relieved the defendant of liability. Tompkins (P) argued that no Pennsylvania statute addressed the issue, leaving the federal court to apply general federal law. Erie Railroad (D) responded that section 34 of the Federal Judiciary Act of 1789 required the court to apply the laws of the state as the "rules of decision." The court refused to apply Pennsylvania law and judgment was entered for Tompkins (P). On appeal, the court affirmed.

■ ISSUE

In a suit brought in federal court under diversity jurisdiction, does general federal law govern the rights and liabilities of the parties?

■ DECISION AND RATIONALE

(Brandeis, J.) No. Under *Swift v. Tyson*, a federal court sitting with diversity jurisdiction must apply only the written laws of the state in which a claim arose. Under this rule, the unwritten common law need not be followed or enforced, but rather a federal court is free to determine the substantive rights of the parties according to federal common law. *Swift* had fallen under some criticism following a case in which the Court enforced a contract under federal common law that would have been unenforceable had the action been filed in state court. Experience in enforcing the *Swift* rule demonstrates that the purposes of diversity jurisdiction—to eliminate state discrimination against nonresidents—had not been achieved. Rather than protecting nonresidents from discrimination, *Swift* created discrimination against citizens by enabling a nonresident to avoid laws applicable in the state merely by asserting a claim under federal common law in a diversity action. The original intent of the *Swift* doctrine to create uniformity of law actually prevented uniformity by encouraging forum shopping. Because of the gross inadequacies of the *Swift* doctrine in practice and the resulting violations of equal protection to state citizens, the doctrine is abolished as unconstitutional.

In abolishing the *Swift* doctrine, federal courts sitting in diversity must apply both the written and unwritten laws of the state. "There is no federal common law." The Constitution permits neither Congress nor the courts to disregard enforceable laws of the states merely by asserting federal jurisdiction over a state-law claim. Because the court failed to consider the proper duty placed upon Erie Railroad (D) under Pennsylvania law, the matter is reversed and remanded for such a determination.

■ DISSENT

(Butler, J.) The Court exceeded the scope of the appeal by declaring *Swift* unconstitutional because the parties raised no constitutional issue on appeal. Yet, because neither party has challenged the constitutionality of the Federal Judiciary Act of 1789, the Court has denied the parties the opportunity to present their arguments for the Court's deliberation. Nor has Congress been afforded the opportunity to support its authority to determine the rules of decisions to be applied in the federal courts. By statute, Congress is afforded that right. Furthermore, even if *Swift* is unconstitutional, the Court has been reluctant to resolve constitutional questions when other grounds are available to resolve the case. Here, the decisions of Pennsylvania courts clearly establish that Tompkins (P) was negligent and that his negligence contributed to his injuries. On that basis alone, the judgment should be reversed.

■ CONCURRENCE IN PART

(Reed, J.) Although the Court correctly disapproved of the *Swift* doctrine and appropriately reversed the judgment below, it is unnecessary to declare the "course pursued" by the federal court unconstitutional. Instead, the Court needs merely to establish that the laws of the state to be applied by a federal court include those decisions of the state's highest court. This Court need not engage in constitutional interpretation to reach the appropriate result, but rather needs only to clarify the construction of the Federal Judiciary Act of 1789.

Analysis:

Erie is one the most important cases in American jurisprudence. By requiring a federal court exercising diversity jurisdiction to apply the law of the state in which the claim arose, the Court eliminated the possibility of a different outcome in a case depending on where the suit was brought. Note that although the Court stated that there is no federal general common law, there is judge-made law from the federal courts, including the body of decisional law derived from adjudicating federal questions and other matters of federal concern, such as the law applying to disputes between two states ...

■ CASE VOCABULARY

ERIE DOCTRINE: The principle that a federal court exercising diversity jurisdiction over a case that does not involve a federal question must apply the substantive law of the state where the court sits.

FEDERAL COMMON LAW: The judge-made law of federal courts, excluding the law in all cases governed by state law; specifically, the body of decisional law derived from federal courts adjudicating federal questions and other matters of federal concern, such as the law applying to disputes between two states, as well as foreign-relations law.

GENERAL FEDERAL COMMON LAW: In the period before *Erie v. Tompkins*, the judge-made law developed by federal courts in deciding disputes in diversity cases. Since *Erie* was decided in 1938, a federal court has been bound to apply, as a general matter, the law of the state in which it sits. Thus, although there is a "federal common law," there is no *general* federal common law applicable to all disputes heard in federal court.

Guaranty Trust Co. v. York

(*Bond Trustee*) v. (*Note–Holder*)

326 U.S. 99, 65 S.Ct. 1464, 89 L.Ed. 2079 (1945)

FEDERAL COURTS MUST APPLY STATE PROCEDURAL RULES IF THE RULES DETERMINE THE OUTCOME OF THE CASE

■ **INSTANT FACTS** York (P) sued Guaranty Trust (D) in federal court in order to avoid the application of the state's statute of limitations, which would have barred the claim.

■ **BLACK LETTER RULE** Federal courts with diversity jurisdiction must apply the state's statute of limitations or other procedural rules if they have a significant effect on the outcome of the case.

■ **PROCEDURAL BASIS**

Certiorari to review the reversal of summary judgment based on a state statute of limitations in a federal court diversity-of-jurisdiction case.

■ **FACTS**

York (P) sued Guaranty Trust (D) in a federal diversity action for breach of fiduciary duty, allegedly arising out of Guaranty Trust's (D) failure to protect the plaintiff's interest in the trust. Guaranty Trust (D) appealed the reversal of summary judgment that barred York (P) from bringing a breach of trust action against Guaranty Trust (D). The court of appeals held that the suit could be brought on the equity side of a federal district court because the federal court was not required to apply the state statute of limitations that would govern the suit had it been filed in state court. Guaranty Trust (D) argued that because the suit was time barred under state law, York (P) should not be able to use diversity jurisdiction to circumvent the state statute of limitations and obtain a result that would not be available under the applicable state law.

■ **ISSUE**

Are federal courts sitting in diversity bound by the state statute of limitations in an equity suit based on state law?

■ **DECISION AND RATIONALE**

(Frankfurter, J.) Yes. In diversity actions, federal courts have generally not distinguished actions at law from actions in equity with respect to the application of state substantive law. Although section 34 of the Federal Judiciary Act of 1789 directed that state law is the rule of decisions "in trials of common law," this language has not been strictly construed to exclude suits in equity. Equitable relief in federal courts, however, is limited to that relief historically available before the English Court of Chancery in which an adequate remedy at law is unavailable, and may not be extended on the basis of state law. Similarly, state law cannot limit equitable relief available in federal courts merely because it would not be available in the courts of the state. However, when state equity actions are brought in federal courts merely because of diversity of citizenship, the federal court acts as another court of the state and cannot "afford recovery if the right to recover is made unavailable by the State nor can it substantially affect the enforcement of the right as given by the State." The policy underlying *Erie v. Tompkins* was not to

---

create bright lines between substantive and procedural laws, but rather to ensure that a state cause of action brought in federal court by reason of diversity results in substantially the same outcome as it would have if adjudicated in state court. Whether a statute of limitations may be characterized as substantive or procedural is immaterial. Instead, the appropriate inquiry is whether the statute of limitations represents the manner in which a state right is enforced or whether it substantially affects the outcome of the litigation. Clearly, a state law that would entirely preclude an action in state court substantially affects the outcome of the litigation before the federal court. To carve an exception out of the *Erie* doctrine merely because the case sounds in equity rather than at law would violate the spirit and intent of *Erie* and result in different outcomes merely because the parties maintain diverse citizenship. The state statute of limitations governs the case. Reversed and remanded.

Analysis:

Guaranty Trust expanded *Erie* to provide that if the federal court's jurisdiction is based on diversity, a federal court should reach the same outcome as a state court, regardless of whether the remedy sought was legal or equitable. The case also addresses the issue of whether a state statute of limitations is effectively substantive, so that it should be controlling in federal court. However, the court did not rely on the terms "substantive" and "procedural" because of their different meanings in different contexts. Instead, the court established what is now known as the "outcome-determinative" test, so that a federal court should follow a state rule that is outcome-determinative whether it is labeled procedural or substantive.

■ CASE VOCABULARY

DIVERSITY OF CITIZENSHIP: A basis for federal-court jurisdiction that exists when (1) a case is between citizens of different states, or between a citizen of a state and an alien; and (2) the matter in controversy exceeds a specific value (now $75,000). For purposes of diversity jurisdiction, a corporation is considered a citizen of both the state of incorporation and the state of its principal place of business. An unincorporated association, such as a partnership, is considered a citizen of each state where at least one of its members is a citizen.

EQUITABLE REMEDY: A nonmonetary remedy, such as an injunction or specific performance, obtained when monetary damages cannot adequately redress the injury.

OUTCOME–DETERMINATIVE TEST: A test used to determine whether an issue is substantive for purposes of the *Erie* doctrine by examining the issue's potential effect on the outcome of the litigation.

Byrd v. Blue Ridge Rural Electric Cooperative, Inc.

(Injured Worker) v. *(Electric Company)*

356 U.S. 525, 78 S.Ct. 893, 2 L.Ed.2d 953 (1958)

FEDERAL PROCEDURAL LAW CONTROLS

■ **INSTANT FACTS** Byrd (P) sued Blue Ridge Rural Electrical Cooperative (D) in South Carolina federal court for injuries allegedly caused by the defendant's negligence.

■ **BLACK LETTER RULE** When federal law is not substantially likely to affect the outcome of a case, federal law applies.

■ **PROCEDURAL BASIS**

Certiorari to review a decision of the Fourth Circuit Court of Appeals reversing a judgment for the plaintiff.

■ **FACTS**

Byrd (P) was working on the construction crew of a construction contractor when he was injured on the job due to the alleged negligence of the Blue Ridge Rural Electrical Cooperative (D). Byrd (P) sued Blue Ridge (D) in South Carolina federal court, alleging diversity of citizenship. Blue Ridge (D) asserted as an affirmative defense that the plaintiff was performing tasks of the kind typically done by its employees, making the plaintiff a statutory employee and barring his claim under state workers' compensation laws. After Blue Ridge's (D) motion to dismiss was denied, a jury entered a verdict for Byrd (P). On appeal, the federal appeals court reversed and directed that judgment be entered for Blue Ridge (D).

■ **ISSUE**

Should the question of a right to a jury trial on the issue of statutory immunity be decided as a matter of state law?

■ **DECISION AND RATIONALE**

(Brennan, J.) No. The Court of Appeals determined that the South Carolina statute afforded Blue Ridge (D) immunity upon proof that the activities engaged in by Byrd (P) at the time of his injury were similar to those engaged in by Blue Ridge's (D) crews as part of the construction operation. This determination requires the weighing of evidence after considering the positions of both parties. Based on the court's conclusion, the matter should have been remanded for a new trial rather than directing judgment for the defendant. On remand, the federal court need not submit the question to a jury. While a federal court exercising diversity jurisdiction must apply state law when determining the rights and liabilities of the parties, issues concerning the judge-jury function are not "bound up" with the determination of those rights and liabilities. Accordingly, differences of state law must yield to federal policies addressing the judge-jury function when federal interests outweigh the interests of the state. After weighing the interests, if it is not substantially likely that application of federal law would affect the outcome of the suit, federal law applies.

Here, although the law of South Carolina generally declares that the availability of an affirmative defense in workers' compensation case is a matter within the court's discretion, nothing in state law indicates that such a conclusion is anything more than past custom and practice. There is nothing to suggest that the rule is bound up in the parties' rights and liabilities. Furthermore, although the outcome of the case may indeed be different if decided by a jury than by a judge, the distribution of trial functions lies within the power of the federal court. State laws and rules cannot usurp that power from the federal court. Finally, there is no assurance that the outcome of the litigation will be different if considered by a jury than by a trial judge. There is no countervailing reason to disturb the federal policy of submitting such issues to a jury determination. Reversed and remanded.

Analysis:

Byrd has been widely credited with reconciling the Federal Rules of Civil Procedure with the *Erie* doctrine, applying state substantive law and federal procedural law in federal diversity actions based on strong federal policy. On the other hand, many courts had difficulty applying *Byrd* given the absence of an objective test with which to balance state and federal interests.

Hanna v. Plumer

(Injured Plaintiff) v. *(Alleged Tortfeasor)*

380 U.S. 460, 85 S.Ct. 1136, 14 L.Ed.2d 8 (1965)

FEDERAL SERVICE OF PROCESS RULES APPLY IN FEDERAL DIVERSITY ACTIONS

■ **INSTANT FACTS** Hanna (P), an Ohio citizen, sued Plumer (D), the executor of a deceased Massachusetts citizen, in Massachusetts federal court for injuries sustained as a result of an automobile accident in South Carolina.

■ **BLACK LETTER RULE** A federal court exercising diversity jurisdiction must apply state substantive law and federal procedural law.

■ **PROCEDURAL BASIS**

Certiorari to review a decision of the First Circuit Court of Appeals, affirming the trial court's grant of summary judgment.

■ **FACTS**

Hanna (P), an Ohio citizen, suffered personal injuries as a result of an automobile accident caused by the negligence of Osgood, a Massachusetts citizen. Plaintiff sued Osgood's executor, Plumer (D), in Massachusetts federal court, as Osgood had passed away prior to filing. The plaintiff served Plumer (D) by leaving a copy of the summons and complaint with Plumer's (D) wife at his residence in compliance with the Federal Rules of Civil Procedure. Massachusetts law, however, requires personal service upon an executor or administrator. The defendant successfully moved for summary judgment for ineffective service of process, and the plaintiff appealed. The First Circuit Court of Appeals affirmed.

■ **ISSUE**

In a federal diversity action, must service of process be made in accordance with the Federal Rules of Civil Procedure?

■ **DECISION AND RATIONALE**

(Warren, C.J.) Yes. While state law may provide different standards for service of process, the Federal Rules of Civil Procedure govern the adequacy of service of process in federal diversity actions. Federal courts are to apply federal procedural law and state substantive law to diversity actions, consistent with the *Erie* doctrine. In determining which body of law to apply, a federal court must determine, first, whether federal law is substantially likely to affect the outcome of the case and, if so, whether the application of federal law will discourage forum shopping or create an inequitable administration of the laws.

Here, service of process was made in compliance with Rule 4(d)(1) of the Federal Rules of Civil Procedure, which permits substituted service by leaving papers with any person of suitable age and discretion at the person's usual place of abode. Because the manner in which a person may be notified of a suit is a matter of practice and procedure of the court, the federal standard need not yield to the more restrictive state standard. Although the line between substantive law and procedural law may not always be clear, the issue is easily resolved when it directly involves a Federal Rule of Civil Procedure. The Federal Rules of Civil Procedure were adopted and are enforced to provide a uniform system of procedural laws in the federal courts, while *Erie* ensures that the substantive outcome of the litigation will be decided on the same body of law whether in state or federal court. Although state-created rights must be enforced in federal diversity actions, Congress is within its power to adopt the means by which federal courts do so. Because the Federal Rules of Civil Procedure are constitutionally within Congress's authority and govern procedural affairs in federal courts, conflicting state requirements must yield. Reversed.

■ **CONCURRENCE**

(Harlan, J.) The *Erie* doctrine, in addition to discouraging forum shopping and avoiding an inequitable administration of the law, highlights principles of federalism set forth in the U.S. Constitution. By compelling federal courts to apply state substantive law in diversity suits, *Erie* reinforces the constitutional mandate that the federal government may not invade the province of the states to define the rights and liabilities of their citizens. The proper test to determine which rule to apply, whether substantive or procedural, is whether the choice of rule by the plaintiff would "substantially affect those primary decisions respecting human conduct which our constitutional system leaves to state regulation." Accordingly, federal courts should not blindly assume that enforcement of the Federal Rules of Civil Procedure is required by the *Erie* doctrine, but must determine whether enforcement of the rule would substantially infringe upon a state's constitutional right to govern the affairs of its citizens. Despite the Court's apparent adoption of the sanctity of the Federal Rules of Civil Procedure, little is sacrificed by enforcement of Rule 4(d)(1) in this instance. While the Massachusetts rule is designed to protect an executor from unknown claims at the time he distributes the assets of an estate, Rule 4(d)(1) merely requires that he check his home, the courthouse, and the registry of probate before acting. Because Rule 4(d)(1) does not significantly frustrate the purpose of the Massachusetts rule, the Court's decision is correct.

Analysis:

Despite Justice Harlan's concurring opinion, the majority opinion has been praised for providing a clear and simple test for considering when a federal law should be applied and for promoting a uniform application of the Federal Rules of Civil Procedure in the face of state law alternatives.

■ **CASE VOCABULARY**

FORUM SHOPPING: The practice of choosing the most favorable jurisdiction or court in which a claim might be heard.

Burlington Northern Railroad Co. v. Woods

(Railroad) v. *(Injured Plaintiff)*

480 U.S. 1, 107 S.Ct. 967, 94 L.Ed.2d 1 (1987)

STATE LAWS MAY NOT DEPRIVE FEDERAL COURTS OF THEIR DISCRETION

■ **INSTANT FACTS** After a trial court judgment for Woods (P) was affirmed, the federal appeals court applied a mandatory affirmance penalty as required by a state statute.

■ **BLACK LETTER RULE** When a state procedural statute and a federal procedural statute conflict, a federal court sitting in diversity must apply the federal standard.

■ **PROCEDURAL BASIS**

Certiorari to review a decision of the Eleventh Circuit Court of Appeals applying a state statute imposing a mandatory affirmance penalty on appeal.

■ **FACTS**

Woods (P) sued Burlington Northern Railroad Co. (D) for personal injuries in an Alabama state court. After the defendant removed the case to federal court on the basis of diversity jurisdiction, a jury awarded the plaintiff $300,000. Burlington Northern (D) posted a bond to stay the judgment pending appeal to the Eleventh Circuit Court of Appeals. On appeal, the Eleventh Circuit affirmed and granted the plaintiff's motion to impose a mandatory ten-percent affirmance penalty as required by Alabama law to prevent frivolous appeals. Burlington Northern (D) petitioned for certiorari.

■ **ISSUE**

Must a federal court sitting in diversity apply a state rule requiring a mandatory ten-percent affirmance penalty upon affirming a trial court's judgment?

■ **DECISION AND RATIONALE**

(Marshall, J.) No. Under Rule 38 of the Federal Rules of Appellate Procedure, an appeals court has discretion to award "just damages" upon a finding that an appeal is frivolous. The Alabama mandatory affirmance penalty deprives the federal court of that discretion. If the federal rule is reasonable and falls within Congress's rule-making authority, however, the federal rule must apply. Congress's rule-making authority extends to all procedural matters before federal courts and may not "abridge, enlarge, or modify any substantive right" under the laws of the states. Here, the purposes of the state and federal rules are the same—to prevent the filing of frivolous appeals for purposes of delay in the execution of a judgment. Because strict enforcement of the state rule forbids a federal court from imposing less than ten percent as a "just award," the state rule conflicts with the federal rule. The discretionary authority of the federal courts must be preserved as intended by Congress. Reversed.

Analysis:

The Court's decision relies on the considerable strength of Congress's rule-making authority. Although the Court acknowledges that the state and federal rules serve the same purpose, the Court presumes

---

that the deference afforded to federal judges under the Federal Rules of Appellate Procedure better serves those purposes. Nowhere in the decision does the Court discuss the state policies behind the mandatory affirmance penalty. As a result, the Court implies that it is immaterial in federal court whether the state practice is the more sound approach, at least when it irreconcilably conflicts with the federal practice established by Congress.

■ **CASE VOCABULARY**

REMOVAL: The transfer of an action from state to federal court.

Walker v. Armco Steel Corp.

(Carpenter) v. *(Nail Manufacturer)*
446 U.S. 740, 100 S.Ct. 1978, 64 L.Ed.2d 659 (1980)

WHEN THERE IS NO CONFLICT, FEDERAL COURTS MAY APPLY STATE RULES

■ **INSTANT FACTS** Walker's (P) federal diversity action was dismissed for failure to serve the defendant within the statute of limitations as required by state law.

■ **BLACK LETTER RULE** When federal rules do not directly conflict with state rules, the state rules will be enforced.

■ **PROCEDURAL BASIS**

Certiorari to review a decision dismissing the plaintiff's suit on the basis of state law.

■ **FACTS**

Walker (P) was injured on August 22, 1975, when a nail manufactured by Armco Steel Corp. (D) shattered. Walker (P) filed suit against Armco Steel Corp. (D) in Oklahoma federal court on August 19, 1977, asserting diversity jurisdiction, but did not serve Armco Steel's (D) registered agent until December 1, 1977. Armco Steel (D) moved to dismiss the complaint as barred by Oklahoma's applicable two-year statute of limitations. Under Oklahoma law, a suit is commenced when the defendant receives service of process, whereas under the Federal Rules of Civil Procedure, the filing of a complaint commences an action. The district court applied state law and dismissed Walker's (P) action. After appeal, Walker petitioned for certiorari.

■ **ISSUE**

Must a federal court sitting in diversity apply state law in determining when a suit is commenced for purposes of the statute of limitations?

■ **DECISION AND RATIONALE**

(Marshall, J.) Yes. Although the federal rule provides that an action is commenced upon the filing of the complaint, nothing in the rule suggests that it was intended to toll a state statute of limitations. Instead, Rule 3 indicates the beginning of timing requirements contained elsewhere in the Federal Rules of Civil Procedure. A statute of limitations contains the substantive requirements for filing an action, after which a defendant may have the peace of mind that no action may be brought and that it will not be required to defend its actions. The notice requirement furthers this purpose by ensuring that a defendant is informed of the claims against it within the prescribed period. Read in this way, Rule 3 and state statutes of limitations can coexist without direct conflict. Because no direct conflict exists, the reasoning of *Hanna v. Plumer* does not apply and the issue is governed by *Erie Railroad Co. v. Tompkins*. Applying the federal rule in this instance would create a federal cause of action where no state cause of action exists, merely because of diversity of citizenship. Affirmed.

Analysis:

In 1987, the Supreme Court complicated the issue considered in *Walker*. In *West v. Conrail*, 481 U.S. 35 (1987), the Court concluded that in a federal action under federal-question jurisdiction, the filing of a lawsuit was sufficient to toll a federal statute of limitations, although service of process had not been perfected. In essence, the Court reasoned that although Federal Rule of Civil Procedure 3 does not affect the timing of a state statute of limitations applicable in a diversity action, it does affect the timing of a federal statute of limitations in a federal-question action. Because the federal statute of limitations contained no service of process requirement, Federal Rule of Civil Procedure 4, permitting service within 120 days of the filing of the complaint, applied.

■ CASE VOCABULARY

PROCESS: A summons or writ, especially to appear or respond in court.

STATUTE OF LIMITATIONS: A statute establishing a time limit for suing in a civil case, based on the date when the claim accrued (as when the injury occurred or was discovered). The purpose of such a statute is to require diligent prosecution of known claims, thereby providing finality and predictability in legal affairs and ensuring that claims will be resolved while evidence is reasonably available and fresh.

Gasperini v. Center for Humanities, Inc.

(Photographer) v. *(Educational Organization)*

518 U.S. 415, 116 S.Ct. 2211, 135 L.Ed.2d 659 (1996)

SOME STATE PROCEDURAL LAWS *ARE* APPLIED IN FEDERAL COURT

■ **INSTANT FACTS** Gasperini (P) obtained a jury verdict in New York federal court against the Center for Humanities, Inc. (D) for breach of contract, conversion, and negligence after the defendant lost 300 photographs lent to it by the plaintiff.

■ **BLACK LETTER RULE** When state law interests relating to the division of the judge-jury function can be furthered in a federal diversity action without frustrating federal interests, state law will apply.

■ **PROCEDURAL BASIS**

Certiorari to review Second Circuit Court of Appeals' decision vacating the district court judgment entered on a jury verdict.

■ **FACTS**

Gasperini (P) was a journalist covering events in Central America when he agreed to lend 300 photographs to the Center for Humanities, Inc. (D) to be used in an educational video. The defendant lost the photographs and the plaintiff sued in New York federal court on the basis of diversity of citizenship. After a jury valued each photograph at $1500 and issued a verdict for the plaintiff, the defendant moved for a new trial, arguing the verdict was excessive. The district court denied the motion and the Second Circuit vacated the judgment, applying New York state law.

■ **ISSUE**

Does state law determine the standard to be used by a federal court exercising diversity jurisdiction to measure the excessiveness of a federal jury verdict entered on the basis of state law?

■ **DECISION AND RATIONALE**

(Ginsburg, J.) Yes. While federal courts generally review a jury award to determine if its "shocks the conscience of the court," a New York statute requires a court to determine whether the verdict "deviates materially from what would be reasonable compensation," a stricter standard than that used by federal courts. Under *Erie*, a federal court sitting in diversity must apply state substantive law and federal procedural law. To determine whether a state law is substantive or procedural, it must be examined to determine whether it will determine the outcome of the case in light of *Erie*'s twin aims of discouraging forum shopping and avoiding the inequitable distribution of the laws. Although a statutory cap on damages is indisputably substantive law, the New York statute is not a statutory cap since it provides no maximum value above which a plaintiff's damages may not extend. However, the scope of the statute is predominantly substantive. If the federal court were to apply the less restrictive federal standard, a larger award for a plaintiff would be likely, which in turn affects the outcome of the case. The New York statutory scheme, however, also contains a procedural directive to New York courts to state the reasons for the size of the award and the factors considered. When a state statute, such as that at issue, contains both substantive and procedural components, a federal court must determine whether application of the substantive component offends the re-examination clause of the Seventh Amendment.

Gasperini (P) argues that because the statute contains an instruction to appellate courts, the Re–Examination Clause precludes the federal court from enforcing the New York standard.

In *Byrd v. Blue Ridge Electrical Cooperative, Inc.*, the Court determined that when a state statute affects an "essential characteristic" of the federal court system, the federal court should not apply it. There, the Court held that a state law requiring an issue of fact to be considered by a judge would not be enforced by a federal court because the distribution of the judge-jury trial functions was an essential characteristic of federal procedure under the Seventh Amendment. The present case, however, deals not with the right to a jury trial under the Seventh Amendment, but the Re-examination Clause, which precludes a federal court from re-examining an issue of fact determined by a jury other than pursuant to the rules of common law. Under Federal Rule of Civil Procedure 59(c), a federal judge has the authority to grant new trials if the verdict appears to be against the weight of the evidence. The Seventh Amendment does not forbid appellate review of the verdict.

The New York statute was enacted to provide some scrutiny and stability to the state's tort law and ensure fairness to defendants throughout the state. Although the federal standard arguably frustrates that purpose, the state interests can be preserved by the federal court's application of the state standards. When state law interests can be furthered without frustrating coexisting federal interests, state law will apply. To hold otherwise would promote forum shopping and inequitable administration of the law between state and federal courts.

Because the district court failed to review the verdict against the state statute to determine whether it deviates materially from what would be reasonable compensation, the decision is vacated and remanded for such a determination.

■ DISSENT

(Stevens, J.) The Court's *Erie* analysis correctly determines that the state statute is substantive law that must be applied by the federal court. There is no need, however, to vacate the district court's judgment because there is no reason to believe it would disagree with the Second Circuit's determination under the correct standard. The decision of the Second Circuit should be affirmed.

■ DISSENT

(Scalia, J.) The Court's decision inescapably collapses under the weight of its own reason. The Court's decision to remand the matter to the district court for a determination of the excessiveness of the verdict under state law contradicts the principle that the judge-jury function is a matter of federal law. If the judge-jury function is an essential characteristic of the federal court system, the state standard should not be used to determine the judge's scope of review over a jury's verdict. To do so necessarily disrupts the federal system and frustrates its essential characteristics, and implicitly overrules longstanding Court precedent. Like the standards of appellate review, the standards under which a federal court must evaluate the excessiveness of a jury verdict does not implicate a rule of law, which defines a party's rights, but rather merely determines whether the law has been complied with.

The Court made the "classic *Erie* mistake." By requiring a federal court to apply state law rules governing the excessiveness of jury verdicts, the Court offends the fundamental interests of the federal court system as set forth in the Federal Rules of Civil Procedure. The state law at issue in this case is procedural in nature and should not be forced upon the federal courts.

Analysis:

Commentators generally criticize this opinion for a lack of a reasoned discussion of all the factors presented by *Erie* and its progeny, relying instead on those principles most favorable to the Court's decision. For example, the Court failed to consider the first question presented by *Erie*—whether the state standard should be applied at all—as mentioned in *Byrd v. Blue Ridge Electric Cooperative, Inc.* Also, the Court does not explain a principal consideration raised in *Hanna v. Plumer*—whether application of the state standard endangers the Seventh Amendment. Critics claim the Court's reasoning fails to indicate why this case is governed by a different *Erie* analysis than in those cases.

■ CASE VOCABULARY

REMITTITUR: The process by which a court reduces or proposes to reduce the damages awarded in a jury verdict.

Mason v. American Emery Wheel Works

(Injured Worker) v. *(Product Manufacturer)*

241 F.2d 906 (1st Cir. 1957)

OUTDATED STATE LAW DOES NOT APPLY IN FEDERAL COURT

■ **INSTANT FACTS** Mason (P) was injured in Mississippi by an emery wheel manufactured by American Emery Wheel Works (D), a Rhode Island corporation.

■ **BLACK LETTER RULE** A federal court sitting in diversity need not strictly enforce the substantive state law if there is sufficient indication that a state court, given the opportunity to consider the case, would not enforce the law as stated.

■ **PROCEDURAL BASIS**

On appeal to review a federal district court decision to grant the defendant's motion to dismiss.

■ **FACTS**

Mason (P), a Mississippi citizen, sued American Emery Wheel Works (D), a Rhode Island corporation, in a Rhode Island federal court for injuries caused by a defective emery wheel manufactured by the defendant. In its answer, American Emery Wheel Works (D) claimed lack of privity as required by Mississippi law and it moved to dismiss. Applying Mississippi law, the Rhode Island court found that the emery wheel had passed through several owners before it was sold to the plaintiff's employer, destroying privity with the defendant. The court granted the defendant's motion to dismiss.

■ **ISSUE**

Must a federal court sitting in diversity jurisdiction strictly apply the substantive law of the state in which an action arose?

■ **DECISION AND RATIONALE**

(Magruder, C.J.) No. Although the Rhode Island court correctly chose Mississippi law as the applicable substantive standard controlling the case, the only Mississippi case relied upon is a 1928 case requiring privity of contract between a manufacturer and an end-user to sustain a products liability action. While the rule set forth in that case was once the majority rule, the prevailing view across the country has changed. No longer is privity generally required to sustain the plaintiff's action, so the Mississippi law is in the minority. Of course, if the Supreme Court of Mississippi had occasion to consider and reaffirm the minority rule established in 1928, the court would be obligated to apply the minority view in accordance with the governing state law. However, a case need not be explicitly overruled to lose its precedential value. The Supreme Court of Mississippi discussed the minority rule in a recent case and acknowledged the trend of other jurisdictions away from the Mississippi rule. Although the court determined the outcome of that case on other grounds, it is apparent that the Supreme Court of Mississippi would reverse the 1928 case and adopt the majority trend if given the opportunity. The Rhode Island federal court erred in applying Mississippi's antiquated minority privity requirement under the circumstances. Vacated and remanded.

■ **CONCURRENCE**

(Hartigan, J.) Although the dicta relied upon clearly implies the Supreme Court of Mississippi's intention to depart from the minority rule when given the opportunity, the court's message provides little assistance to federal judges when considering whether to apply state law as required by *Erie* or to rely upon dicta tending to conflict with established state law. When the situation is less clear than here, the choice between conflicting holdings and dicta is not easy.

Analysis:

Five years after Judge Magruder's conclusion that the Supreme Court of Mississippi would depart from its minority approach requiring privity if given the opportunity, the court got that opportunity. Despite acknowledging Judge Magruder's prediction, the Supreme Court of Mississippi declined to overrule the 1928 case. Instead, the Court decided the issue on different grounds, although the opportunity existed to apply the majority rule. Given this decision, it is questionable whether *Mason* was correctly decided under Mississippi law.

■ CASE VOCABULARY

STARE DECISIS: The doctrine of precedent, under which it is necessary for a court to follow earlier judicial decisions when the same points arise again in litigation.

Dice v. Akron, Canton & Youngstown R.R.

(Railroad Fireman) v. *(Railroad)*

342 U.S. 359, 72 S.Ct. 312, 96 L.Ed. 398 (1952)

THE VALIDITY OF A FELA RELEASE IS DETERMINED BY FEDERAL LAW

■ **INSTANT FACTS** Dice (P) sued Akron, Canton & Youngstown R.R. (D) in Ohio state court for negligence under the Federal Employers' Liability Act.

■ **BLACK LETTER RULE** When a substantive right is created by federal statute, states may not fashion state-law defenses to defeat the federal right.

■ **PROCEDURAL BASIS**

Certiorari to review a decision of the Ohio Supreme Court upholding a trial court's judgment notwithstanding the verdict.

■ **FACTS**

Dice (P) was a railroad fireman injured when the train on which he was riding jumped the track. Dice (P) filed a negligence action in an Ohio state court under the Federal Employer's Liability Act (FELA). The defendant asserted that the claim should be dismissed based on a release signed by Dice (P). Dice (P) claimed the release was signed as a result of the defendant's fraudulent representations that the paper was merely an acknowledgement of backpay. After a jury returned a verdict for the plaintiff, the trial court entered a judgment notwithstanding the verdict, finding that Dice (P) was negligent in failing to read the document he was signing. A state court of appeals reversed the judgment, applying FELA and concluding that under federal law there was ample evidence of fraud to support the jury's verdict. On appeal the Ohio Supreme Court reversed, holding that Ohio law governed the case, that Ohio law required Dice (P) to read the release, and that a judge under Ohio law decided issues of fact related to fraud. Dice (P) petitioned for certiorari.

■ **ISSUE**

Must a state court presiding over an action under the Federal Employer's Liability Act apply federal law in determining the validity of a release?

■ **DECISION AND RATIONALE**

(Black, J.) Yes. The validity of releases under the Federal Employers' Liability Act (FELA) is governed by federal law. Because Dice's (P) substantive right to recover arises out of federal law, so too must defenses related to Dice's (P) claims be governed by federal law. If a state were permitted to fashion state-law defenses to a federal right, the state would necessarily control the availability of relief to the plaintiff. The uniform national right created by FELA would be destroyed.

Furthermore, FELA was enacted to afford railroad workers a right to recover for injuries resulting from their employers' negligence. The rule applied by the Ohio Supreme Court would protect an employer committing active fraud because of the employee's mere negligence in failing to read a release. Accordingly, a release is void if an employee is induced to sign it by the fraudulent representations of an employer intended to deceive the employee.

Finally, Ohio law provides that Dice (P) is entitled to a jury determination of all factual issues surrounding his claims. Yet, the court treats the factual determination of the validity of a release differently. Because Ohio law affords plaintiffs the right to a trial by jury in all negligence actions, it may not separate one factual issue from the others and submit it to the court for determination. The trial court erred in directing a judgment notwithstanding the verdict. Reversed and remanded.

■ CONCURRENCE IN PART

(Frankfurter, J.) Under Ohio law, the judge is the trier of fact on all issues pertaining to fraud. Yet, the Court requires these issues to be determined by a jury because the negligence case arises under FELA. In the process, the Court disregards the principles of federalism that preserve the judicial power of the States. Although a state court may not treat negligence actions under FELA any differently than other negligence actions available under state law, neither must a state be compelled to treat a FELA case differently because it arises under federal law. The Ohio system does not seek to evade the requirements of FELA, but rather merely enforces the same system applicable to other negligence actions in the plaintiff's FELA action. However, if state courts are to properly assert concurrent jurisdiction over federal claims, they must afford the substantive rights of the federal standard. Because the Ohio Supreme Court applied the state standard, its judgment should be reversed.

Analysis:

Just as federal courts must apply state substantive law in the enforcement of state-created rights and liabilities, states must apply federal substantive law for federally created rights and liabilities. Many statutes afford states concurrent jurisdiction over federal causes of action. To permit states to fashion their own laws relative to those federal rights would frustrate the need for national uniformity of federal laws, encourage forum shopping, and violate constitutional provisions of federalism.

■ CASE VOCABULARY

CONCURRENT JURISDICTION: Jurisdiction exercised simultaneously by more than one court over the same subject matter and within the same territory, with the litigant having the right to choose the court in which to file the action.

FEDERAL EMPLOYERS' LIABILITY ACT: A workers'-compensation law that provides death and disability benefits for employees of railroads engaged in interstate and foreign commerce.

JUDGMENT NOTWITHSTANDING THE VERDICT: A judgment entered for one party even though a jury verdict has been rendered for the opposing party.

RELEASE: Liberation from an obligation, duty, or demand; the act of giving up a right or claim to the person against whom it could have been enforced.

CHAPTER TWELVE

Appeals

Bowles v. Russell

Instant Facts: A criminal defendant filed an appeal from the denial of a habeas petition within the time period allowed by the district court's order, but outside the time limits prescribed by federal statute and rule, and the federal court of appeals declined to hear the case.

Black Letter Rule: Time limits for filing a notice of appeal are jurisdictional in nature, and the untimely filing of notice, even if filed in reliance on a district court order, deprives the court of appeals of jurisdiction.

Quackenbush v. Allstate Insurance Co.

Instant Facts: Quackenbush (P) sued Allstate Insurance Co. (D) for breach of contract in state court and the case was removed to federal court but subsequently remanded back to state court.

Black Letter Rule: A party is entitled to a single appeal, to be deferred until final judgment has been entered, in which claims of district court error at any stage of the litigation may be asserted.

Cohen v. Beneficial Industrial Loan Corp.

Instant Facts: Beneficial Industrial Loan Corp. (D) appealed from a federal district court order refusing to enforce a state statute requiring the plaintiff to post bond.

Black Letter Rule: Interlocutory decisions are immediately appealable if, although they do not bring the litigation to an end, they have a final and irreparable effect on the rights of the parties.

Will v. Hallock

Instant Facts: U.S. Customs Agents argued that the case against them should have been dismissed once the case against the government was dismissed, but the court denied their motion and they appealed.

Black Letter Rule: The requirements for a collateral order appeal are that an order (1) conclusively determine the disputed question, (2) resolve an important issue completely separate from the merits of the action, and (3) be effectively unreviewable on appeal from the final judgment.

Carson v. American Brands, Inc.

Instant Facts: A group of black employees and job applicants sued a tobacco company for discrimination; the parties reached a proposed settlement, but the court refused to approve their consent decree because it would have required the employer to give preferential treatment to black employees and applicants, and the plaintiffs appealed.

Black Letter Rule: An appeal as of right may be taken from interlocutory orders of federal district courts granting, continuing, modifying, refusing, or dissolving injunctions.

Nystrom v. TREX, Inc.

Instant Facts: The federal district court issued a ruling partially resolving the parties' dispute but staying the resolution of certain claims, and the plaintiff appealed from the decision.

Black Letter Rule: Interlocutory appeals are within the court's discretion, and will be granted only when the court certifies that each ruling presented for appeal involves a controlling question of law as to which there is substantial ground for difference of opinion, and that an immediate appeal from the order may materially advance the ultimate termination of the litigation.

Will v. United States

Instant Facts: The United States (P) petitioned for a writ of mandamus to compel Judge Will (D) to vacate an order on a bill of particulars.

Black Letter Rule: A writ of mandamus is traditionally appropriate only in extraordinary circumstances to confine an inferior court to a lawful exercise of its prescribed jurisdiction or to compel it to exercise its authority when it is its duty to do so.

Bose Corp. v. Consumers Union of United States, Inc.

Instant Facts: Bose Corp. (P) obtained a judgment in a defamation action against Consumers Union of United States, Inc. (D), but the First Circuit Court of Appeals reversed after conducting an independent review of the record to redetermine questions of fact.

Black Letter Rule: In a First Amendment case, an appellate court may conduct an independent review of the record to determine questions of fact bearing on a party's constitutional rights.

Bowles v. Russell

(Convicted Murderer) v. *(Prison Warden)*

551 U.S. 205, 127 S.Ct. 2360, 168 L.Ed.2d 96 (2007)

STATUTES AND RULES, NOT COURT ORDERS, DETERMINE APPROPRIATE TIME LIMITS

WARNING

Do NOT rely on a judge to correctly tell you a time limit. His mistake will be your misfortune.

stus.com

■ **INSTANT FACTS** A criminal defendant filed an appeal from the denial of a habeas petition within the time period allowed by the district court's order, but outside the time limits prescribed by federal statute and rule, and the federal court of appeals declined to hear the case.

■ **BLACK LETTER RULE** Time limits for filing a notice of appeal are jurisdictional in nature, and the untimely filing of notice, even if filed in reliance on a district court order, deprives the court of appeals of jurisdiction.

■ **PROCEDURAL BASIS**

Supreme Court review of a federal court of appeals decision declining to hear the case.

■ **FACTS**

In 1999, a state jury convicted Bowles (P) of murder and sentenced him to imprisonment for fifteen years to life. Bowles (P) filed an unsuccessful appeal and then filed a federal habeas corpus application, which was denied. Bowles (P) had thirty days to appeal from that denial, but he failed to do so. Later, he moved to reopen the period during which he could file his notice of appeal pursuant to Fed. R. App. P. 4(a)(6), which allows a fourteen-day extension under certain conditions. The federal district court granted the motion, but for some reason gave Bowles (P) seventeen rather than the fourteen days allowed by federal rule and statute. Bowles (P) filed his notice of appeal within the seventeen days, but after the fourteen days allowed by statute and rule had expired. Russell (D) argued that the notice was untimely and that the court therefore lacked jurisdiction to hear the appeal. The court of appeals agreed, and the Supreme Court granted certiorari.

■ **ISSUE**

Did the court of appeals have jurisdiction to entertain an appeal filed after the statutory period but within the period allowed by the district court's order?

■ **DECISION AND RATIONALE**

(Thomas, J.) No. Time limits for filing a notice of appeal are jurisdictional in nature, and the untimely filing of notice, even if filed in reliance on a district court order, deprives the court of appeals of jurisdiction. Jurisdictional treatment of time limits makes good sense. Because Congress decides whether federal courts can hear cases at all, it can also determine when, and under what conditions, federal courts can hear them. The timely filing of a notice of appeal is a jurisdictional requirement, and the court has no authority to make exceptions, no matter what "unique circumstances" may be presented. If this result is deemed too inequitable, Congress may authorize courts to promulgate new rules that excuse compliance with statutory time limits. Affirmed.

■ DISSENT

(Souter, J.) It is intolerable for the court to treat people this way. This criminal defendant complied with a court order, yet was denied an appeal. We have warned several times that "jurisdiction" has too many meanings. The time limit here is more like a statute of limitations than a definition of the set of cases that may be adjudicated, which is what jurisdiction really is. We have the authority to recognize equitable exceptions to the fourteen-day time limit, and this seems like an appropriate case in which to do so, where the untimely filing of the notice of appeal was based on reliance on an error by a district court, but resulted in no prejudice to the other party. I would vacate the decision of the court of appeals and remand for a consideration of the merits.

Analysis:

The dissent argued here that the majority wrongfully viewed the concept of jurisdiction as it had "in the days when we used the term imprecisely." The majority argued that if its treatment of its own jurisdiction was simply a relic of the old days, it was a relic with severe consequences. In what seems to be more a justification of the dissent's viewpoint than its own, the majority points out an example of the effects of a brightline standard in cases like this. Just a few months prior to this decision, the Supreme Court Clerk, pursuant to S. Ct. R. 13.2, had refused to accept a petition for certiorari submitted by Ryan Heath Dickson because it was filed just one day late. As a result, Dickson was executed. In the letter sent to Dickson's counsel, the Clerk explained that once the time to file a petition for a writ of certiorari has expired, the Court no longer has the power to review the petition. "The rejected certiorari petition was Dickson's first in this Court," the majority observed, "and one can only speculate as to whether denial of that petition would have been a foregone conclusion."

■ CASE VOCABULARY

EQUITABLE: Just; consistent with principles of justice and right; existing in equity; available or sustainable by an action in equity, or under the rules and principles of equity.

HABEAS CORPUS: [Law, Latin: "that you have the body."] A writ employed to bring a person before a court, most frequently to ensure that the party's imprisonment or detention is not illegal (*habeas corpus ad subjiciendum*). In addition to being used to test the legality of an arrest or commitment, the writ may be used to obtain review of (1) the regularity of the extradition process, (2) the right to or amount of bail, or (3) the jurisdiction of a court that has imposed a criminal sentence.

Quackenbush v. Allstate Insurance Co.

(California Insurance Commissioner) v. *(Insurance Company)*
517 U.S. 706, 116 S.Ct. 1712, 135 L.Ed.2d 1 (1996)

A REMAND ORDER IS APPEALABLE

■ **INSTANT FACTS** Quackenbush (P) sued All-state Insurance Co. (D) for breach of contract in state court and the case was removed to federal court but subsequently remanded back to state court.

■ **BLACK LETTER RULE** A party is entitled to a single appeal, to be deferred until final judgment has been entered, in which claims of district court error at any stage of the litigation may be asserted.

■ **PROCEDURAL BASIS**

Certiorari to review a decision of the Ninth Circuit Court of Appeals, vacating a district court judgment on appeal.

■ **FACTS**

Quackenbush (P), the Insurance Commissioner for California, was appointed trustee over the assets of Mission Insurance Company and its affiliates after they were ordered liquidated by a California court. As trustee, Quackenbush (P) filed suit against Allstate Insurance Co. (D) for breach of contract based on Allstate's (D) refusal to honor its obligations under reinsurance contracts. Allstate (D) removed the suit to federal court and filed a motion to compel arbitration. Quackenbush (P) moved to remand, arguing that the federal court should abstain from the matter because its decision may interfere with the state's regulation of the insolvent Mission companies. The district court concluded that abstention was appropriate and remanded the case to state court. On appeal, the Ninth Circuit Court of Appeals vacated the decision and ordered arbitration, ruling that abstention is appropriate only when equitable relief is sought.

■ **ISSUE**

Is an abstention-based remand order, sending a case that had been removed to federal court back to state court, appealable as a final order?

■ **DECISION AND RATIONALE**

(O'Connor, J.) Yes. While under 28 U.S.C. § 1291, federal appellate courts have appellate jurisdiction over "final decisions" of the district courts, "a party is entitled to a single appeal, to be deferred until final judgment has been entered, in which claims of district court error at any stage of the litigation may be ventilated." Accordingly, only those district court orders that effectively end the litigation will trigger appellate jurisdiction. By its nature, a remand order does not end the litigation, but rather transfers it to another forum. However, the practical effect of an abstention-based remand order is to dispel the federal court of jurisdiction and end the federal litigation. The only avenue of appeal of a final judgment ending the litigation in state court would be through the state appellate courts. Therefore, the remand order was appealable as a final order under § 1291. Affirmed.

Analysis:

Under the Court's reasoning, any federal court decision ending the federal litigation is a final decision within the meaning of 28 U.S.C. § 1291. Other examples would be a dismissal for failure to state a claim and a dismissal and remand for lack of supplemental jurisdiction. When federal claims are dismissed, leaving only state claims for consideration by a state court, the litigation is far from at an end. When such a decision is issued and an appeal is filed, the state court generally should stay the proceedings in the state court to allow the appeals court to determine the proper forum.

■ CASE VOCABULARY

ABSTENTION: A federal court's relinquishment of jurisdiction when necessary to avoid needless conflict with a state's administration of its own affairs.

APPEAL: A proceeding undertaken to have a decision reconsidered by bringing it to a higher authority, especially the submission of a lower court's or agency's decision to a higher court for review and possible reversal.

APPELLATE JURISDICTION: The power of a court to review and revise a lower court's decision.

FINAL JUDGMENT: A court's last action that settles the rights of the parties and disposes of all issues in controversy, except for the award of costs (and, sometimes, attorney's fees) and enforcement of the judgment.

FINAL–JUDGMENT RULE: The principle that a party may appeal only from a district court's final decision that ends the litigation on the merits. Under this rule, a party must raise all claims of error in a single appeal.

REMAND: To send (a case or claim) back to the court or tribunal from which it came for some further action.

Cohen v. Beneficial Industrial Loan Corp.

(Shareholder) v. *(Corporation)*

337 U.S. 541, 69 S.Ct. 1221, 93 L.Ed. 1528 (1949)

AN ORDER REFUSING TO REQUIRE A BOND IS APPEALABLE

■ **INSTANT FACTS** Beneficial Industrial Loan Corp. (D) appealed from a federal district court order refusing to enforce a state statute requiring the plaintiff to post bond.

■ **BLACK LETTER RULE** Interlocutory decisions are immediately appealable if, although they do not bring the litigation to an end, they have a final and irreparable effect on the rights of the parties.

■ **PROCEDURAL BASIS**

Certiorari to determine the appealability of a federal district court order holding state law inapplicable in a federal proceeding.

■ **FACTS**

Cohen's (P) decedent, a minority shareholder in Beneficial Industrial Loan Corp. (D), filed a derivative action in New Jersey federal court alleging a breach of fiduciary duty against the defendant, its managers, and directors by unjustly enriching themselves at the corporation's expense. Two years later, New Jersey enacted a statute making derivative-action plaintiffs liable for a corporation's legal costs if the plaintiffs held less than a specified number of shares and the defendant ultimately prevailed. The statute further required such plaintiffs to post a bond upon filing to cover such costs and specifically stated that it applied to pending actions. Although Beneficial (D) moved to compel Cohen's (D) decedent to post the required bond, the federal court determined that the state statute was inapplicable in federal suits. Beneficial (D) appealed, contending the district court's order was appealable as a final order.

■ **ISSUE**

Is a federal district court order refusing to apply a state law requiring the posting of a bond appealable as a final order?

■ **DECISION AND RATIONALE**

(Jackson, J.) Yes. Although 28 U.S.C. § 1291 permits appeals only from final decisions of the district courts, § 1292 allows appeals from certain interlocutory decisions that, while not bringing the litigation to an end, have a final and irreparable effect on the rights of the parties. While the types of decisions referenced in § 1292 are not material to this case, the statute indicates a congressional intent to allow appeals from orders in which a particular issue is decided and, in that sense, is final.

Here, the district court's order is conclusive of the bond issue and is not likely to be incorporated in the court's final appealable judgment. Therefore, by the time the right to appeal is perfected, it will be too late to appeal the effects of the order and the defendant will be irreparably damaged. While the issue is collateral to the merits of the case, it is a final disposition of the issue decided and too important to require the defendant to wait until a judgment on the merits is rendered. Affirmed.

Analysis:

While the district court's order does not affect the defendant's interests in the merits of the suit, it does affect an important issue—the payment of legal fees. The statute suggests a state policy reflecting the importance of securing the plaintiff's ability to pay such legal fees, which is entitled to considerable deference. If the defendant were not entitled to appeal the issue because it was not incorporated into the court's final decision, the plaintiff would successfully avoid state policy by filing the action in federal court rather than state court. Such forum shopping must be discouraged.

■ **CASE VOCABULARY**

COLLATERAL–ORDER DOCTRINE: A doctrine allowing appeal from an interlocutory order that conclusively determines an issue wholly separate from the merits of the action and effectively unreviewable on appeal from a final judgment.

DERIVATIVE ACTION: A suit by a beneficiary of a fiduciary to enforce a right belonging to the fiduciary, especially a suit asserted by a shareholder on the corporation's behalf against a third party (usually a corporate officer) because of the corporation's failure to take some action against the third party.

INTERLOCUTORY APPEAL: An appeal that occurs before the trial court's final ruling on the entire case.

Will v. Hallock

(*Customs Agent*) v. (*Owner of Seized Computers*)

546 U.S. 345, 126 S.Ct. 952, 163 L.Ed.2d 836 (2006)

THE FINAL JUDGMENT RULE APPLIES IN ALL BUT EXCEPTIONAL CASES

Sorry, the final judgment rule applies in all but exceptional cases.

stus.com

■ **INSTANT FACTS** U.S. Customs Agents argued that the case against them should have been dismissed once the case against the government was dismissed, but the court denied their motion and they appealed.

■ **BLACK LETTER RULE** The requirements for a collateral order appeal are that an order (1) conclusively determine the disputed question, (2) resolve an important issue completely separate from the merits of the action, and (3) be effectively unreviewable on appeal from the final judgment.

■ **PROCEDURAL BASIS**

Certiorari to the United States Court of Appeals for the Second Circuit.

■ **FACTS**

U.S. Customs Agents, acting on a warrant, seized computer equipment from the plaintiff's home. No charges were brought, and the equipment was returned, albeit in a very damaged condition. The plaintiff brought suit against the United States under the Federal Tort Claims Act, and while that suit was pending, she brought a second suit against the agents, alleging negligence. After the suit against the United States was dismissed, the agents moved for dismissal of the case against them, arguing that the action was barred by a federal statute, 28 U.S.C. § 2676 (the "judgment bar" urged by the defendants), once the first case was dismissed. The trial court denied the agents' motion and they appealed, despite the lack of a final judgment on the merits. On appeal, the Second Circuit held that the collateral order doctrine justified the appeal, even though there had been no final judgment.

■ **ISSUE**

Did the court properly consider the appeal in this case despite the lack of a final judgment on the merits?

■ **DECISION AND RATIONALE**

(Souter, J.) No. The requirements for a collateral order appeal are that an order (1) conclusively determine the disputed question, (2) resolve an important issue completely separate from the merits of the action, and (3) be effectively unreviewable on appeal from the final judgment. There is only a small class of collaterally appealable orders, and the requirements are stringent. An order rejecting immunity, for instance, may be immediately appealable. If, through rigorous application of the final judgment requirement, the value of the interests that would be lost supersedes the value of applying the general rule, a collateral order appeal may be allowed. Honoring the separation of powers, preserving the efficiency of government, respecting a state's dignitary interests, and mitigating the government's advantage over an individual are examples of such interests. Does the claim of the customs agents in this case serve such a weighty public objective? There is no such public interest at stake simply because the "judgment bar" is said to be applicable. The judgment bar at issue in this case is no more important than the typical defense of claim preclusion, and it justifies no immediate appeal of right. The judgment of the court of appeals is vacated and the case is remanded with instructions to dismiss the appeal for lack of jurisdiction.

Analysis:

Section 2676 of Title 28 of the United States Code provides that "[t]he judgment in an action under section 1346 (b) of this title [against the United States or its agents acting within the scope of their office] shall constitute a complete bar to any action by the claimant, by reason of the same subject matter, against the employee of the government whose act or omission gave rise to the claim." Here, the claim against the government was dismissed. The trial court held that the bar of § 2676 did not apply, however, and refused to dismiss the case against the agents. According to the Supreme Court, the judgment bar of the statute was not the kind of interest that would justify an exception to the application of the final judgment rule.

■ CASE VOCABULARY

COLLATERAL ORDER DOCTRINE: A doctrine allowing appeal from an interlocutory order that conclusively determines an issue wholly separate from the merits of the action and effectively unreviewable on appeal from a final judgment. Also termed *Cohen* doctrine.

FINAL JUDGMENT RULE: The principle that a party may appeal only from a district court's final decision that ends the litigation on the merits. Under this rule, a party must raise all claims of error in a single appeal.

Carson v. American Brands, Inc.

(*Class Representative/Employee*) v. (*Tobacco Company/Employer*)

450 U.S. 79, 101 S.Ct. 993, 67 L.Ed.2d 59 (1981)

INTERLOCUTORY ORDERS INVOLVING INJUNCTIVE RELIEF ARE APPEALBLE

■ **INSTANT FACTS** A group of black employees and job applicants sued a tobacco company for discrimination; the parties reached a proposed settlement, but the court refused to approve their consent decree because it would have required the employer to give preferential treatment to black employees and applicants, and the plaintiffs appealed.

■ **BLACK LETTER RULE** An appeal as of right may be taken from interlocutory orders of federal district courts granting, continuing, modifying, refusing, or dissolving injunctions.

■ **PROCEDURAL BASIS**

Supreme Court review of a federal circuit court's refusal to consider an appeal.

■ **FACTS**

A group of black employees and applicants for employment at the Richmond Leaf Department of the American Tobacco Company brought suit for violations of their civil rights. They argued that the employer had discriminated against them on the basis of their race. The parties negotiated a settlement and moved the court to approve it and enter their proposed consent decree, which would have required the employer to give hiring and promotional preference to black employees. The court denied the motion, concluding that preferential treatment on the basis of race violated Title VII and the Constitution. The plaintiffs appealed, but the Fourth Circuit dismissed the appeal for want of jurisdiction, holding that the interlocutory order was not appealable. The Supreme Court, based on a disagreement among the federal circuits, granted certiorari to review the case.

■ **ISSUE**

Is an interlocutory order of the federal district court denying a joint motion of the parties to enter a consent decree containing injunctive relieve an appealable order?

■ **DECISION AND RATIONALE**

(Brennan, J.) Yes. An appeal as of right may be taken from interlocutory orders of federal district courts granting, continuing, modifying, refusing, or dissolving injunctions. This is a limited exception to the final judgment rule, however, and it is available only when allowing an appeal will further the statutory purpose of permitting litigants to effectually challenge interlocutory orders of serious, and perhaps irreparable, consequence. Here, unless the order is appealable, the plaintiffs will lose their opportunity to challenge an interlocutory order that denies them injunctive relief and that has a serious and perhaps irreparable consequence. First, they might lose their opportunity to settle their case on the negotiated terms. Settlement agreements and consent decrees are predicated on an express or implied condition that the parties will, by their agreement, avoid the costs and uncertainties of litigation. By refusing to enter the proposed consent decree, the district court has effectively ordered the parties to proceed to trial, thus denying them the right to compromise their dispute on mutually agreeable terms. Second, the

---

plaintiffs will be denied the immediate application of new hiring, transfer, and promotion policies, and will thereby suffer additional serious and perhaps irreparable consequences. Accordingly, the order is essentially an order "refusing" an "injunction," and it is therefore appealable under 28 U.S.C. § 1291. Reversed.

Analysis:

In this case, the federal appellate court had held that the order of the district court refusing to enter the consent decree was not appealable. The Supreme Court reversed, holding that the order of the district court refusing to enter the consent decree was an order "refusing an injunction" and was therefore appealable under 28 U.S.C. § 1292(a)(1). The Court remanded the case for further proceedings in conformity with its decision, and the appeal was then considered on its merits. On remand, a majority of the circuit court was of the view that the district court should be directed to enter the consent decree, and it so ordered.

■ CASE VOCABULARY

CONSENT DECREE: A court decree that all parties agree to.

INJUNCTION: A court order commanding or preventing an action. To get an injunction, the complainant must show that there is no plain, adequate, and complete remedy at law and that an irreparable injury will result unless the relief is granted.

INTERLOCUTORY: (Of an order, judgment, appeal, etc.) Interim or temporary, not constituting a final resolution of the whole controversy.

Nystrom v. TREX, Inc.

(Patent Holder) v. *(Alleged Infringer)*

339 F.3d 1347 (Fed. Cir. 2003)

PARTIAL JUDGMENTS ARE NOT FINAL FOR PURPOSES OF APPEAL

That's my final order!

Okay, *NOW* It's time to appeal to Mom.

stus.com

■ **INSTANT FACTS** The federal district court issued a ruling partially resolving the parties' dispute but staying the resolution of certain claims, and the plaintiff appealed from the decision.

■ **BLACK LETTER RULE** Interlocutory appeals are within the court's discretion, and will be granted only when the court certifies that each ruling presented for appeal involves a controlling question of law as to which there is substantial ground for difference of opinion, and that an immediate appeal from the order may materially advance the ultimate termination of the litigation.

■ **PROCEDURAL BASIS**

On appeal from the federal district court's partial resolution of the parties' claims.

■ **FACTS**

Nystrom (P) filed a patent infringement suit against TREX (D). TREX (D) counterclaimed, seeking a declaratory judgment of non-infringement, and further claiming that the patent was invalid and unenforceable. TREX (D) also raised antitrust counterclaims, which it voluntarily dismissed and reinstated more than once, prompting Nystrom (P) to move for sanctions based on TREX's (D) unnecessarily complicating and prolonging the litigation. That motion was denied. Thereafter, TREX moved for summary judgment, which was granted in part as to some counts of the plaintiff's complaint, but stayed in part as to other counts. Nystrom (P) appealed.

■ **ISSUE**

Did the judgment below, granting the defendant summary judgment as to some of the plaintiff's claims and some of the defendant's counterclaims, constitute a final judgment for purposes of appeal?

■ **DECISION AND RATIONALE**

(Linn, J.) No. Interlocutory appeals are within the court's discretion, and will be granted only when the court certifies that each ruling presented for appeal involves a controlling question of law as to which there is substantial ground for difference of opinion, and that an immediate appeal from the order may materially advance the ultimate termination of the litigation. Such appeals are rarely granted.

Every federal appellate court has a special obligation to satisfy itself of its own jurisdiction even thought the parties are prepared to concede it. That is, even though the parties here raised no objection to our jurisdiction over this appeal, we must consider whether there has been a final judgment of the district court or there is a basis for jurisdiction over an interlocutory order. There is neither. Parties may generally only appeal from a final order of the district court—an order that ends the litigation on the merits and leaves nothing more for the court to do than execute the judgment. In this case, the district court reserved certain issues and stayed the resolution of certain claims. Stay orders generally are not final for purposes of an appeal. Moreover, a judgment that does not dispose of pending counterclaims is not a final judgment. Without finality at the district court level, this court declines to entertain the present appeal. Because TREX's (D) invalidity and unenforceability counterclaim remains pending at the district court level, the judgment appealed from is not final, and the court therefore dismisses the appeal for lack of jurisdiction.

Analysis:

In this case, Nystrom (P) had appealed from the grant of summary judgment of non-infringement, the grant of summary judgment of invalidity of claims 18–20, and the district court's denial of sanctions. That appeal was dismissed for lack of finality in light of the stayed invalidity and unenforceability counterclaims regarding claims 1–17. Ultimately, however, the district court entered a retroactive Amended Final Judgment that repeated the previously entered judgments of non-infringement and of invalidity of claims 18–20, but also dismissed without prejudice the remainder of TREX's (D) declaratory judgment counterclaims regarding claims 1–17. The appeal was then reinstated.

■ CASE VOCABULARY

DECLARATORY JUDGMENT: A binding adjudication that establishes the rights and other legal relations of the parties without providing for or ordering enforcement. Declaratory judgments are often sought, for example, by insurance companies in determining whether a policy covers a given insured or peril.

INFRINGEMENT: An act that interferes with one of the exclusive rights of a patent, copyright, or trademark owner.

PATENT: The governmental grant of a right, privilege, or authority.

STAY: The postponement or halting of a proceeding, judgment, or the like; an order to suspend all or part of a judicial proceeding or a judgment resulting from that proceeding.

Will v. United States

(*District Court Judge*) v. (*Federal Government*)
389 U.S. 90, 88 S.Ct. 269, 19 L.Ed.2d 305 (1967)

A WRIT OF MANDAMUS REQUIRES EXTRAORDINARY JUSTIFICATION

■ **INSTANT FACTS** The United States (P) petitioned for a writ of mandamus to compel Judge Will (D) to vacate an order on a bill of particulars.

■ **BLACK LETTER RULE** A writ of mandamus is traditionally appropriate only in extraordinary circumstances to confine an inferior court to a lawful exercise of its prescribed jurisdiction or to compel it to exercise its authority when it is its duty to do so.

■ **PROCEDURAL BASIS**

Certiorari to review a decision of the Seventh Circuit Court of Appeals granting a writ of mandamus.

■ **FACTS**

Horowitz, a defendant in a tax evasion case pending before Judge Will (D), filed a motion for a bill of particulars requesting information. After the scope of the bill of particulars had been narrowed, a dispute arose over the defendant's request for certain information concerning oral statements relied upon by the Government (P) to support the charges. The request asked for the names and addresses of the persons to whom the statements were allegedly made, the times and places they were made, whether the witnesses were government agents, and whether the witnesses prepared any transcripts or memoranda of the statements. After considering the request, Judge Will (D) ordered the Government (P) to comply with the request. The Government (P) refused to comply with the order, stating that Judge Will (D) had no authority to require the Government (P) to provide a list of prosecution witnesses. After Judge Will (D) indicated his intention to dismiss the indictment against Horowitz because of the Government's (P) refusal to comply, the Government (P) petitioned to the Seventh Circuit Court of Appeals for a writ of mandamus compelling Judge Will (D) to strike the request from the bill of particulars. Although the court initially denied the writ, the writ was issued on reconsideration without a decision, requiring Judge Will (D) "to vacate his order directing the Government to answer question 25 in defendant's motion for bill of particulars."

■ **ISSUE**

May a court of appeals grant a writ of mandamus without a reasoned decision establishing the extraordinary circumstances justifying the writ?

■ **DECISION AND RATIONALE**

(Warren, C.J.) No. A writ of mandamus is traditionally appropriate only "to confine an inferior court to a lawful exercise of its prescribed jurisdiction or to compel it to exercise its authority when it is its duty to do so." Given the judicial policy of limiting appeals until the litigation has reached its termination, a writ of mandamus is proper under only the most extraordinary circumstances. This is particularly true when, as here, the underlying litigation is criminal in nature, for piecemeal appeals threaten the defendant's constitutional right to a speedy trial and risk double jeopardy. With these considerations, the writ in this matter does not involve such extraordinary circumstances.

The Government (P) contends that mandamus is appropriate here because Judge Will (D) ordered it to, in effect, produce a list of its witnesses prior to trial and this action was a result of a deliberate court policy in disregard of the Federal Rules of Criminal Procedure. The record, however, does not support these assertions. In granting the writ, the Court of Appeals provided no justification for its order. Similarly, the Government (P) has provided no evidence that Judge Will's (D) order was a result of an adopted policy in violation of the Federal Rules, nor that Judge Will (D) had similarly acted in other cases with like circumstances. Although a deliberate policy intended to contravene the Federal Rules is relevant in a mandamus proceeding, the Government (P) bears the burden of establishing such a policy as the court's motivation for its order.

While mandamus serves a corrective function, it is incumbent upon the court granting the writ to establish its reasoning and demonstrate the existence of extraordinary circumstances. Without so doing, the court of appeals exceeds the bounds of its authority to grant the writ as much as the district court in issuing the order under review. While mandamus may have been appropriate on a fully developed record, the writ cannot issue without demonstrating extraordinary circumstances. Vacated and remanded.

Analysis:

The writ was denied not because the Supreme Court determined Judge Will (D) acted appropriately, but because the court of appeals failed to demonstrate that Judge Will (D) acted inappropriately. If the court of appeals had issued a clear order finding that Judge Will (D) exceeded his authority due to a policy implemented in the Northern District of Illinois, the writ would likely have been granted given those extraordinary circumstances.

■ CASE VOCABULARY

DOUBLE JEOPARDY: The fact of being prosecuted twice for substantially the same offense.

MANDAMUS: A writ issued by a superior court to compel a lower court or a government official to perform mandatory or purely ministerial duties correctly.

Bose Corp. v. Consumers Union of United States, Inc.

(Electronics Manufacturer) v. *(Publisher)*

466 U.S. 485, 104 S.Ct. 1949, 80 L.Ed.2d 502 (1984)

THE *NEW YORK TIMES* RULE APPLIES TO APPEALS WITH FIRST AMENDMENT IMPLICATIONS

■ **INSTANT FACTS** Bose Corp. (P) obtained a judgment in a defamation action against Consumers Union of United States, Inc. (D), but the First Circuit Court of Appeals reversed after conducting an independent review of the record to redetermine questions of fact.

■ **BLACK LETTER RULE** In a First Amendment case, an appellate court may conduct an independent review of the record to determine questions of fact bearing on a party's constitutional rights.

■ PROCEDURAL BASIS

Certiorari to review a decision of the First Circuit Court of Appeals affirming a judgment for the defendant.

■ FACTS

In its magazine "Consumer Reports," Consumers Union of United States, Inc. (D) issued a disparaging report on a stereo system manufactured by Bose Corp. (P). Bose (P) filed a product disparagement action in federal court. Following a bench trial, the court issued an opinion in the defendant's favor, finding that Bose (P) was a public figure and that Bose (P) failed to prove the actual malice required to support its claims. The court, however, specifically found that clear and convincing evidence demonstrated that one sentence in the report contained a false fact concerning the system, which the defendant reported with knowledge of its falsity, and that the fact was disparaging. This determination was made after consideration of testimony from an expert sound engineer who tested the stereo and wrote the report on which the article was based. The First Circuit Court of Appeals affirmed after a de novo examination of the record, finding that there was no clear and convincing evidence that the report was made with knowledge of its falsity.

■ ISSUE

In a First Amendment case, may an appellate court conduct an independent review of the record evidence to determine questions of fact established by a trial court's judgment?

■ DECISION AND RATIONALE

(Stevens, J.) Yes. Under Rule 52(a), "[f]indings of fact shall not be set aside unless clearly erroneous, and due regard shall be given to the opportunity of the trial court to judge the credibility of the witnesses." However, in First Amendment cases, *New York Times v. Sullivan*, 376 U.S. 254 (1964), obliges the appellate court to conduct an independent examination of the record to ensure that the judgment does not violate free expression. The Supreme Court's standard of review must, therefore, reconcile the two conflicting approaches. The *New York Times* rule requires an independent review of the record evidence, and Rule 52(a) does not forbid such a review. Rule 52(a) merely requires the appellate court to respect the trial court's determinations of witnesses' credibility while determining whether the trial court's ruling is clearly erroneous nonetheless.

The rule of deference to the trial court's factual findings underscores the harmony between the two rules. Although the clearly erroneous standard applies in all circumstances, the strength of the presumption of correctness depends on the strength of the evidence considered by the trial court. For instance, when the trial court relies upon documentary evidence, the presumption "has lesser force" than when the trial court considers purely oral testimony. Likewise as the complexity and length of the trial increases, so too is the appellate court's reluctance to question the trial court's findings of fact increased. Rule 52(a) merely precludes reexamination of the facts affecting the outcome of the litigation, not errors of law or of mixed law and fact.

In First Amendment cases, the facts surrounding the utterance at issue impact the constitutional rights of the individual making the utterance. While the trial court may determine whether an utterance was made, whether it was true or false, and whether it was made with sufficient knowledge to establish a cause of action of libel, those factual determinations carry with them questions of constitutional law that fall within the *New York Times* rule. A trier of fact, whether judge or jury, may not reliably determine the legal effect of the factual findings because of the danger that such legal decisions may be affected by personal views. Accordingly, on appellate review, the court must conduct an independent review of the factual findings to determine their legal consequences. Because "actual malice" is a legal conclusion, the appellate court must consider the factual findings on an independent review to ensure that the established facts constitute actual malice and safeguard First Amendment liberties. Here, the court of appeals was correct that proof of falsity does not establish proof of malice and that the record failed to establish the defendant's malice. Affirmed.

■ DISSENT

(Rehnquist, J.) A finding of actual malice depends on no more than the mens rea of the author of the challenged statement, and appellate courts are insufficiently capable of determining the mens rea from the record on appeal. Here, the trial court concluded by clear and convincing evidence that the author wrote the disparaging report with knowledge that it was false based on its view of the witness's credibility at trial. The issue on appeal is not whether the trial court misunderstood its legal requirements, but rather whether the trial court's determination was correct. The court of appeals did not challenge the correctness of the court's conclusion, instead deeming the witness's language as imprecise and incapable of raising an inference of actual malice. The precision of the witness's statement, however, bears no relation to his knowledge of the falsity of the statement.

The problem with the Court's decision lies in the elevation of a pure question of fact, such as the witness's actual knowledge and recklessness, to a question of constitutional fact. While independent review is appropriate in matters in which questions of law are "so intermingled" with questions of fact, state-of-mind determinations have generally been afforded substantial deference on appeal, especially in criminal matters when the burden of proof is higher than *New York Time*'s clear-and-convincing standard. Independent review exists not so an appellate court may redetermine questions of fact, but to remedy incorrect determinations affected by bias or other influences. Appellate courts cannot reliably make determinations of a witness's malice without a consideration of the witness's credibility at trial. Instead, the trial court's determination after considering the witness's demeanor at trial is more reliable than an appellate court's decision based on the record on appeal. Such second-guessing does not protect free expression, but increases skepticism of the credibility determinations of trial courts. The court of appeals' decision should be reversed and remanded to allow the court to apply the clearly erroneous standard as set forth in Rule 52(a).

Analysis:

In its 1984 decision, the Court indicated that in some instances the presumption of the correctness of a trial court's factual determination is stronger than in others. For instance, the Court stated that when a determination is based upon oral testimony rather than documentary evidence, the court's opportunity to view the witness's in-court credibility is entitled to some deference. In 1985, however, Federal Rule of Civil Procedure 52(a) was amended to specifically provide that a trial court's findings of fact "whether based on oral or documentary evidence" are subject to the clearly erroneous standard.

■ **CASE VOCABULARY**

ACTUAL MALICE: Knowledge (by the person who utters or publishes a defamatory statement) that a statement is false, or reckless disregard about whether the statement is true.

CLEARLY ERRONEOUS STANDARD: The standard of review that an appellate court usually applies in judging a trial court's treatment of factual issues. Under this standard, a judgment will be upheld unless the appellate court is left with the firm conviction that an error has been committed.

DE NOVO JUDICIAL REVIEW: A court's nondeferential review of an administrative decision, usually through a review of the administrative record plus any additional evidence the parties present.

MENS REA: The state of mind that the prosecution, to secure a conviction, must prove that a defendant had when committing a crime; criminal intent or recklessness.

CHAPTER THIRTEEN

Preclusive Effects of Judgments

Manego v. Orleans Board of Trade

Instant Facts: After Manego (P) lost his suit against the defendants for civil rights violations, he filed a subsequent action alleging antitrust violations arising out of the same facts.

Black Letter Rule: Under the doctrine of res judicata, a final judgment on the merits precludes parties or their privies from relitigating issues that were or could have been raised in that action.

Federated Department Stores, Inc. v. Moitie

Instant Facts: After failing to appeal adverse judgments against them, Moitie (P) and Brown filed subsequent state court actions under state anti-trust laws.

Black Letter Rule: Res judicata bars relitigation of a final adjudication on the merits and is not affected by the fact that the judgment may have been wrong or rested on a legal principle subsequently overruled in another case.

Rinehart v. Locke

Instant Facts: Rinehart (P) filed a complaint against Locke (D) and others one year after a nearly identical complaint had been dismissed by the district court.

Black Letter Rule: Unless otherwise provided, a court order dismissing a complaint for failure to state a claim is an adjudication on the merits, which bars any subsequent litigation on the issue.

Marrese v. American Academy of Orthopedic Surgeons

Instant Facts: After Marrese's (P) state-law suit was dismissed, he filed a subsequent action in federal court under federal antitrust law.

Black Letter Rule: In determining the preclusive effect of a state court judgment on subsequent federal litigation, a federal court must look to the law of the state to determine whether the judgment would preclude relitigation in state courts.

Semtek International, Inc. v. Lockheed Martin Corp.

Instant Facts: After a California federal court dismissed the plaintiff's action on the basis of the state statute of limitations, a Maryland state court dismissed a subsequent suit brought by the plaintiff on the same grounds.

Black Letter Rule: The claim-preclusive effect of a judgment on the merits in a federal diversity action is governed by the law of the state in which the federal court sits.

Little v. Blue Goose Motor Coach Co.

Instant Facts: After Blue Goose Motor Coach Co. (D) obtained a verdict against Dr. Little for property damage resulting from his negligence, Little (P) obtained a verdict against Blue Goose (D) for personal injuries resulting from its negligence.

Black Letter Rule: Estoppel by verdict arises when a material fact in any litigation has been determined in a former suit between the same parties or between parties with whom the parties to the subsequent suit are in privity, when the fact was also material to the issue.

Hardy v. Johns–Manville Sales Corp.

Instant Facts: Hardy (P) and other plaintiffs sued Johns–Manville Sales Corp. (D) and eighteen other asbestos manufacturers, sellers, and distributors for injuries sustained due to defendants' alleged breach of the duty to warn of the harmful effects of asbestos exposure.

Black Letter Rule: Unless a subsequent suit shares common issues of fact or law with a prior suit, a judgment of the prior suit does not bar litigation of related issues in the later action.

Commissioner of Internal Revenue v. Sunnen

Instant Facts: The Commissioner of Internal Revenue (P) sought to declare payments from a patent contract assigned to Sunnen's (D) wife as income to him, although a court had previously determined that they were not.

Black Letter Rule: An intervening change of law or circumstances may render the doctrine of collateral estoppel inapplicable to a subsequent determination of identical issues of law and fact.

Halpern v. Schwartz

Instant Facts: After a court determined that Halpern (D) transferred property to avoid creditors, Schwartz (P) moved for summary judgment in the bankruptcy proceeding based on the court's findings.

Black Letter Rule: Although an issue was fully litigated and a finding on the issue was made in the prior litigation, the prior judgment will not foreclose reconsideration of the same issue if that issue was not necessary to the rendering of the prior judgment and hence was incidental, collateral, or immaterial to that judgment.

Taylor v. Sturgell

Instant Facts: After on antique aircraft enthusiast's Freedom of Information lawsuit proved unsuccessful, Taylor (P), a friend and fellow enthusiast, brought suit seeking the same information, and the court similarly denied his request based on the judgment in the first case; Taylor (P) appealed.

Black Letter Rule: The rule against nonparty preclusion is subject only to certain recognized exceptions: (1) a nonparty may agree to be bound by a judgment, (2) certain substantive relationships may justify preclusion (e.g., privity), (3) a nonparty's interests may have been adequately represented in the prior litigation (e.g., class actions and suits by trustees or guardians), (4) a nonparty may have assumed control over the earlier lawsuit, (5) a nonparty may have colluded to avoid the preclusive effect of an earlier judgment by litigating through a proxy, or (6) special statutory schemes (such as bankruptcy) may apply.

Parklane Hosiery Co. v. Shore

Instant Facts: Shore (P) sued Parklane Hosiery Co. (D) for issuing an illegal proxy statement in connection with a merger.

Black Letter Rule: When the plaintiff in a later suit could easily have joined in an earlier action, or when the application of offensive estoppel would be unfair to a defendant, the doctrine of offensive collateral estoppel does not apply.

Stephenson v. Dow Chemical Co.

Instant Facts: Vietnam veterans sued the manufacturers of Agent Orange many years after the approval of a class action settlement covering their injuries.

Black Letter Rule: Class action judgments bind only those absent class members whose interests are of the same class as the class members such that their interests have been adequately represented.

United States v. Mendoza

Instant Facts: Mendoza (P), a Filipino national living in the United States, filed a naturalization petition under a World War II statute more than thirty years after its repeal.

Black Letter Rule: Nonmutual offensive collateral estoppel does not apply against the government in such a way as to preclude relitigation of issues of law determined by a federal district court.

Manego v. Orleans Board of Trade

(*License Applicant*) v. (*Private Organization*)

773 F.2d 1 (1st Cir. 1985)

A TRANSACTIONAL APPROACH DETERMINING WHETHER THE UNDERLYING FACTS ARE THE SAME IN TWO SEPARATE ACTIONS

■ **INSTANT FACTS** After Manego (P) lost his suit against the defendants for civil rights violations, he filed a subsequent action alleging antitrust violations arising out of the same facts.

■ **BLACK LETTER RULE** Under the doctrine of res judicata, a final judgment on the merits precludes parties or their privies from relitigating issues that were or could have been raised in that action.

■ **PROCEDURAL BASIS**

On appeal to review a decision of a federal district court granting summary judgment to the defendants.

■ **FACTS**

Following a mortgage foreclosure, the Cape Cod Five Cents Savings Bank owned an ice skating rink used primarily by children. The Bank's vice-president, Willard, served as general manager. At that time, Willard was also the president of the Orleans Board of Trade (D), a private organization acting as a chamber of commerce. Intending to build a disco on a vacant lot adjoining the rink, Manego (P) sought liquor and entertainment licenses from the Orleans Board of Selectmen. Because it was feared that the disco would threaten the safety of the children using the rink, the Orleans Board of Trade (D) voted to oppose the disco. Thereafter, the Orleans Board of Selectmen held a public hearing on Manego's (P) application for a liquor license, which drew considerable public disapproval. At the hearing, Willard announced the Board of Trade's (D) opposition to the disco. After the Selectmen denied the application, Manego (P) appealed the denial to the Board of Appeals. Willard wrote a letter to the Board of Appeals asserting the bank's disapproval of the disco because of its safety concerns. The Board of Appeals denied the appeal. At the Board of Trade's (D) monthly meeting shortly thereafter, the denial of the liquor license and a hearing scheduled for the following day on Manego's (P) amusement license were discussed. After that hearing, the Selectmen denied Manego's (P) amusement license application as well. The Orleans Board of Appeals, however, granted Manego (P) a permit to build the disco. The bank then filed suit in a state court challenging the issuance of the building permit. The bank dismissed its suit after the rink was sold while the suit was pending.

At the time of the sale, the rink's entertainment license had expired and no renewal was sought until after the sale was completed. Because the license had lapsed, the Selectmen treated the application as a request for a new license, and a public hearing was held. Because changes to the rink attracted an older crowd, the application sought a broader license than previously granted for the rink. Citing the rink's status as the only local skating establishment and its safe and "noncorrupting" environment for young people, the Selectmen granted the license.

Manego (P) filed suit in federal court against the Selectmen, the bank, and Willard, alleging they conspired to deny him his licenses because of his race in violation of federal and state laws. After several counts were dismissed for failure to state a claim, the district court granted summary judgment against Manego (P) on the remaining claims because Manego (P) had failed to conduct the necessary discovery to support his position with sufficient evidence to create a genuine issue of material fact. The First Circuit Court of Appeals affirmed, holding that the fact that the Board of Trade (D) unanimously voted to oppose the license does not permit the inference of a conspiracy given the Selectmen's rationale for its denial.

Thereafter, Manego (P) filed a second suit against the bank, Willard, and the Board of Trade (D), alleging violations of the federal Sherman Antitrust Act. This time, Manego (P) offered depositions and other information obtained through discovery indicating that Willard simultaneously served as an officer of the bank, the rink's general manager, and the president of the Board of Trade (D); that members of the Board of Trade (D) also served on the Board of Selectmen; that the Board of Trade (D) was present at the hearing before the Selectmen; that the Selectmen granted the rink's new application for a license; and that the bank challenged Manego's (P) building permit in court until it no longer had an interest in the rink. This interest, Manego (P) alleged, was the motivation for the Board of Trade's (D) actions. The defendants moved for summary judgment on the basis of res judicata. The district court granted the motion for summary judgment filed by the bank and Willard because the facts forming the basis for Manego's (P) antitrust claim were the same as those supporting his earlier civil rights action. On the Board of Trade's (D) motion, the court granted summary judgment because, although res judicata did not apply, there was no genuine issue of material fact supporting the Board of Trade's (D) liability.

■ **ISSUE**

After dismissal of a plaintiff's cause of action, may the plaintiff bring a subsequent action on a different legal theory based on the same transaction from which the first claim arose?

■ **DECISION AND RATIONALE**

(Bownes, J.) No. Under the doctrine of res judicata, "a final judgment on the merits of an action precludes parties or their privies from relitigating issues that were or could have been raised in that action." Necessarily, the subsequent action must involve the same cause of action or claim. Under Restatement (Second) of Judgments § 24, which the court adopts, a transactional definition establishes that "[w]hen a valid or final judgment rendered in an action extinguishes the plaintiff's claim pursuant to the rules of merger or bar ... , the claim extinguished includes all rights of the plaintiff to remedies against the defendant with respect to all or any part of the transaction, or series of connected transactions, out of which the action arose." Where the facts involved "are related in time, space, origin, or motivation, ... form a convenient trial unit, and ... their treatment as a unit conforms to the parties' expectations or business understanding or usage," a single transaction exists. Here, the fact that Manego (P) alleged different legal theories in his two actions does not create separate transactions. Nor is it material that different defendants were named in the two actions. Willard's common involvement with both defendants indicates the facts involve the same transaction.

Similarly, the omission of the bank's intent to offer live music and dancing at the rink does not create a separate transaction. While res judicata will not generally apply where facts are unavailable through the discovery process, Manego (P) failed to reasonably take advantage of discovery to uncover the bank's entertainment intentions. This failure cannot be the basis for establishing separate transactions. While a failure to assert different facts that may be possible and convenient to assert in a single proceeding does not bar a plaintiff from later asserting those facts in a subsequent action, a plaintiff must assert all claims when the underlying facts are the same for all. Here, the two causes of action rely on the same underlying actions of the bank and Willard; only their alleged motive differs. Whether Manego (P) claims the action resulted in a restraint of trade or racial discrimination, the facts giving rise to both actions are the same. Accordingly, Manego (P) was required to litigate both claims in the same action and is barred by res judicata from pursuing them separately.

As for the Board of Trade (D), the court's decision that res judicata does not apply but that Manego (P) failed to demonstrate a genuine issue of material fact to avoid application of a legal exception to the defendant's liability was appropriate. Affirmed.

Analysis:

The transactional approach of the Restatement (Second) of Judgments broadens the application of res judicata beyond the specific cause of action asserted to reach all causes of action that could have been asserted under a specific set of facts. This approach was brought on by the change in the Federal Rules of Civil Procedure to enable plaintiffs to assert all claims arising out of common facts in a single action by original or supplemental jurisdiction.

■ CASE VOCABULARY

RES JUDICATA: An issue that has been definitively settled by judicial decision; an affirmative defense barring the same parties from litigating a second lawsuit on the same claim, or any other claim arising from the same transaction or series of transactions and that could have been—but was not—raised in the first suit.

Federated Department Stores, Inc. v. Moitie

(*Department Store*) v. (*Retail Consumer*)

452 U.S. 394, 101 S.Ct. 2424, 69 L.Ed.2d 103 (1981)

A CHANGE IN THE LAW DOES NOT REVIVE A FINAL JUDGMENT

■ **INSTANT FACTS** After failing to appeal adverse judgments against them, Moitie (P) and Brown filed subsequent state court actions under state anti-trust laws.

■ **BLACK LETTER RULE** Res judicata bars relitigation of a final adjudication on the merits and is not affected by the fact that the judgment may have been wrong or rested on a legal principle subsequently overruled in another case.

■ PROCEDURAL BASIS

Certiorari to review a decision of the Ninth Circuit Court of Appeals reversing a federal court's dismissal of the plaintiffs' actions on res judicata grounds.

■ FACTS

Seven consumers, including Moitie (P) and Brown, filed separate class action suits in Northern California against Federated Department Stores, Inc. (D), alleging illegal price fixing. Moitie (P) filed her suit in California state court, which was subsequently removed to federal court and consolidated with the other six actions, including Brown's. The district court dismissed all seven actions in their entirety because, under the law, consumers had no standing to sue without damage to their "business or property" under federal anti-trust statutes. Five of the plaintiffs appealed the decision to the Ninth Circuit, which reversed following a subsequent United States Supreme Court decision establishing the consumers' standing to sue. Rather than appealing the adverse judgments against them, Moitie (P) and Brown filed separate actions in California state court relying on California state law. Federated (D) again removed the cases to federal court, which refused to remand, citing the "essentially federal" character of the claims. The federal court dismissed the claims on the basis of res judicata. On appeal, the Ninth Circuit reversed, refusing to apply res judicata on public policy grounds.

■ ISSUE

Does res judicata bar relitigation of an unappealed adverse judgment where other plaintiffs in similar actions against common defendants successfully appealed the judgments against them?

■ DECISION AND RATIONALE

(Rehnquist, J.) Yes. Res judicata bars relitigation of a final adjudication on the merits and is not affected "by the fact that the judgment may have been wrong or rested on a legal principle subsequently overruled in another case." Instead, errors in a court's judgment must be corrected only by a direct attack to the appropriate court of appeals. Parties may not seek a windfall by enforcing a subsequent reversal of a case in which the party has no interest after the party has made a calculated decision to forgo direct appeal in favor of other tactical decisions.

Enforcement of res judicata in this instance will cause no grave injustice to the plaintiffs when the law is applied even-handedly. Principles of res judicata have been consistently enforced for many years and further the public policies of bringing cases to a final determination to avoid overcrowding of court dockets and ensuring the litigants the peace of mind that they will not be called to face the issues presented in the future. Although the first actions relied solely on federal law and the second complaints allege state-law claims not addressed by the first judgments, it is necessary only to determine that the earlier judgments foreclose the plaintiffs' suits on federal law claims. Reversed and remanded.

■ CONCURRENCE

(Blackmun, J.) While there may be cases in which res judicata should give way to simple justice and public policy, this is not one of them. In an appropriate case, equity may require that an adverse litigant have the opportunity to raise issues incorrectly determined in a prior judgment. Here, however, the plaintiffs made the intentional choice to file a subsequent state court action rather than appealing the judgments against them. When, as here, the litigation is complex, res judicata ensures the matter is decided in a single proceeding rather than risking "break-away" litigation. Contrary to the majority's decision, however, the earlier judgments determining the plaintiffs' federal claims serve as res judicata against the plaintiffs' subsequent state-law claims. Res judicata bars not only claims that were actually raised in an initial suit, but those claims that could have been raised as well. Because the plaintiffs' state-law suits are essentially federal claims in disguise, the plaintiffs could have raised their state-law claims in the initial suit. Despite their failure to do so, res judicata precludes litigation of those claims.

■ DISSENT

(Brennan, J.) The case should have been remanded to state court upon the plaintiffs' request. The plaintiffs are free to choose whether to pursue claims under federal or state law, and since federal law did not preempt the state law claims, the matter involves no triable federal issue to establish federal question jurisdiction.

Analysis:

The Court's decision establishes that a litigant with claims of a federal character may not avoid federal jurisdiction merely by asserting them under state law in state court. Critics, however, point to issues of comity and federalism and suggest that a plaintiff is free to assert its rights under any law available. If the plaintiff, therefore, asserts a valid claim under state law, it must be allowed to proceed distinct from any federal claims. With supplemental jurisdiction, however, res judicata would bar any later claims arising out of the same facts, whether based on state or federal grounds.

■ CASE VOCABULARY

REMAND: To send (a case or claim) back to the court or tribunal from which it came for some further action.

REMOVAL: The transfer of an action from state to federal court.

Rinehart v. Locke

(Alleged Victim) v. *(Police Detective)*

454 F.2d 313 (7th Cir. 1971)

FAILING TO APPEAL THE DISMISSAL OF A CLAIM EXTINGUISHES THE SUIT

■ **INSTANT FACTS** Rinehart (P) filed a complaint against Locke (D) and others one year after a nearly identical complaint had been dismissed by the district court.

■ **BLACK LETTER RULE** Unless otherwise provided, a court order dismissing a complaint for failure to state a claim is an adjudication on the merits, which bars any subsequent litigation on the issue.

■ **PROCEDURAL BASIS**

On appeal to review a decision of a federal district court dismissing the plaintiff's complaint on res judicata grounds.

■ **FACTS**

In 1964, Locke (D) and other private detectives falsely reported Rinehart (P) for impersonating a police officer. Rinehart (P) was arrested without a warrant and falsely charged with the unlawful use of a weapon and resisting arrest. He was convicted and imprisoned, but the conviction was overturned in 1967. In 1969, the plaintiff filed a complaint in federal court for damages resulting from the unconstitutional arrest. The court dismissed the complaint for failure to state a claim because the plaintiff failed to allege an absence of probable cause, and the court denied leave to amend the complaint. The plaintiff did not appeal the dismissal. Instead, the plaintiff filed a subsequent complaint in 1970, alleging constitutional violations and an absence of probable cause. The defendants asserted that the issue was barred as res judicata by the 1969 dismissal order. The district court agreed and dismissed the complaint.

■ **ISSUE**

Does the dismissal of the plaintiff's complaint for failure to state a claim bar a subsequent complaint on similar grounds that validly states the claim as amended?

■ **DECISION AND RATIONALE**

(Fairchild, J.) Yes. Under Federal Rule of Civil Procedure 41(b), "[u]nless the court in its order for dismissal otherwise specifies, a dismissal . . . , other than a dismissal for lack of jurisdiction, for improper venue, or for failure to join a party under rule 19, operates as an adjudication on the merits." The rule demonstrates that unless a district court specifically provides that a dismissal is without prejudice to the plaintiff's rights to refile the action, the order is an adjudication on the merits, which bars the plaintiff from relitigating the action in a subsequent proceeding. A plaintiff facing dismissal bears the burden of convincing the judge to enter dismissal without prejudice to his rights. If unsuccessful, his available avenue of relief is a direct appeal. Because the 1969 order did not indicate otherwise, it was an adjudication on the merits barring the plaintiff's 1970 complaint. Affirmed.

Analysis:

The preclusive effect of a 12(b)(6) dismissal as a judgment on the merits seems harsh under some circumstances. In situations such as *Rinehart*, where the complaint was insufficient for failure to allege an element of the offense, dismissal seems more severe than when a complaint is correctly drafted but fails to state a claim. In many cases, the court will grant the plaintiff leave to amend his or her complaint, but in this instance that avenue of relief was not available.

■ CASE VOCABULARY

MERITS: The elements or grounds of a claim or defense; the substantive considerations to be taken into account in deciding a case, as opposed to extraneous or technical points, especially of procedure.

Marrese v. American Academy of Orthopedic Surgeons

(Orthopedic Surgeon) v. *(Professional Association)*

470 U.S. 373, 105 S.Ct. 1327, 84 L.Ed.2d 274 (1985)

FEDERAL COURTS LOOK TO STATE LAW TO DETERMINE THE PRECLUSIVE EFFECT OF A STATE COURT JUDGMENT

■ **INSTANT FACTS** After Marrese's (P) state-law suit was dismissed, he filed a subsequent action in federal court under federal antitrust law.

■ **BLACK LETTER RULE** In determining the preclusive effect of a state court judgment on subsequent federal litigation, a federal court must look to the law of the state to determine whether the judgment would preclude relitigation in state courts.

■ **PROCEDURAL BASIS**

Certiorari to review a decision of the Seventh Circuit Court of Appeals affirming a dismissal by a federal district court.

■ **FACTS**

Marrese (P) and another orthopedic surgeon sued the American Academy of Orthopedic Surgeons (D) in Illinois state court alleging violations of their common law associational rights under state law when their applications for membership were summarily dismissed without a hearing. No state antitrust claims were alleged. When the state court dismissed the complaints for failure to state a claim upon which relief could be granted, the plaintiffs filed suit in federal court under federal antitrust law. The district court dismissed the complaint on the basis of res judicata, holding that the federal suit was barred by the dismissal of the state action. On appeal, the Seventh Circuit Court of Appeals affirmed, recognizing that state antitrust law was substantially similar to federal antitrust law.

■ **ISSUE**

May a state court judgment have a preclusive effect on a federal antitrust claim that could not have been raised in the state proceeding?

■ **DECISION AND RATIONALE**

(O'Connor, J.) Yes. Under 28 U.S.C. § 1738, state judgments "shall have the same full faith and credit in every court in the United States . . . as they have by law or usage in the courts of such State . . . from which they are taken." Accordingly, in determining the preclusive effect of a state court judgment, a federal court must look to the law of the state to determine whether the judgment would preclude relitigation in state courts. Although federal antitrust claims are within the exclusive jurisdiction of the federal courts, the law of the state applies and may establish the preclusive effect of the state judgment on a subsequent federal complaint. When a state judgment would bar relitigation of an action in state court, it implicitly bars relitigation in federal court as well, even though the statutory claim could not fall within the state court's jurisdiction. Only when a later statute expressly or implicitly repeals the federal statute, or some other exception to § 1738 exists, will relitigation be appropriate.

As with all matters involving exclusive federal jurisdiction, the state court will have no occasion to actually consider a plaintiff's federal claims. Nonetheless, a federal court should look at the general preclusive effect of the state court judgment on future litigation. Generally, however, if "[t]he plaintiff was unable to rely on a certain theory of the case or to seek a certain remedy because of the limitations on the subject matter jurisdiction of the courts," a state court judgment will not bar litigation of the issue in the federal courts. Only after the preclusive effect of the judgment under state law has been established may a federal court determine whether an exception to § 1738 exists to permit the federal litigation to proceed. Because the Seventh Circuit failed to apply this approach to determine whether Illinois law establishes the preclusive effect of the state court judgment, the matter must be remanded for further proceedings.

Because the American justice system is separated into state and federal courts, matters of comity and federalism require a federal court to respect the States' ability to determine the preclusive effect of judgments handed down by their courts. While the burden on the court system may be greater by requiring a litigant to bring his claims initially in the court of most general jurisdiction, litigants have the right to choose the court in which they bring their claims. Because of this respect for the state courts' authority, a federally created exception to § 1738 that an action brought initially in state court forgoes litigation in federal court on separate federal grounds that could not have been raised in the state court is improper. Reversed and remanded.

■ CONCURRENCE

(Burger, C.J.) While generally a federal court must respect the preclusive effect of a state court judgment under state law, when the plaintiff had available adequate state-law theories substantially identical to federal theories later asserted in a federal action, the federal claims should be barred as res judicata. In such circumstances, a plaintiff has a "full and fair opportunity" to raise the claims, whether in state or federal court, and should be barred from asserting them after failing to do so in the initial state court action.

It is likely that state law may not sufficiently determine the preclusive effects of a judgment such as that at issue here. Because the federal interests of eliminating harassment of defendants in subsequent litigation and avoiding the burden imposed upon the federal courts are strong, a federal rule barring those claims in which a plaintiff had a "full and fair opportunity" to litigate would be appropriate, regardless of the outcome under state law.

Analysis:

Although the Court's decision suggests that state courts have the power to preclude federal proceedings based on the same transaction as that presented in the state proceeding, that is not likely the case when the federal claims involves exclusive federal jurisdiction. In many states, one key consideration for the application of res judicata is the litigants' opportunity to present their claims or defenses in an earlier proceeding. When the federal claims could not have been considered by the state court, therefore, res judicata would not bar the subsequent federal action.

■ CASE VOCABULARY

EXCLUSIVE JURISDICTION: A court's power to adjudicate an action or class of actions to the exclusion of all other courts.

Semtek International, Inc. v. Lockheed Martin Corp.

(Plaintiff) v. *(Defendant)*

531 U.S. 497, 121 S.Ct. 1021, 149 L.Ed.2d 32 (2001)

A CLAIM DISMISSED AS TIME–BARRED MAY BE BROUGHT IN ANOTHER JURISDICTION WITH A LONGER STATUTORY PERIOD

■ **INSTANT FACTS** After a California federal court dismissed the plaintiff's action on the basis of the state statute of limitations, a Maryland state court dismissed a subsequent suit brought by the plaintiff on the same grounds.

■ **BLACK LETTER RULE** The claim-preclusive effect of a judgment on the merits in a federal diversity action is governed by the law of the state in which the federal court sits.

■ **PROCEDURAL BASIS**

Certiorari to review a decision of the Maryland Court of Special Appeals affirming a trial court dismissal of the plaintiff's action.

■ **FACTS**

Semtek International, Inc. (P) sued Lockheed Martin Corp. (D) in California state court for breach of contract and various torts. Lockheed Martin (D) removed the case to California federal court on the basis of diversity of citizenship and successfully moved for dismissal of the action with prejudice on the merits as barred by the state-law statute of limitations. Thereafter, Semtek (P) refiled its case against Lockheed Martin (D) in Maryland state court within the Maryland statute of limitations. On the defendant's motion, the Maryland court dismissed the complaint on the basis of res judicata, reasoning that the decision of the California federal court was on the merits and precluded the subsequent suit. After a Maryland court of appeals affirmed, Semtek (P) sought a writ of certiorari.

■ **ISSUE**

Is the claim-preclusive effect of a federal judgment dismissing a diversity action on statute-of-limitations grounds determined by the law of the state in which the federal court sits?

■ **DECISION AND RATIONALE**

(Scalia, J.) Yes. Under Federal Rule of Civil Procedure 41(b), a court order dismissing a plaintiff's complaint "operates as an adjudication on the merits" unless otherwise specified. While an adjudication on the merits generally has a claim-preclusive effect on the relitigation of those claims, not all adjudications on the merits are barred by res judicata. "On the merits" is generally understood as a determination of the substance of the claim. While traditionally judgments on the merits have invoked the doctrines of res judicata and claim preclusion, no longer do all adjudications on the merits have a claim-preclusive effect under Rule 41(b). In this instance, Rule 41(b) governs the internal procedures of the California federal court, declaring its decision on the merits by default. To hold this procedural declaration binding upon the plaintiff's substantive state-law rights to pursue its claims in another jurisdiction, though not in California, would violate the principles of the Rules Enabling Act, which specifically preserves a party's substantive rights. Further, any claim-preclusive effect of the federal court judgment on the plaintiff's state-law rights would give rise to conflicting decisions based on the forum in which the decision is rendered. For instance, under California state law, a party may not recover a desired remedy after the expiration of the state statute of limitations. Yet, the claims remain viable for consideration in an appropriate foreign jurisdiction. If a defendant in a diversity action could defeat the law of the state by merely removing the action to federal court for a decision on the merits under state law, the result of the action would be determined not by the law of the state, but by the forum in which the law is applied. Accordingly, the reasonable understanding of the default language of Rule 41(b) is that "adjudication on the merits" is the opposite of "dismissal without prejudice" as discussed in Rule 41(a). Although a dismissal with prejudice may, under certain circumstances, bar a party from relitigating his claims in other courts, the default provisions of Rule 41(b) should be construed only to preclude relitigation of the claims in the same court in which the adjudication on the merits was decided. Rule 41(b) does not determine the claim-preclusive effect of the California federal court judgment in the Maryland state court.

Since Rule 41(b) does not control the preclusive effect of the federal court judgment, the Court must fashion a rule to be applied. In *Dupasseur v. Rochereau*, the Court applied a since-repealed statute to determine that the claim-preclusive effect of a federal diversity judgment is properly determined by the law of the state in which the federal court sits. Although *Dupasseur* does not apply to this matter given its reliance upon a repealed statute, its reasoning continues to be appropriate in diversity actions. Because the substantive rights involved in a federal diversity action are governed by state law, the claim-preclusive effect of a federal court judgment applying state law should similarly be governed by state law. As mentioned, any uniform federal rule would create forum shopping and promote removal, when available, for a tactical advantage. Only when federal interests directly conflict with the state-law interests will the federal interests prevail.

Here, because the California federal court granted dismissal on the merits only because state law so required, California state law governs the issue of claim preclusion. Because California does not forbid the plaintiff from bringing its claims in another jurisdiction, the Maryland court erred in dismissing the plaintiff's claims. Reversed and remanded.

Analysis:

Semtek is controversial, in part, because it endeavors to apply state procedural law in a federal diversity case. Under *Erie v. Tompkins* and its progeny, a federal court sitting in diversity generally applies the substantive law of the state in which the action arose and the procedural rules of the federal court, most notably the Federal Rules of Civil Procedure. The problem encountered in *Semtek*, however, is that the Federal Rules of Civil Procedure fail to discuss the claim-preclusive effect of federal diversity judgments. With no procedural rule to enforce, the Court created federal common law to resolve the issue.

■ CASE VOCABULARY

CLAIM PRECLUSION: "[T]he principal distinction between claim preclusion and issue preclusion is . . . that the former forecloses litigation of matters that have never been litigated. This makes it important to know the dimensions of the 'claim' that is foreclosed by bringing the first action, but unfortunately no precise definition is possible." Charles Alan Wright, *The Law of Federal Courts* § 100A, at 723 (5th ed. 1994).

STATUTE OF LIMITATIONS: A law that bars claims after a specified period; specifically, a statute establishing a time limit for suing in a civil case, based on the date when the claim accrued (as when the injury occurred or was discovered). The purpose of such a statute is to require diligent prosecution of known claims, thereby providing finality and predictability in legal affairs and ensuring that claims will be resolved while evidence is reasonably available and fresh.

Little v. Blue Goose Motor Coach Co.

(Injured Motorist's Widow) v. *(Bus Owner)*
346 Ill. 266, 178 N.E. 496 (1931)

A FINDING OF NEGLIGENCE PRECLUDES RELITIGATION OF THAT ISSUE IN A SUBSEQUENT
ACTION

■ **INSTANT FACTS** After Blue Goose Motor Coach Co. (D) obtained a verdict against Dr. Little for property damage resulting from his negligence, Little (P) obtained a verdict against Blue Goose (D) for personal injuries resulting from its negligence.

■ **BLACK LETTER RULE** Estoppel by verdict arises when a material fact in any litigation has been determined in a former suit between the same parties or between parties with whom the parties to the subsequent suit are in privity, when the fact was also material to the issue

---

■ **PROCEDURAL BASIS**

On appeal to review a decision of the Illinois Appellate Court reversing a city court verdict for the plaintiff.

■ **FACTS**

Blue Goose Motor Coach Co. (D) initially sued Dr. Little before a justice of the peace for damages caused to its passenger bus as a result of a collision between the bus and Dr. Little's vehicle. The justice of the peace awarded judgment to Blue Goose (D) for the amount of its property damage, which was appealed to the county court. While the case was pending, however, Dr. Little filed suit against Blue Goose (D) in city court for personal injuries suffered in the collision. After Little died and his widow (P) succeeded him, Blue Goose (D) claimed the suit was estopped by the earlier verdict, which resulted from a presentation of witnesses and evidence to determine the plaintiff's fault. The court rejected the defense and ultimately awarded Little (P) judgment on her claim. The Illinois Appellate Court reversed, finding that the earlier proceeding had determined that Dr. Little was negligent in causing the collision.

■ **ISSUE**

Is a finding of negligence in an earlier property damage suit binding upon the parties or those in privity with the parties in a subsequent proceeding on a different cause of action?

■ **DECISION AND RATIONALE**

(Per curiam) Yes. "Estoppel by verdict arises when a material fact in any litigation has been determined in a former suit between the same parties or between parties with whom the parties to the subsequent suit are in privity, where the fact was also material to the issue." The Appellate Court determined that the justice of the peace had established Dr. Little's negligence in the collision, which was the same issue presented before the city court. When the decision of the justice of the peace became final, it was binding not only on Dr. Little, but on his widow (P), who stood in privity with him. Since Dr. Little was estopped to relitigate the issue in the same or subsequent proceeding, so too is his widow (P), whether the subsequent proceeding involved a different cause of action or not. The justice of the peace's decision that Dr. Little's negligence was the cause of the collision applies to both the widow's (P) wrongful death and claims and her willful and wanton conduct claims, each of which rely upon the defendant's negligence as a prerequisite for recovery. Affirmed.

Analysis:

This early case predates the adoption of the transactional approach to determining the scope of the litigation suggested in the Restatement (Second) of Judgments. Yet, the court's reasoning suggests a similar approach. It was the issue of negligence arising from the action that guided the court's decision, rather than the legal theories involved or the parties asserting them. Once the issue of negligence was determined in the first action, all other claims of negligence are barred.

■ CASE VOCABULARY

ESTOPPEL: A bar that prevents one from asserting a claim or right that contradicts what one has said or done before or what has been legally established as true; a bar that prevents relitigation of issues.

PRIVITY: A connection or relationship between two parties, each having a legally recognized interest in the same subject matter (such as a transaction, proceeding, or piece of property); mutuality of interests.

Hardy v. Johns–Manville Sales Corp.

(Injured Plaintiff) v. *(Asbestos Manufacturer)*

681 F.2d 334 (5th Cir. 1982)

NOT ALL ASBESTOS MAKERS ARE LIABLE IN EVERY ASBESTOS SUIT

■ **INSTANT FACTS** Hardy (P) and other plaintiffs sued Johns–Manville Sales Corp. (D) and eighteen other asbestos manufacturers, sellers, and distributors for injuries sustained due to defendants' alleged breach of the duty to warn of the harmful effects of asbestos exposure.

■ **BLACK LETTER RULE** Unless a subsequent suit shares common issues of fact or law with a prior suit, a judgment of the prior suit does not bar litigation of related issues in the later action.

■ **PROCEDURAL BASIS**

Appeal from a trial court judgment for the plaintiff.

■ **FACTS**

In a first suit, several plaintiffs sued six asbestos manufacturers for personal injuries caused by the manufacturers' breach of the duty to warn of the health risks associated with asbestos exposure. The plaintiffs obtained a judgment finding the six defendants breached their duty to warn. In a subsequent suit, Hardy (P) and other plaintiffs not involved in the earlier suit sued the six manufacturers and thirteen others for similar damages, alleging negligence, breach of implied warranty, and strict liability. The trial court concluded that the doctrine of issue preclusion barred all defendants from denying the plaintiffs' claims.

■ **ISSUE**

Does a prior judgment entered on related issues of fact and law collaterally estop a defendant in a subsequent suit from asserting a defense when the prior judgment may have been based on different issues than those presented in the subsequent action?

■ **DECISION AND RATIONALE**

(Gee, Cir. J.) No. In the earlier suit, the jury determined that the defendants there had failed to sufficiently warn the plaintiffs of the dangers associated with its asbestos products, but issues of strict liability were never formally presented to the jury in the court's instructions. The defendants claim that because the jury was never instructed on strict liability, the prior judgment has no preclusive effect against the defendants in the instant suit.

The jury's verdict in the first suit does not preclude the defendants' asserted defenses because it was sufficiently ambiguous. Although the jury determined that the defendants had a duty to warn, it failed to establish when that duty arose. Moreover, the verdict is unclear whether any warnings given were appropriate and does not address plaintiffs exposed to asbestos well after the warnings were given. Strict liability for failure to warn requires the question of the manufacturer's reasonable knowledge of the dangers. Accordingly, the failure to warn does not determine that the product was so unreasonably dangerous as to require warnings. Furthermore, the plaintiffs' injuries in the instant matters occurred in different periods than those suffered in the first suit. The defendants' knowledge may be different in each period and the hazardous materials at issue may be different. Collateral estoppel applies only to those issues of fact or law necessarily decided by the prior verdict. Since it is uncertain whether the first jury decided that case on the questions of fact and law presented in the instant case, collateral estoppel is inapplicable. Reversed.

Analysis:

The court's decision places the burdens on trial courts not only to determine *what* an earlier jury determined, but *why*. However, jurors often weigh many considerations in reaching a verdict, some of which may not merit mention in its ultimate verdict. While the primary issues of a case will often be established, the court faces a difficult burden when attempting to decipher all of the nuances of an earlier suit.

■ CASE VOCABULARY

COLLATERAL ESTOPPEL: An affirmative defense barring a party from relitigating an issue determined against that party in an earlier action, even if the second action differs significantly from the first one.

OFFENSIVE COLLATERAL ESTOPPEL: Estoppel asserted by a plaintiff to prevent a defendant from relitigating an issue previously decided against the defendant and for another plaintiff.

Commissioner of Internal Revenue v. Sunnen

(Tax Authority) v. *(Taxpayer)*

333 U.S. 591, 68 S.Ct. 715, 92 L.Ed. 898 (1948)

COLLATERAL ESTOPPEL DOES NOT VEST RIGHTS THAT WOULD BE UNAVAILABLE UNDER CURRENT LAW

■ **INSTANT FACTS** The Commissioner of Internal Revenue (P) sought to declare payments from a patent contract assigned to Sunnen's (D) wife as income to him, although a court had previously determined that they were not.

■ **BLACK LETTER RULE** An intervening change of law or circumstances may render the doctrine of collateral estoppel inapplicable to a subsequent determination of identical issues of law and fact.

■ **PROCEDURAL BASIS**

Certiorari to review a decision of the United States Tax Court.

■ **FACTS**

In 1928, Sunnen (D) assigned the rights under a patent contract to his wife, who received payments under the contract over the next three years. In 1935, the Board of Tax Appeals determined that the payments received by the wife were not taxable to Sunnen (D). Nonetheless, the Commissioner of Internal Revenue (P) later brought suit against Sunnen (D) to tax him on payments received by the wife after 1935 under the same contract and other contracts patterned after the 1928 contract. The Tax Court determined that the payments made on the other contracts were taxable to Sunnen (D), relying on a series of Supreme Court decisions in 1940, but held that the earlier decision was res judicata as to any income from the 1928 contract.

■ **ISSUE**

Does an intervening change of law or circumstances render the doctrine of collateral estoppel inapplicable to a subsequent determination on identical issues of law and fact that were previously determined?

■ **DECISION AND RATIONALE**

(Murphy, J.) Yes. Generally, each tax year stands on its own concerning the taxpayer's liability to pay taxes on income generated. A determination of a taxpayer's status in one year is res judicata only as it applies to his or her liability in that year, since tax liability in subsequent years is generally not the issue determined in such disputes. However, in the income tax arena, a decision on tax liability that is capable of repetition without substantial variation in subsequent years will generally preclude a subsequent relitigation of the taxpayer's liability to avoid an inequitable impact on the taxpayer. When the circumstances under which the initial judgment was decided change, however, the preclusive effect of the judgment must be examined. To permit a taxpayer who has obtained a judicial determination under different circumstances would place the taxpayer on different footing from others similarly situated whose liability arose after the circumstances have changed, leading to inequalities in the administration of tax laws. Collateral estoppel serves to avoid repetitious lawsuits over the same disputes, but cannot be used to vest rights that would no longer be afforded to others in the taxpayer's situation.

Here, the Tax Court's conclusion that the other contracts patterned after the 1928 contract were not affected by the initial judgment was correct. Even though those contracts are identical to the 1928 contract in all material respects, liability under those contracts was not at issue in the initial determination. Regarding the issue of subsequent liability for payments received under the 1928 contract, however, there is complete identity of issues, facts, and parties as the prior determination. Since the initial determination, however, the legal landscape on tax liability has significantly changed such that Sunnen (D), as transferor of taxable income, would incur tax liability on the transfers. Because this change of law makes clear the errors of perpetuating the prior determination, collateral estoppel does not require the court to honor the prior judgment. Reversed in part.

Analysis:

The principle underlying the reasoning of the Court's decision is the equitable administration of the laws. Sunnen (D) should be afforded the benefit of the tax determination in 1928 for as long as the contract threatens to impose tax liability because to relitigate the issue against him would result in significant unfairness. On the other hand, should Sunnen (D) receive an extended benefit from the earlier tax determination to the exclusion of others similarly situated, different inequities would arise.

■ CASE VOCABULARY

COLLATERAL ESTOPPEL: An affirmative defense barring a party from relitigating an issue determined against that party in an earlier action, even if the second action differs significantly from the first one.

RES JUDICATA: An issue that has been definitively settled by judicial decision; an affirmative defense barring the same parties from litigating a second lawsuit on the same claim, or any other claim arising from the same transaction or series of transactions and that could have been—but was not—raised in the first suit.

Halpern v. Schwartz

(Bankruptcy Debtor) v. *(Bankruptcy Trustee)*
426 F.2d 102 (2d Cir. 1970)

AN ISSUE THAT IS NOT NECESSARILY DETERMINED IN A PRIOR JUDGMENT CAN BE RELITIGATED

■ **INSTANT FACTS** After a court determined that Halpern (D) transferred property to avoid creditors, Schwartz (P) moved for summary judgment in the bankruptcy proceeding based on the court's findings.

■ **BLACK LETTER RULE** Although an issue was fully litigated and a finding on the issue was made in the prior litigation, the prior judgment will not foreclose reconsideration of the same issue if that issue was not necessary to the rendering of the prior judgment and hence was incidental, collateral, or immaterial to that judgment.

■ **PROCEDURAL BASIS**

On appeal to review an order of the district court affirming a referee's decision granting summary judgment for Schwartz (P).

■ **FACTS**

Creditors filed an involuntary bankruptcy petition against Halpern (D), alleging she improperly transferred a bond and mortgage to her son to obstruct the creditors' claims, transferred the property as an insolvent without fair consideration, and made a preferential payment on an antecedent debt. After trial, the bankruptcy court found she committed the three acts alleged and adjudged her bankrupt. The judgment was affirmed on appeal and referred to Schwartz (P), the bankruptcy trustee. Thereafter, Schwartz (P) opposed Halpern's (D) discharge from bankruptcy because she improperly transferred the bond and mortgage to her son to obstruct creditors, and moved for summary judgment because the court's judgment determined the issue and res judicata prohibited its relitigation. After a referee granted summary judgment, the district court affirmed.

■ **ISSUE**

When a prior judgment rested on several independent, alternative grounds, is that judgment conclusive as to the facts that were necessarily found in order to establish only one separate ground?

■ **DECISION AND RATIONALE**

(Smith, J.) No. A prerequisite finding for granting Schwartz's (P) motion for summary judgment is a determination that Halpern (D) transferred the bond and mortgage with the actual intent to defraud creditors. Of the three findings of the bankruptcy court, only the finding that she transferred property with the intent to hinder or delay creditors occasioned the issue of Halpern's (P) intent. This finding alone was the basis for the appeal court's decision that the issue of intent had been established.

"[A]lthough an issue was fully litigated and a finding on the issue was made in the prior litigation, the prior judgment will not foreclose reconsideration of the same issue if that issue was not necessary to the rendering of the prior judgment, and hence was incidental, collateral, or immaterial to that judgment." This is so because the issue may not have received full deliberation because it was not essential to the outcome of the judgment, and an inessential issue may not have received full attention by the litigants on appeal because more essential issues will ultimately affect the case's disposition.

When the issue is not essential to the judgment, neither party may challenge or defend the court's decision in that respect because its affirmance or reversal will not alter the lower court's judgment.

Here, the Bankruptcy Code infers intent when a transfer is made by an insolvent without fair consideration. Accordingly, once the bankruptcy court determined that Halpern (D) was insolvent and the transfer was without fair consideration, the necessary acts existed to support the court's order. So too did the court's decision that the transfer was preferential support its order. Once these findings were made, there was no need to scrutinize the evidence of Halpern's (D) intent at either the bankruptcy court or appellate court level. Sound judicial policy forbids a requirement that a litigant appeal all inessential issues, when other grounds exist to affirm the judgment against her, simply out of fear for the preclusive effects of the inessential findings in a later proceeding. Because alternative grounds existed to support the bankruptcy court's earlier decision, its finding of actual intent is not res judicata in a later proceeding on the issue. Reversed.

Analysis:

The Restatement (Second) of Judgments recognizes the principle of *Halpern v. Schwartz*. In comment (i) to § 27, the Restatement provides, "If a judgment of a court of first instance is based on determinations of two issues, either of which standing independently would be sufficient to support the result, the judgment is not conclusive with respect to either issue standing alone."

■ **CASE VOCABULARY**

DISCHARGE: The release of a debtor from monetary obligations upon adjudication of bankruptcy.

INSOLVENCY: The condition of being unable to pay debts as they fall due or in the usual course of business.

INTENT: The state of mind accompanying an act, especially a forbidden act.

INVOLUNTARY BANKRUPTCY: A bankruptcy proceeding initiated by creditors (usually three or more) to force the debtor to declare bankruptcy or be legally declared bankrupt.

Taylor v. Sturgell

(Antique Aircraft Enthusiast) v. *(FAA Administrator)*

533 U.S. 880, 128 S.Ct. 2161, 171 L.Ed.2d 155 (2008)

NONPARTIES ARE RARELY BOUND BY EARLIER JUDGMENTS IN SIMILAR CASES

Seriously?!? You climbed all the way up here to ask the same question your friend just asked?

stus.com

■ **INSTANT FACTS** After on antique aircraft enthusiast's Freedom of Information lawsuit proved unsuccessful, Taylor (P), a friend and fellow enthusiast, brought suit seeking the same information, and the court similarly denied his request based on the judgment in the first case; Taylor (P) appealed.

■ **BLACK LETTER RULE** The rule against non-party preclusion is subject only to certain recognized exceptions: (1) a nonparty may agree to be bound by a judgment, (2) certain substantive relationships may justify preclusion (e.g., privity), (3) a nonparty's interests may have been adequately represented in the prior litigation (e.g., class actions and suits by trustees or guardians), (4) a nonparty may have assumed control over the earlier lawsuit, (5) a nonparty may have colluded to avoid the preclusive effect of an earlier judgment by litigating through a proxy, or (6) special statutory schemes (such as bankruptcy) may apply.

■ **PROCEDURAL BASIS**

Certiorari to the United States Court of Appeals for the District of Columbia.

■ **FACTS**

Taylor (P), a vintage aircraft enthusiast, filed a lawsuit under the Freedom of Information Act, seeking documents relating to a vintage airplane. Herrick, a friend of Taylor's (P), had previously filed an unsuccessful suit seeking the same documents. The court denied Taylor's (P) request, concluding that Taylor's (P) interests had been virtually represented by Herrick, despite the fact that there was no evidence that Taylor (P) controlled, financed, participated in, or even had notice of Herrick's lawsuit.

Different federal circuit courts had applied different standards to determine whether a unity of interests existed such that a judgment in one case had preclusive effect in another. In this case, the Court of Appeals for the District of Columbia rejected the tests applied in other circuits and devised its own five-factor test. Under the D.C. test, the first two factors—identity of interest and adequacy of representation—were *necessary*, but not *sufficient*, for virtual representation. In addition, the court concluded, one of three additional factors must be established: either a close relationship between the present party and his or her putative representative, or substantial participation by the present party in the first case, or tactical maneuvering on the part of the present party to avoid preclusion by the prior judgment. Applying that test to Taylor's (P) case, the court concluded that the necessary conditions for "virtual representation" were met. Taylor (P) appealed, and the Supreme Court granted certiorari to resolve the disagreement among the circuits over the permissibility and scope of preclusion based on so-called virtual representation.

■ **ISSUE**

Did the District of Columbia Court of Appeals apply the correct test to determine whether Taylor's (P) lawsuit was precluded by the earlier judgment in his friend Herrick's case?

■ **DECISION AND RATIONALE**

(Ginsburg, J.) No. The rule against nonparty preclusion is subject only to certain recognized exceptions: (1) a nonparty may agree to be bound by a judgment, (2) certain substantive relationships may justify preclusion (e.g., privity), (3) a nonparty's interests may have been adequately represented in the prior litigation (e.g., class actions and suits by trustees or guardians), (4) a nonparty may have assumed control over the earlier lawsuit, (5) a nonparty may have colluded to avoid the preclusive effect of an earlier judgment by litigating through a proxy, or (6) special statutory schemes (such as bankruptcy) may apply. Beyond these established exceptions, some courts recognize a "virtual representation" exception. We find none of the reasons in support of such an exception persuasive.

First, we must once again emphasize the importance of the general rule that a litigant is not bound by a judgment to which he or she was not a party. Second, "adequate representation," to suffice as "virtual representation," requires that (1) the interests of the nonparty and her representative are aligned; and (2) either the party understood herself to be acting in a representative capacity, or the original court took care to protect the interest of the nonparty. Adequate representation sometimes also requires actual notice of the original suit to the persons alleged to have been represented. Third, a balancing approach to nonparty preclusion, like that applied by the appellate court, would create more headaches than it relieves. Preclusion doctrine is intended to reduce the courts' burden, not increase it. The doctrine of stare decisis already allows courts to swiftly dispose of repetitive lawsuits. Human tendency as well will generally prevent a litigant from bringing an identical claim to one that has already proven to be fruitless.

Turning to Taylor's (P) case, there is nothing in the record to suggest that Taylor (P) agreed to be bound by Herrick's litigation, that they have any legal relationship, that Taylor (P) controlled Herrick's lawsuit, or that Taylor (P) was adequately represented by Herrick. Nor did Herrick bring suit as a representative or agent of Taylor (P). As to the argument that Herrick and Taylor (P) have colluded to avoid the preclusive effect of the first judgment (or that Taylor (P) was the agent of Herrick), we have never enunciated a clear standard, but courts should be cautious before finding collusion. A remand is appropriate for further determination as to whether Taylor (P) was acting as Herrick's agent in bringing the second lawsuit—an issue on which the defendant will bear the burden of proof. Vacated and remanded.

Analysis:

Virtual representation generally refers to the bringing of an action on behalf of an unnamed party or parties, as in a class action, where a number of people have similar interests to the named party, and upon whom the court's judgment will be binding. It can also refer to representation by guardians ad litem or trustees, for instance, who represent the interests of others more than themselves. In the present case, the defendants argued that once Herrick's claims proved unsuccessful, he engaged his friend to try again on his behalf, essentially tricking the court into giving them another shot at the defendants. The court was unpersuaded that this case presented a proper scenario for application of an exception to the rule against nonparty preclusion, but it gave the defendants one more chance, on remand, to show that Taylor (P) and Herrick colluded to avoid the preclusive effect of the judgment in Herrick's case.

■ **CASE VOCABULARY**

ADEQUATE REPRESENTATION: A close alignment of interests between actual parties and potential parties in a lawsuit, so that the interests of potential parties are sufficiently protected by the actual parties. The concept of adequate representation is often used in procedural contexts. For example, if a case is to be certified as a class action, there must be adequate representation by the named plaintiffs of all the potential class members. And if a nonparty is to intervene in a lawsuit, there must not already be adequate representation of the nonparty by an existing party.

STARE DECISIS: [Latin, "to stand by things decided."] The doctrine of precedent, under which it is necessary for a court to follow earlier judicial decisions when the same points arise again in litigation.

VIRTUAL REPRESENTATION: A party's maintenance of an action on behalf of others with a similar interest, as a class representative does in a class action.

VIRTUAL–REPRESENTATION DOCTRINE: The principle that a judgment may bind a person who is not a party to the litigation if one of the parties is so closely aligned with the nonparty's interests that the nonparty has been adequately represented by the party in court. Under this doctrine, for instance, a judgment in a case naming only the husband as a party can be binding on his wife as well.

Parklane Hosiery Co. v. Shore

(Publicly Traded Corporation) v. *(Stockholder)*

439 U.S. 322, 99 S.Ct. 645, 58 L.Ed.2d 552 (1979)

OFFENSIVE COLLATERAL ESTOPPEL DIFFERS FROM DEFENSIVE COLLATERAL ESTOPPEL

■ **INSTANT FACTS** Shore (P) sued Parklane Hosiery Co. (D) for issuing an illegal proxy statement in connection with a merger.

■ **BLACK LETTER RULE** When the plaintiff in a later suit could easily have joined in an earlier action, or when the application of offensive estoppel would be unfair to a defendant, the doctrine of offensive collateral estoppel does not apply.

■ **PROCEDURAL BASIS**

Certiorari to review a Second Circuit Court of Appeals decision reversing a district court order denying the plaintiff's motion for summary judgment.

■ **FACTS**

Shore (P) sued Parklane Hosiery Co. (D) for issuing a materially false and misleading proxy statement in connection with a merger, in violation of federal securities laws, praying for damages, rescission of the merger, and costs. Thereafter, but before the plaintiff's suit came to trial, the Securities and Exchange Commission (SEC) sued Parklane Hosiery (D) in federal court on essentially the same grounds, requesting injunctive relief. After trial in the SEC suit, the district court entered a declaratory judgment against Parklane Hosiery (D). Shore (P) then moved for summary judgment, arguing the issue of liability had been decided in the SEC suit and that Parklane Hosiery (D) was collaterally estopped to relitigate the issue. The district court denied the motion, holding that collateral estoppel would violate Parklane Hosiery's (D) Seventh Amendment right to a jury trial. The Second Circuit Court of Appeals reversed, holding that Parklane Hosiery (D) had a full and fair opportunity to litigate the issues and was not entitled to relitigation by jury trial.

■ **ISSUE**

When the plaintiff could easily have joined in an earlier action, or when the application of offensive estoppel would be unfair to a defendant, is it error to apply the doctrine of collateral estoppel?

■ **DECISION AND RATIONALE**

(Stewart, J.) Yes. Collateral estoppel serves both to protect litigants from the burden of relitigating issues already determined and promoting judicial economy. Generally, collateral estoppel required mutuality of parties such that a nonparty could not offensively enforce an initial judgment in a separate proceeding. Over time, the mutuality requirement was abandoned when the party against whom enforcement of the prior judgment is sought has had a full and fair opportunity to litigate the issue. Permitting the party to relitigate the issue would waste both the court's and the litigant's time and money to determine an issue previously established as a matter of law. However, defensive collateral estoppel, in which a defendant seeks to prevent a plaintiff from relitigating an issue it previously litigated against a different defendant, is distinguishable from offensive collateral estoppel, in which a plaintiff seeks to enforce a finding against a defendant from an earlier suit brought by a different plaintiff. But

---

both prevent the same demands on judicial economy. While defensive collateral estoppel forbids a plaintiff from relitigating an adverse judgment against other defendants, offensive collateral estoppel prevents a plaintiff from waiting for the outcome of a related suit before enforcing his rights. Similarly, offensive collateral estoppel may be unfair to a defendant initially faced with a small nominal claim and choosing not to allocate sufficient resources to its defense after a cost-benefit analysis. Also, a defendant in a subsequent action may have different procedural opportunities that may lead to a different result. These problems can be overcome, however, by permitting the court broad discretion in the application of offensive collateral estoppel. "The general rule should be that in cases where a plaintiff could easily have joined in the earlier action or where ... the application of offensive estoppel would be unfair to a defendant, a trial judge should not allow the use of offensive collateral estoppel."

Here, the plaintiff could not have easily joined the prior action, since it was brought by the SEC under its regulatory authority. Further, the seriousness of the government investigation gave Parklane Hosiery (D) every incentive to fully litigate the issues. That determination is not inconsistent with any prior decisions, and the defendant has no available procedural opportunities that may result in a different outcome. Because Parklane Hosiery (D) had a full and fair opportunity to litigate, offensive collateral estoppel bars it from relitigating the issues. The Seventh Amendment is not violated in the absence of mutuality of parties. Affirmed.

■ **DISSENT**

(Rehnquist, J.) Because the Seventh Amendment applies to those actions in which a jury trial was afforded at common law at the time of its 1791 enactment, Parklane Hosiery (D) was denied its Seventh Amendment right to a jury trial. In 1791, application of collateral estoppel required mutuality of parties, which would require a jury trial in this case had it occurred at that time. The changes in the law of collateral estoppel that developed because of the abandonment of the mutuality requirement cannot deprive the defendant of its constitutional right to a jury trial.

Even if the Seventh Amendment is not violated, offensive collateral estoppel should not be permitted in this case. Collateral estoppel is unfair to defendants who, like Parklane Hosiery (D), have not had the opportunity to have their claims decided by a jury. There is a strong federal policy in favor of jury trials, and the availability of a jury trial in a private action presents an important procedural opportunity that may lead to a different result than in the SEC suit, in which no jury trial was available. Furthermore, the benefit of estopping Parklane Hosiery (D) from relitigating the issue decided in the SEC action is minimal, since a jury must still be impaneled to determine to what extent the plaintiffs have been damaged.

Analysis:

The Court's opinion deals with the traditional doctrine of mutuality. Under that doctrine, neither party to a suit could use a prior judgment against the other unless both were parties in the initial suit. While the Court departs from the doctrine of mutuality, it does so only after granting a trial court broad discretion to determine whether the plaintiff could have joined the prior suit and whether offensive collateral estoppel will prejudice the defendant and interfere with judicial economy.

■ **CASE VOCABULARY**

DEFENSIVE COLLATERAL ESTOPPEL: Estoppel asserted by a defendant to prevent a plaintiff from relitigating an issue previously decided against the plaintiff.

MUTUALITY DOCTRINE: The collateral estoppel principle that a judgment is not conclusively in favor of someone unless the opposite decision would also be conclusively against that person.

OFFENSIVE COLLATERAL ESTOPPEL: Estoppel asserted by a plaintiff to prevent a defendant from relitigating an issue previously decided against the defendant and for another plaintiff.

Stephenson v. Dow Chemical Co.

(Vietnam Veteran) v. *(Chemical Manufacturer)*

273 F.3d 249 (2d Cir. 2001), *aff'd*, 539 U.S. 111, 123 S.Ct. 2161 (2003)

CLASS ACTION SUITS DO NOT FORECLOSE ALL SIMILAR CLAIMS

■ **INSTANT FACTS** Vietnam veterans sued the manufacturers of Agent Orange many years after the approval of a class action settlement covering their injuries.

■ **BLACK LETTER RULE** Class action judgments bind only those absent class members whose interests are of the same class as the class members such that their interests have been adequately represented.

■ **PROCEDURAL BASIS**

On appeal to consider a decision from the Eastern District of New York dismissing the plaintiffs' actions as a collateral attack on a final judgment.

■ **FACTS**

In 1983, the Eastern District of New York certified a class consisting of "all persons who were in the United States, New Zealand, or Australian Armed Forces at any time from 1961 to 1972 who were injured while in or near Vietnam by exposure to Agent Orange" or other specified chemicals, including their spouses, parents, and children born before 1984. All potential class members were given notice by mail or through the media, indicating their right to opt out of the class action. On the eve of trial for negligent manufacture, strict liability, breach of warranty, intentional tort, and nuisance, the action settled, requiring the defendants to pay $180 million into a settlement fund, with $10 million assigned to indemnify the defendants against future state court actions on the same claims. The settlement specifically bound all persons who had not yet manifested any injuries. After extensive hearings, the court approved the settlement. Seventy-five percent of the settlement funds were distributed to injured class members through December 1994, with the remainder allotted to a government agency providing grants to agencies serving Vietnam veterans and their families. After challenges to the class certification before the United States Supreme Court, the Court approved the class certification, the settlement, and the distribution plan.

Several years later, two class actions were filed in Texas state court against the same defendants, relying exclusively on state law and alleging the injuries did not manifest until after the settlement. The case was referred to jointly as the *Ivy/Hartman* action. The defendants removed the action to federal court, arguing that the issues had already been litigated and decided in the initial class action. After the case was transferred to the Eastern District of New York, the plaintiffs argued that it was unfair to bind them to the earlier settlement when their injuries were unknown at that time. The district court dismissed the *Ivy/Hartman* action, reasoning that the initial settlement contemplated the emergence of previously unknown injuries and accounted for that fact by extending payments under the distribution plan through 1994. Accordingly, the plaintiffs were entitled to recover under the prior settlement. The Second Circuit Court of Appeals affirmed the dismissal, concluding that the injury arose at the time Agent Orange entered their bodies and they were included in the earlier class as "at-risk" plaintiffs. Further, the Second Circuit determined that the *Ivy/Hartman* plaintiffs had not been deprived of due process because they were adequately represented in the first action and they received adequate notice of their opt-out rights.

Approximately five years later, Isaacson sued the manufacturers of Agent Orange, including Dow Chemical (D), under state law in New Jersey state court after he was diagnosed with non-Hodgkins Lymphoma. Several months later, Stephenson (P) sued the same defendants in Louisiana federal court after he was diagnosed with bone marrow cancer. Again, the defendants removed the Isaacson action to federal court and both cases were transferred to the Eastern District for New York, which consolidated the claims. The court granted the defendants' motion to dismiss based on the prior settlement and subsequent final judgment, concluding that the action was an impermissible collateral attack on the settlement.

■ ISSUE

Are plaintiffs bound by an earlier class action settlement when their interests were not adequately represented?

■ DECISION AND RATIONALE

(Parker, J.) No. The defendants contend that collateral attacks on class action judgments are permitted "only where there has been no prior determination of the absent class members' due process rights." Because the plaintiffs' rights were adequately represented in the Agent Orange litigation, the defendant claims the collateral attack is improper. However, although Ivy/Hartman determined that the Agent Orange settlement adequately represented the interests of the absent class members there, it did not specifically address whether absent members whose injuries had not yet manifested before the settlement funds had been distributed were adequately represented. Therefore, this issue has not been decided and may be considered on a collateral attack. Class action judgments bind only those absent class members whose interests are of the same class as the class members, such that their interests have been adequately represented. After a court determines that a class representative is capable of adequately representing the class, due process also requires a determination of whether the representative adequately protected the interests of the class members after the termination of the litigation. While the first determination is not subject to a collateral attack, the second may be, since it is not required to be made by the trial court.

The plaintiffs do not challenge the merits of the final judgment in the Agent Orange litigation, but rather argue that they were not proper parties to that judgment. If the plaintiffs were not proper parties, res judicata does not bar their claims and the defendants are not threatened by double liability. Res judicata bars relitigation of claims that were or could have been adjudicated in a prior final judgment. One central element of res judicata is that the case involve "the same parties or their privies." The plaintiffs rely on two cases, Amchem Products, Inc. v. Windsor, 521 U.S. 591 (1997) and Ortiz v. Fibreboard Corp., 527 U.S. 815 (1999), to demonstrate that they were not parties bound by the Agent Orange settlement. In Amchem, the Supreme Court established that the interests of class members suffering asbestos-related injuries were sufficiently distinct from those who had merely been exposed to asbestos to defeat class certification. Additionally, the Court reasoned that individuals whose injuries had not yet manifested lacked the necessary knowledge to protect their interests in the class action by submitting a claim or opting out. In Ortiz, the Court relied upon Amchem to further illustrate that the interests of members with present claims and those of members with future claims are not the same, requiring distinct subclasses with separate representation to protect each interest.

Due process requires that all absent members have adequate representations at all times, with reasonable notice of the action and with the opportunity to opt out. Although both Stephenson (P) and Isaacson fall within the definition of the earlier class, their interests are in conflict with those represented in the earlier litigation. The settlement protected those absent class members whose injuries had manifested before the 1994 final distribution date without adequately providing for absent members whose injuries had not. Under Amchem and Ortiz, the plaintiffs were not adequately represented in the initial settlement and are not bound by its final judgment. Whether Stephenson and Issacson would have lost on the merits of their claims in the earlier litigation is immaterial. Instead, the focus is whether the plaintiffs were afforded due process in the earlier action. Because they were not adequately represented in the class action, the plaintiffs were not proper parties and are not bound by the settlement. Vacated and remanded.

Analysis:

Although the court distinguished plaintiffs with latent injuries from plaintiffs with current injuries for purposes of ensuring adequate representation for each group, such a solution appears not to address another of the court's primary concerns. In addition to the adequacy of representation, the court was concerned that plaintiffs with latent injuries that did not manifest until after the settlement fund was terminated received no notice of their rights to participate or opt-out. And even if such persons did receive notice of a pending suit, such notice would be meaningless given their lack of symptoms and injuries at the time.

■ CASE VOCABULARY

CLASS ACTION: A lawsuit in which a single person or a small group of people represents the interests of a larger group. Federal procedure has several requirements for maintaining a class action: (1) the class must be so large that individual suits would be impracticable, (2) there must be legal or factual questions common to the class, (3) the claims or defenses of the representative parties must be typical of those of the class, and (4) the representative parties must adequately protect the interests of the class.

COLLATERAL ATTACK: An attack on a judgment entered in a different proceeding.

OPT OUT: To choose not to participate in (something).

United States v. Mendoza

(Federal Government) v. *(Filipino National)*

464 U.S. 154, 104 S.Ct. 568, 78 L.Ed.2d 379 (1984)

IMPORTANT QUESTIONS OF FEDERAL LAW REQUIRE REEXAMINATION

YOU CAN'T HOLD THAT PRIOR DECISION AGAINST ME, YOUR HONOR!

■ **INSTANT FACTS** Mendoza (P), a Filipino national living in the United States, filed a naturalization petition under a World War II statute more than thirty years after its repeal.

■ **BLACK LETTER RULE** Nonmutual offensive collateral estoppel does not apply against the government in such a way as to preclude relitigation of issues of law determined by a federal district court.

■ PROCEDURAL BASIS

Certiorari to review a decision of a federal court of appeals binding the Government (D) to an earlier judgment.

■ FACTS

Under a World War II federal statute, all foreign citizens serving honorably in the U.S. military were entitled to petition for naturalization before December 31, 1946. The statute was repealed after the war, but the U.S. immigration office in the Philippines had been closed from October 1945 to August 1946. In 1978, Mendoza (P), a Filipino national residing in the United States, petitioned for naturalization under the wartime act. Mendoza (P) sought to excuse his delay by the immigration office's closure, relying on a 1975 decision of a U.S. district court acknowledging the office's closure as a violation of individual due process rights. Mendoza (P) claimed the question had been resolved against the United States Government (D), estopping it to relitigate the issue. A federal court of appeals held the Government (D) was bound by the earlier decision.

■ ISSUE

Is the Government (D) barred by collateral estoppel from relitigating issues of law previously determined against the Government (D) in a prior suit involving different parties?

■ DECISION AND RATIONALE

(Rehnquist, J.) No. The Government (D) is not in the same position as a private litigant because of the importance of the issues involved in government litigation. In fact, due to the subject matter, most litigation in which the Government (D) is a party is of a kind that *only* the Government (D) can be a party. Because of this, the Government (D) is more likely to be involved in litigation concerning the same issues previously litigated in former suits. To hold the Government (D) bound to a rule of law established in a prior adjudication would hinder the development of important questions of law through additional exposure to the reasoned decisions of courts of appeals. Additionally, collateral estoppel would compel the Solicitor General to pursue appeals of all unfavorable decisions against the Government (D) regardless of the strain on public resources and court dockets. Similarly, the court of appeals did not determine that collateral estoppel would bar all successive relitigation of questions of law, but rather that on the record evidence there was no significant showing of a crucial need to reevaluate American immigration laws. The court, however, failed to establish what record evidence would be necessary to establish such a need so as to put other courts and the Government (D) on notice as to which decisions are likely to preclude further litigation and which decisions are not. "[N]onmutual offensive collateral estoppel simply does not apply against the government in such a way as to preclude relitigation of issues such as those involved in this case." Res judicata, however, does prohibit the Government (D) from relitigating issues resolved in a prior suit involving the same litigants on the same issues. Such mutuality alleviates the concerns associated with nonmutual collateral estoppel because the Government (D) is still free to relitigate the issue in later actions involving different parties. Reversed.

Analysis:

In an abstract sense, collateral estoppel is both a shield from an adverse judgment against the Government and a sword available to the Government against private parties. When the Government is the defendant in an action, it is not bound by adverse judgments previously involving another party. Yet, when Government action is supported by a court decision, it effectively becomes the law of the land, binding others who are not parties to the action. This is so, however, not because of the authority of the prior judgment, but because the government action is properly within its authority.

■ CASE VOCABULARY

COLLATERAL ESTOPPEL: An affirmative defense barring a party from relitigating an issue determined against that party in an earlier action, even if the second action differs significantly from the first one.

MUTUALITY DOCTRINE: The collateral estoppel principle that a judgment is not conclusively in favor of someone unless the opposite decision would also be conclusively against that person.

OFFENSIVE COLLATERAL ESTOPPEL: Estoppel asserted by a plaintiff to prevent a defendant from relitigating an issue previously decided against the defendant and for another plaintiff.

RES JUDICATA: An issue that has been definitively settled by judicial decision; an affirmative defense barring the same parties from litigating a second lawsuit on the same claim, or any other claim arising from the same transaction or series of transactions and that could have been—but was not—raised in the first suit.